iMovie™ 2
For Dummies™

MW00844438

Tricks for Better Video

✔ **Lock the camera down.** Use a tripod or a steadying device to keep the camera from bouncing or rotating during filming.

✔ **Pan and zoom with authority.** Shoot for a few seconds without panning or zooming, then move the camera or perform your zoom, and then shoot steady footage again. It's important not to have too much movement in your shots — constantly "seeking" the shot with panning and zooming is the quickest way to make your video look like *America's Funniest Videos*.

✔ **Choose simple backgrounds.** This is especially true if you're filming action that you eventually want to turn into a QuickTime movie for playback on a computer screen or over the Internet.

✔ **Get handles.** Begin taping a few seconds before you yell "Action!" and get a few seconds after the point where you yell "Cut!" This ensures that you'll have a little extra video to work with when you're editing in iMovie.

✔ **Get good sound.** Get your microphone as close to the action as possible (without interfering with the video of the shot). In many cases, this means getting add-on microphones that your actors can hold or clip to their shirts.

✔ **Get good light.** Make sure your *key light* source is behind the camera and to one side — not in the actor's eyes, but not behind the actor, either. Then, fill in shadows with a *fill light* or a *reflector*, if you have one.

✔ **Use a filter.** A simple UV filter keeps the lens safe from ultraviolet light and dust or cracking. (A busted filter is $20; a busted lens usually means buying a new camcorder.) Other filters offer interesting effects, as outlined in Chapter 18.

Miscellaneous iMovie Shortcuts

Command	Shortcut	Use it to
File⇨New Project	⌘+N	Create a new iMovie project
File⇨Open Project	⌘+O	Open an existing project
File⇨Save Project	⌘+S	Save changes to your current project
File⇨Export Movie	⌘+E	Export the movie to a camcorder or to a QuickTime computer file
File⇨Save Frame As	⌘+F	Save the selected frame as a PICT or JPEG file
File⇨Import File	⌘+I	Import an image, QuickTime movie, or audio file into the current project
File⇨Get Clip Info	⌘+Shift+I	Get information about the selected clip
File⇨Quit	⌘+Q	Quit iMovie
Edit⇨Undo	⌘+Z	Undos the last action (iMovie has multiple undo capabilities)
Edit⇨Redo	⌘+Shift+Z	Redo the command you just undid (this reverses the Edit⇨Undo command)
Edit⇨Select All	⌘+A	In the Shelf or Clip Viewer, select all clips
Edit⇨Select None	⌘+D	De-select (un-highlight) all currently selected clips
Advanced⇨Extract Audio	⌘+J	Extract audio from selected clip (on the Timeline)
Advanced⇨Paste Over at Playhead	⌘+Shift+V	Paste video starting at the playhead (but leave the underlying audio of the original clip)
Advanced⇨Lock Audio Clip at Playhead	⌘+L	Lock audio to a particular portion of the video clip
Move to Home	Home key	Move to the beginning of your iMovie project

iMovie™ 2 For Dummies®

Cheat Sheet

Rules of Video Composition

- **Split the screen into thirds.** Unless your actor is speaking directly to the video's audience (as in a presidential speech or a PBS telethon), place the person in the left or right third of the frame. In most cases, you also want people in your videos to be looking toward the center of the frame, not off camera. (If the person is in the leftmost third of the frame, he or she should be looking to the right.)

- **Don't amputate.** Don't cut off your actor at his chin, neck, waist, knees, or ankles. Instead, compose the shot so you see a little shirt collar or belt buckle or shoes, even if you can't show the whole person — the audience fills in the rest with their minds.

- **Consider the background.** Take careful note that you don't have palm trees that appear to be growing out of your actor's head, for example, and try to ensure that the background isn't *so* busy that it distracts from the video. One trick is to change the *depth of field* so that the background is less focused than the foreground (see Chapter 1.)

- **Get different shots.** Get the three basic shots: establishing, medium, and close up. Each shot should be from a slighty different angle (usually a change of more than 30 degrees) or even different locales; the combination of shots can make for effective video.

Monitor Editing Commands

Command	Shortcut	With the playhead or crop markers
Play	Spacebar	Play the clip
Move forward	Right arrow	Move forward one frame
Move back	Left arrow	Move backward one frame
Jump forward	Shift+right arrow	Move forward ten frames
Jump back	Shift+Left arrow	Move backward ten frames
Volume up/down	Up/down arrow	Change the volume of playback
Edit⇨Cut	⌘+X	Select the footage you want to cut from the clip (and place on clipboard for pasting)
Edit⇨Copy	⌘+C	Select the footage you want to copy to the clipboard
Edit⇨Paste	⌘+V	Place playhead at point where you want cut or copied footage to reappear
Edit⇨Clear	n/a	Select the portion of video you want to remove
Edit⇨Crop	⌘+K	Select the portions of video you want to keep
Edit⇨Split Video at Playhead	⌘+T	Place the playhead at the point in the clip where you want the split
Edit⇨Create Still Clip	⌘+Shift+S	Place the playhead at the frame you want to turn into a Still Clip
Advanced⇨Reverse Clip Direction	⌘+R	Place the playhead anywhere in the clip you want to play backward

IDG BOOKS WORLDWIDE

For Dummies®: Bestselling Book Series for Beginners

iMovie™ 2

FOR

DUMMIES®

by Todd Stauffer

IDG Books Worldwide, Inc.
An International Data Group Company

Foster City, CA ◆ Chicago, IL ◆ Indianapolis, IN ◆ New York, NY

iMovie™ 2 For Dummies®

Published by
IDG Books Worldwide, Inc.
An International Data Group Company
919 E. Hillsdale Blvd.
Suite 300
Foster City, CA 94404
`www.idgbooks.com` (IDG Books Worldwide Web site)
`www.dummies.com` (Dummies Press Web site)

Library of Congress Control Number: 00-112132

ISBN: 0-7645-0748-6

Printed in the United States of America

10 9 8 7 6 5 4 3 2 1

1B/RT/QS/QR/IN

Distributed in the United States by IDG Books Worldwide, Inc.

Distributed by CDG Books Canada Inc. for Canada; by Transworld Publishers Limited in the United Kingdom; by IDG Norge Books for Norway; by IDG Sweden Books for Sweden; by IDG Books Australia Publishing Corporation Pty. Ltd. for Australia and New Zealand; by TransQuest Publishers Pte Ltd. for Singapore, Malaysia, Thailand, Indonesia, and Hong Kong; by Gotop Information Inc. for Taiwan; by ICG Muse, Inc. for Japan; by Intersoft for South Africa; by Eyrolles for France; by International Thomson Publishing for Germany, Austria and Switzerland; by Distribuidora Cuspide for Argentina; by LR International for Brazil; by Galileo Libros for Chile; by Ediciones ZETA S.C.R. Ltda. for Peru; by WS Computer Publishing Corporation, Inc., for the Philippines; by Contemporanea de Ediciones for Venezuela; by Express Computer Distributors for the Caribbean and West Indies; by Micronesia Media Distributor, Inc. for Micronesia; by Chips Computadoras S.A. de C.V. for Mexico; by Editorial Norma de Panama S.A. for Panama; by American Bookshops for Finland.

For general information on IDG Books Worldwide's books in the U.S., please call our Consumer Customer Service department at 800-762-2974. For reseller information, including discounts and premium sales, please call our Reseller Customer Service department at 800-434-3422.

For information on where to purchase IDG Books Worldwide's books outside the U.S., please contact our International Sales department at 317-572-3993 or fax 317-572-4002.

For consumer information on foreign language translations, please contact our Customer Service department at 1-800-434-3422, fax 317-572-4002, or e-mail `rights@idgbooks.com`.

For information on licensing foreign or domestic rights, please phone +1-650-653-7098.

For sales inquiries and special prices for bulk quantities, please contact our Order Services department at 800-434-3422 or write to the address above.

For information on using IDG Books Worldwide's books in the classroom or for ordering examination copies, please contact our Educational Sales department at 800-434-2086 or fax 317-572-4005.

For press review copies, author interviews, or other publicity information, please contact our Public Relations department at 650-653-7000 or fax 650-653-7500.

For authorization to photocopy items for corporate, personal, or educational use, please contact Copyright Clearance Center, 222 Rosewood Drive, Danvers, MA 01923, or fax 978-750-4470.

is a registered trademark under exclusive license to IDG Books Worldwide, Inc., from International Data Group, Inc.

Dedication

To my brothers, Brian and C.J.

About the Author

Todd Stauffer is the author or co-author of more than 20 books on computing, including *Upgrading and Fixing Macs and iMacs For Dummies, Macworld Mac Upgrade and Repair Bible,* and *Macworld Mac OS 9 Bible* (with Lon Poole). He's a contributing editor for MacCentral.com and *Publish* magazine and publishes his own site, Mac-Upgrade.com. Todd contributes to *MacAddict, Silicon Alley Reporter*, and CMP's *PlanetIT*, among other publications. He's worked as a television and radio host, television writer/producer, magazine editor, advertising writer, and documentation specialist, all in technical fields. He'd give it all up in a heartbeat, though, if one of the major studios optioned his screenplay. Of course, he'd have to finish his screenplay, first.

ABOUT IDG BOOKS WORLDWIDE

Welcome to the world of IDG Books Worldwide.

IDG Books Worldwide, Inc., is a subsidiary of International Data Group, the world's largest publisher of computer-related information and the leading global provider of information services on information technology. IDG was founded more than 30 years ago by Patrick J. McGovern and now employs more than 9,000 people worldwide. IDG publishes more than 290 computer publications in over 75 countries. More than 90 million people read one or more IDG publications each month.

Launched in 1990, IDG Books Worldwide is today the #1 publisher of best-selling computer books in the United States. We are proud to have received eight awards from the Computer Press Association in recognition of editorial excellence and three from Computer Currents' First Annual Readers' Choice Awards. Our best-selling *...For Dummies®* series has more than 50 million copies in print with translations in 31 languages. IDG Books Worldwide, through a joint venture with IDG's Hi-Tech Beijing, became the first U.S. publisher to publish a computer book in the People's Republic of China. In record time, IDG Books Worldwide has become the first choice for millions of readers around the world who want to learn how to better manage their businesses.

Our mission is simple: Every one of our books is designed to bring extra value and skill-building instructions to the reader. Our books are written by experts who understand and care about our readers. The knowledge base of our editorial staff comes from years of experience in publishing, education, and journalism — experience we use to produce books to carry us into the new millennium. In short, we care about books, so we attract the best people. We devote special attention to details such as audience, interior design, use of icons, and illustrations. And because we use an efficient process of authoring, editing, and desktop publishing our books electronically, we can spend more time ensuring superior content and less time on the technicalities of making books.

You can count on our commitment to deliver high-quality books at competitive prices on topics you want to read about. At IDG Books Worldwide, we continue in the IDG tradition of delivering quality for more than 30 years. You'll find no better book on a subject than one from IDG Books Worldwide.

John Kilcullen
Chairman and CEO
IDG Books Worldwide, Inc.

*Eighth Annual
Computer Press
Awards ≥1992*

*Ninth Annual
Computer Press
Awards ≥1993*

*Tenth Annual
Computer Press
Awards ≥1994*

*Eleventh Annual
Computer Press
Awards ≥1995*

IDG is the world's leading IT media, research and exposition company. Founded in 1964, IDG had 1997 revenues of $2.05 billion and has more than 9,000 employees worldwide. IDG offers the widest range of media options that reach IT buyers in 75 countries representing 95% of worldwide IT spending. IDG's diverse product and services portfolio spans six key areas including print publishing, online publishing, expositions and conferences, market research, education and training, and global marketing services. More than 90 million people read one or more of IDG's 290 magazines and newspapers, including IDG's leading global brands — Computerworld, PC World, Network World, Macworld and the Channel World family of publications. IDG Books Worldwide is one of the fastest-growing computer book publishers in the world, with more than 700 titles in 36 languages. The "...For Dummies®" series alone has more than 50 million copies in print. IDG offers online users the largest network of technology-specific Web sites around the world through IDG.net (http://www.idg.net), which comprises more than 225 targeted Web sites in 55 countries worldwide. International Data Corporation (IDC) is the world's largest provider of information technology data, analysis and consulting, with research centers in over 41 countries and more than 400 research analysts worldwide. IDG World Expo is a leading producer of more than 168 globally branded conferences and expositions in 35 countries including E3 (Electronic Entertainment Expo), Macworld Expo, ComNet, Windows World Expo, ICE (Internet Commerce Expo), Agenda, DEMO, and Spotlight. IDG's training subsidiary, ExecuTrain, is the world's largest computer training company, with more than 230 locations worldwide and 785 training courses. IDG Marketing Services helps industry-leading IT companies build international brand recognition by developing global integrated marketing programs via IDG's print, online and exposition products worldwide. Further information about the company can be found at www.idg.com.
1/26/00

Author's Acknowledgments

Is it really true that someone can have a job where he gets to play with iMovie and camcorders and computers all day? Is this a good thing or a bad thing?

I'd like to thank everyone at Flying Pig Publications (er, Hungry Minds, Inc.) for their help in getting this book written, bound, and dressed up in a fabulous little yellow ensemble. I'm particularly pleased that I was the person selected to write this book, because otherwise it would have made it awkward for me to write the Author's Acknowledgments.

Thanks to Mike Roney, acquisitions editor, for once again promising me the opportunity to write a book on a fun topic in the ...For Dummies series. I also thank him for not taking back his promise after it was revealed that he'd called me accidentally, thanks to a bug in his handheld computer, and that he hadn't really wanted me for the project after all.

Thanks to Susan Pink, project editor, for making everything run smoothly and for making sure I got paid and, by extension, fed and sheltered. Likewise, thanks to Dennis Cohen, technical editor to the stars, for helpful advice and criticism regarding the accuracy of the book. I'd also like to acknowledge the work performed by Laura Moss and the media development team to put together the fine CD-ROM that accompanies this book.

Wendy Bergen and Jack Pommer of Metrovision Productions taught me what little I know about television production and putting together a TV show during our collaboration on Disk Doctors. I'd also like to thank DVCreators.net and Eric Schultheis, who taught an informative and entertaining DV Revolution Workshop, where I learned quite a bit about digital video cameras, professional lighting, and sound-gathering techniques.

More thanks to David Rogelberg, Sherry Rogelberg, and everyone else at Studio B, the writers' agency with a name that just so happens to fit perfectly into the acknowledgments of a book about movie making. ("Yes, Mr. Lucas, I'll be shooting down in Studio B.")

Huge thanks to Leo Jakobson and Nicola Liebert, who were both graciously (and inexplicably) willing to stand in the winter cold while I fumbled with the camcorder to produce some of the screenshots and QuickTime movies that accompany this book.

Finally, personal thanks to Donna Ladd for the support and love, and special thanks to Daisy for keeping those loose papers from flying all around the living room.

Publisher's Acknowledgments

We're proud of this book; please send us your comments through our IDG Books Worldwide Online Registration Form located at www.dummies.com.

Some of the people who helped bring this book to market include the following:

Acquisitions, Editorial, and Media Development

Project Editor: Susan Pink

Acquisitions Editor: Michael L. Roney

Technical Editor: Dennis Cohen

Permissions Editor: Laura Moss

Media Development Specialist: Jamie Hastings-Smith

Media Development Coordinator: Marisa E. Pearman

Editorial Manager: Kyle Looper

Media Development Manager: Laura Carpenter

Media Development Supervisor: Richard Graves

Production

Project Coordinator: Nicole Doram

Layout and Graphics: Jackie Bennett, LeAndra Johnson, Gabrielle McCann, Jacque Schneider, Rashell Smith, Julie Trippetti, Jeremey Unger

Proofreaders: Laura Albert, Susan Moritz, Charles Spencer, York Production Services, Inc.

Indexer: Liz Cunningham

Special Help
Gabrielle McCann, Rashell Smith

General and Administrative

IDG Books Worldwide, Inc.: John Kilcullen, CEO; Bill Barry, President and COO; John Ball, Executive VP, Operations & Administration; John Harris, CFO

IDG Books Technology Publishing Group: Richard Swadley, Senior Vice President and Publisher; Mary Bednarek, Vice President and Publisher; Walter R. Bruce III, Vice President and Publisher; Joseph Wikert, Vice President and Publisher; Mary C. Corder, Editorial Director; Andy Cummings, Publishing Director, General User Group; Barry Pruett, Publishing Director

IDG Books Manufacturing: Ivor Parker, Vice President, Manufacturing

IDG Books Marketing: John Helmus, Assistant Vice President, Director of Marketing

IDG Books Online Management: Brenda McLaughlin, Executive Vice President, Chief Internet Officer; Gary Millrood, Executive Vice President of Business Development, Sales and Marketing

IDG Books Packaging: Marc J. Mikulich, Vice President, Brand Strategy and Research

IDG Books Production for Branded Press: Debbie Stailey, Production Director

IDG Books Sales: Roland Elgey, Senior Vice President, Sales and Marketing; Michael Violano, Vice President, International Sales and Sub Rights

◆

The publisher would like to give special thanks to Patrick J. McGovern,
without whom this book would not have been possible.

◆

Contents at a Glance

Cartoons at a Glance

By Rich Tennant

page 7

page 163

page 77

page 231

page 307

Cartoon Information:
Fax: 978-546-7747
E-Mail: richtennant@the5thwave.com
World Wide Web: www.the5thwave.com

Table of Contents

Introduction

And then there was iMovie.

I've been in love with camcorders for years. In high school and college, I'd film funny little bits and then sit for hours with my stereo connected to two VCRs, repeatedly punching the pause button, the record button, the play button, rearranging wires, recording again. Loads of fun, but the resulting tapes were muddy, inexact, and clearly amateurish. In brief, they left a little something to be desired.

Later, I got an AV Macintosh model that could digitize pictures from VHS video tape, enabling me to create dinky little QuickTime movies by cutting and pasting scenes together, adding a little narration, and editing it all to taste. Putting together a system that could edit broadcast-quality video and export that video to an actual videotape was too costly. Little computer-window movies were the best I could afford on a hobbyist's budget.

Cue iMovie . . . and, "Action!"

iMovie, combined with modern Mac models that sport special FireWire ports, can directly support the latest raft of camcorders to hit the market: digital camcorders. Not only is image quality better with digital versus regular camcorders, but they're different in one other respect, too: They store images as computer files. Connect the camcorder to your Mac with a simple FireWire cable, fire up iMovie, and you're editing video. Not only that, but you're editing high-quality video that's almost indiscernible from the quality of the footage used on the local evening news. All for only a few thousand dollars — a small percentage of what this would have cost just a few years ago.

This breakthrough in price and quality has led many to proclaim a mini-revolution of sorts. Each of us is a potential videographer, whether for professional purposes, organizational goals, or just kicking around and having a good time. And it so happens that iMovie is an amazing program in that it makes putting together a finished, edited, polished project easy. So easy that, even in this basic text, we can go well beyond the basics and talk about special effects, camera techniques, soundtracks, and visual tricks.

Whether you've always had a strong taste for playing with the video camera or you have specific goals for more serious organizational, educational, or corporate video pursuits, you'll find iMovie will work wonders when teamed with a compatible Mac and a digital camcorder. Welcome to the future.

About This Book

As a video nut, I jumped at the opportunity to write this book. There's so much easy-to-learn information about getting good-quality amateur video with today's camcorders, then turning it around and having a blast editing it into an entertaining and informative end product. It's truly a wonderful new world of movie making for the rest of us. And iMovie is an innovative and friendly program that makes this incredibly powerful application pretty easy to grasp.

But if there's any problem with iMovie — aside from the amount of time it will take you away from things such as meals and family activities — it's that it doesn't come with much of a manual to help you find out the high points. The built-in help functions are good, but they can't cover all the bases. iMovie even has a tutorial, which I certainly recommend you run through, but it can't catch you up on all the options, techniques, and workarounds either.

That's what this book is for: working through the basics of camcorder control and then moving quickly into the iMovie basic and advanced functions. You see how iMovie and QuickTime interact, how to shape your movies for a particular target medium, and some of the easy basics of going from quality footage to a great edited video project. And, of course, the whole thing is packaged in the familiar, friendly, and (I hope) enjoyable *...For Dummies* style.

Oh, and by the end of this book, maybe you'll be persuaded to take time off for those meals and family activities anyway. After all, you have to have *something* to catch on tape, right?

Conventions Used in This Book

Here are a few conventions I use in this book:

- When I refer to an item in a menu, I use something like File⇨Open, which means "Pull down the File menu and choose the Open command."

- New terms show up in *italics*. If it's a term that hasn't appeared in Webster's in the past ten years, I define it, explain it, and in some cases, lambaste and humiliate it before moving on.

- For keyboard shortcuts, something like ⌘+Q means hold down the ⌘ key (the one with the little apple and pretzel on it) and press the letter Q on the keyboard, and then release them at the same time. ⌘+Shift+Q means hold down the ⌘ and Shift keys while pressing the Q key, and then release them all at once.

- Web addresses are shown in a special typeface, such as www.mac-upgrade.com. So too are HTML tags, such as EMBED.

What You're Not to Read

You can take two approaches to reading this book. First, you can read it from beginning to end to find out everything you can about recommended approaches to camcorders and iMovie, moving from the basics of importing video from your camcorder through the concepts of adding titles and transitions, editing sound, and adding special effects. Then it's on to the tasks of exporting the video to tape, CDs, or the Internet.

Second, if you have a specific question as you're working with iMovie, you can head right to that chapter (or the Part of Tens) and start reading. Note in particular that the Part of Tens offers some advice that you may want to know *before* you head out with your camcorder. Also, Chapter 20 covers some troubleshooting issues that you may want to refer to any time you encounter a problem.

Okay, okay — three approaches. Buried deep within this text is another one, hidden by secret code. Jot down the fourth letter in the ninth word of every third sentence of every sixth paragraph and then arrange the letters clockwise. Subtract four. The resulting treatise will uncover the true secrets of the Loch Ness monster, Big Foot, Roswell, the Bermuda Triangle, and the fate of Amelia Earhart, assuming any of those are still secrets by the time you finish.

Foolish Assumptions

This book assumes that you have a basic understanding of how a Macintosh works, how to move around in the Finder, and concepts such as saving and loading files. If you don't know the Macintosh very well, I recommend *Macs For Dummies,* 6th Edition, by David Pogue (published by IDG Books Worldwide, Inc.) or a similar book to help you get up to speed.

Also, as I'm writing, there isn't a version of iMovie that's specifically designed for Mac OS X, so all my foolish assumptions are based on how iMovie currently behaves in Mac OS 9. If you're running iMovie using Mac OS X, you'll find that I discuss how I *think* things will work with a Mac OS X-based version of iMovie, but I can't be sure. That said, the bulk of the differences won't affect this book and you can consult Chapter 20 for help on getting additional information on iMovie through the Internet. (Or, as you see later in this introduction, you can visit my Web site or send me an e-mail if we need to hash something out.)

How This Book Is Organized

iMovie 2 For Dummies is divided into five sections, which are certainly not equal and uniform. (I have my favorites, but I decline to reveal them out of consideration for the feelings of the other parts. They can be rather sensitive.) The chapters progress through the stages of video or filmmaking, from the getting-started elements — getting something on tape, starting up iMovie, and importing video — to the different ways to distribute your iMovie and get it seen. The last part offers lists of additional software and hardware you may want to purchase, strategies for better moviemaking, and troubleshooting tips.

Part I: Getting Started with iMovie

In Part I, you find out about the basics of digital video and iMovie, including a discussion of the technology, system requirements, and some of the hardware involved. You get a quick primer on buying camcorders, lights, and audio equipment as well as other issues involved in getting good video footage and the right computer hardware to deal with that footage. Then you move on to camera operation and filming technique. Next, you launch iMovie and begin importing video into the program so you can edit it.

Part II: In the Editing Bay

Part II offers a full look at all the ways you can edit footage in iMovie. You start with the basic cuts and arrangements, creating a rough idea of what your final video project will look like. Then you move on to building transitions between your clips (wipes, fades, and more sophisticated transitions) and adding titles and credits. After that, you see a powerful new set of features in iMovie 2: the capability to edit audio and video separately using the special Timeline interface, adding a professional touch to your iMovie. After that, you see how to add sound effects and soundtrack music to your iMovie.

Part III: Post Production: Making Your Movie Look Fabulous

After you have your desktop movie imported and edited, you're ready to move into the post-production phase: adding special effects, importing images, and working with add-on tools that enable you to go further than the basics of iMovie. Also in this part is a special chapter (Chapter 13) that goes further into iMovie (and QuickTime) editing techniques that aren't required reading but certainly are fun to explore.

Part IV: Opening Night: Presenting Your Movie

In Part IV, you see the many different things you can do with your desktop movie after you create it. (I like to call this "multiple ways to bore your neighbors," but the editors decided to cut that because it's too negative.) This includes sending your desktop movie back to the camcorder for display on TV (or for taping to VHS tape). You can also create QuickTime movies for a variety of applications, including placing those movies on CD or distributing them over the Internet. And, speaking of the Internet, you can even transfer or post your movies on the Internet using Apple iTools, a set of free Internet-based applications available to Mac OS 9.*x* (and higher) users.

Part V: The Part of Tens

Finally, in the Part of Tens, you're in for some easy reading. Here you see a list of recommended purchases for the card-carrying iMovie addict — everything from additional special effects programs to computer hardware and even video hardware that you may want to add for better movie making. Then, you discover ten ways to improve your movie-making experience, including tips on camera usage and techniques specific to creating Internet movies. Finally, I provide ten tips to help you when iMovie starts acting up, including some of the most common troubleshooting issues and how to solve them.

Icons Used in This Book

Tips are special bits that come from the insider world of a guy whose job it is to spend entirely too much time playing with iMovie. You don't have to read these, but I had to write them, so reading them seems only fair.

When you see this icon, I'm telling you something important or reminding you of an issue already discussed. In many cases these are *redundantly repetitious,* repeating something just stated in the text to try to drive an important point home. They have elegant transitions and impeccably edited grammar, however, so you may be willing to give 'em a gander.

I won't geek out and talk about too much technical stuff, especially given that iMovie and DV camcorders aren't that difficult to use. Still, I feel I must put down on paper the occasional snippet of nerdiness — but you're free to ignore them.

The text has few warnings, but if you see one, soak it up. I issue a warning only if you're in immediate danger of losing data or messing something up. You probably can't harm yourself with iMovie or a camcorder, unless you back over a cliff while filming a particularly beautiful vista, so I'll say, for the record, try not to do that. Otherwise, read any warnings in the text to avoid losing data or messing up your tapes.

I put movie clips and some sample applications on the *iMovie 2 For Dummies* CD-ROM. I refer you to those items throughout the text using this cleverly designed icon.

Where to Go from Here

If issues and questions crop up regarding the book (or if I just have yet another video of my own that I want you all to see), I'll post discussions regarding this book at www.mac-upgrade.com/imovie/ on the Web.

If you still don't get your question answered after visiting the Web site, or if you have a comment, kudos, concern, or criticism, reach me directly at questions@mac-upgrade.com. If you require a response, note the timeframe in your message, such as *1 Week: iMovie Crashing* or something similar. I hope to hear from you!

Part I

Getting Started with iMovie

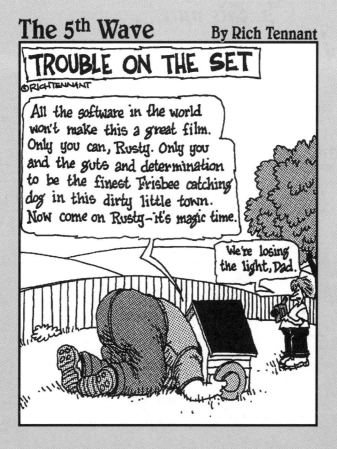

In this part . . .

*i*Movie is a pretty simple application, but there's a lot
you can do with it. One thing you can do, for instance,
is use the editing tools to create a great movie. But a great
movie requires great footage — and getting that footage
can be the tricky part (or, at least, part of the tricky part).
To get good footage, you need to know the basics of digital video, digital cameras, and composition. You might
also want to know a little about preparation for getting
good light and good sound while you're shooting your
footage. Fortunately, I have all that right here in this part,
along with a discussion of how to set up iMovie and how
to begin importing that footage after you've filmed it.

Chapter 1

So You Want to Be a Director

*I*t's tough to think of a better job than film director. You enjoy a multimillion-dollar salary and hobnobbing with Hollywood's elite. And when it comes right down to it, the glory is almost all yours at Oscar time. Plus, you get the house in the hills without being hounded by the paparazzi. Can you beat it?

Okay, so that's not likely to happen to you or me. But, don't despair — that doesn't mean you can't still be a bona fide movie director, even if you remain forever an amateur *auteur*. With a digital camera, iMovie, and a compatible Mac, you have the tools at your disposal to make the next *Diner* meets *Die Hard*, *Titanic* meets *Airplane,* or whatever other stories you have bouncing around in that head of yours.

Who knows, maybe we'll see you on the stage at the Oscars after all. First, though, I present a primer course in the art of digital video production, as well as a look at the computing requirements and equipment needs for creating iMovie projects. If you already have the camcorder and equipment you need, put on your director's cap and jump right into Chapter 2.

Digital Video Explained

These days, it seems that the majority of consumer camcorders (and many professional models) are *digital video,* or *DV,* camcorders. These differ from the more traditional *analog video* camcorders in the way that they store the images you shoot. With an analog camcorder, electronic signal information is written to a magnetic tape, such as a VHS or Hi-8 cassette.

A DV camcorder, on the other hand, immediately translates the images it receives into digital data — ones and zeros — and stores that data as a computer-readable file. Although most DV camcorders still use tape as the storage mechanism, they could just as easily use a hard drive, a memory card, or some other sort of computer storage.

Frankly, most of us who use a camcorder don't care if the images are actually sketched by tiny squirrels, as long as the picture looks good. So why worry over whether or not the camcorder is digital? It turns out that DV offers some significant advantages over analog video. In fact, DV has ushered in a relatively new, exciting use for computers called *desktop video:* the capability to edit and present videos on a typical consumer computer at a reasonable price.

Why DV is a big deal

Editing video on a Macintosh (or a Microsoft Windows computer, for that matter) has been possible for quite some time. As early as 1992, Apple was introducing Macintosh models with special ports designed to turn VHS-type analog video into digital computer files, along with special applications to edit, format, and display that video on a computer screen. Likewise, professionals have been editing video using powerful personal computers and very expensive add-ons and software for well over a decade.

But the advent of digital video has caused a huge fuss over desktop video. In fact, some folks are calling desktop video a *killer application,* or *killer app* — the type of application, such as desktop publishing or Web publishing, that makes people willing to buy a computer for the sole (or primary) purpose of performing that new, *killer* task.

Why all the hoopla? Digital video offers a number of advantages over editing analog video, mostly because of one simple difference: a DV camcorder creates a computer file as you record. How important can that one little technicality be? Here's the list:

✔ **Ease of transfer.** Because a DV camcorder stores its video as a computer file, all you really have to do is copy that file from the camera to a computer. In the past, analog editing required that the images go through a *digitizing process*, in which the computer had to look at the video as it was played back by the camcorder, analyzing each frame and turning it into a series of digital images stored in a single computer file. This was a time-consuming process that required reasonably expensive hardware (usually in the form of internal expansion cards) and a huge amount of computing power. With a DV camera connected via a FireWire cable, you're really just copying the DV data from the camera to the computer, and it all happens pretty quickly.

✔ **Image quality.** The moment you record video images to VHS tape (and, to a lesser degree, Betamax), those images lose some quality. VHS is simply not a medium that thrills the Picasso's of the video world. With DV, on the other hand, the pictures you get from a sub-$1000 DV camera are almost as good as the video used for the evening news. And the more expensive the camera, the better the quality, to the point that a camera that costs only a few thousand dollars can rival the quality of a professional analog camera costing tens of thousands. In fact, feature films and television are being recorded on DV cameras right now, and few people can tell the difference between DV and pro-level analog cameras.

✓ **Copy quality.** When you copy a DV file from one device to another, *signal loss*, which results in lower quality, does not occur. With analog connections, portions of the signal can be lost when the video signal travels through the analog cabling. You know how a taped TV show generally looks worse than the original broadcast? Signal loss is partly to blame. With DV, the taped video is a computer file, so copying it doesn't affect the quality level.

✓ **Cost.** Add everything up — the analog video expansion card, a high-quality analog camera, a powerful Mac — and shooting and editing analog video at anything resembling high quality can be a very expensive proposition. With DV, on the other hand, only a few thousand dollars (including the camera, computer, and software) enables you to put together videos that are absolutely good enough for home, educational, or corporate videos — and probably good enough for the film festival circuit. (Certainly good enough if *Blair Witch Project* was any indication.)

✓ **Distribution (or All the Cool Kids Like It).** A good number of professional documentary, independent, and even Hollywood filmmakers are turning to DV because it offers a revolution not only in the way video is made but also in how it is distributed. That advantage trickles down to those of us using iMovie, too. With digital video, we can put our movies on CDs, on computer desktops, and on the Internet more quickly and cheaply than with analog technologies. That makes it both easy and fun to get your personal video projects distributed as widely as your talent can take them.

So, DV makes analog look like the technology that relies on squirrels, eh? Desktop video's advantages are part of the reason why DV is seen as a killer app. And the killer app is what Apple smelled when it started offering iMac DV, Power Macintosh, Power Macintosh G4 Cube, iBook, and PowerBook models all sporting FireWire ports and a little program called iMovie.

The FireWire phenomenon

That Apple believes desktop video is a killer app is a given — after all, the company now includes iMovie and FireWire ports on nearly every new Mac it sells, including PowerBooks and iBooks. (As of this writing, the lone exception is the FireWire-less base-model iMac.) Part of this is due to Apple's marketing savvy, along with a strong desire to make money. Can't fault the company for that one. But another reason Apple is so keen on desktop video is because the company had a big hand in creating the technology.

For example, Apple invented FireWire. Also called IEEE1394 (*FireWire* is Apple's trademarked name for the technology), FireWire was created to be a new high-speed standard for connecting external devices to computers. Before FireWire, external *ports* for connecting things such as scanners, hard disks, and printers were generally slow and could be tough to configure. FireWire transfers data more quickly than any previous port technology and is also easy to use — in most cases, you simply plug in a device while your Mac is turned on and the device is recognized and configured automatically. FireWire, then, was a welcome introduction on Apple's various Mac models. Under different names, FireWire is a popular option also on Intel-compatible PCs, especially those made by Sony (which calls the technology i.Link).

As it turns out, FireWire is great for transferring digital video from DV camcorders to computers. Digital video files are very large, requiring about 3.5 megabytes per second of storage space. Because of this, a high-speed connection is necessary for transferring video from a DV camcorder to a computer; otherwise, you'd be waiting too long.

Because FireWire is fast (up to 50 megabytes per second) and convenient (it's easy to connect, has small, unobtrusive cables, and can be plugged in and out of the computer at any time), it was an obvious choice as the standard technology for DV camcorders. So, that's what it is: Nearly all DV camcorders have a FireWire-compatible port, which allows it to be connected to a PC or Mac FireWire port (see Figure 1-1). Then, you can use software such as iMovie to connect to the camera and transfer video files from the camera to the computer.

iMovie, everywhere!

Partly because of its investment in FireWire and the success of the original iMac as a home computer, Apple wrote iMovie to ship on its second-generation iMac, the iMac DV. The iMac DV was the first to include FireWire ports and a large enough hard disk to deal with DV files. Coupled with its fast processor and a decent amount of RAM, it was a great platform for a program like iMovie.

iMovie, in turn, was a fairly radical approach to video editing. It was, to put it succinctly, *easy.* No one had thought to make a video-editing program easy before, so iMovie was quite the mini-revolution when it came out. Compared to existing video-editing programs, iMovie was amazing in both its simplicity and, considering that it's included with most Macs, its capabilities.

iMovie is non-linear DV editing software, so you can cut a stream of video into *clips*, which are simply smaller portions of an overall film or video presentation, and then move those clips around like puzzle pieces. With iMovie, you can instantly move backward or forward to any point in your movie, and then edit, add to, or play back that portion of the video.

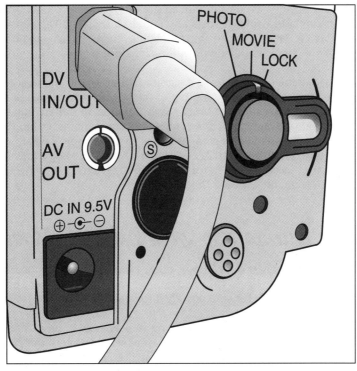

Figure 1-1:
My
camcorder
includes a
FireWire-
compatible
DV port.

iMovie isn't the only non-linear editing application to come along so far; they've been around for years, from the reasonably priced (translation: hundreds of dollars) Adobe Premiere and Apple Final Cut Pro to the pricier (translation: thousands of dollars) Avid and Media 100 systems for professional studio editing.

What really makes iMovie new and special is that it enables you to toss together an impressive video without a college degree in Film Studies. With a point-and-click interface and simple controls for movie creation, iMovie is perfect for the home computer user with a DV video camera. iMovie's drag-and-drop approach to editing makes desktop video about as easy as putting together a slide presentation in AppleWorks and probably a bit easier than building your own Web site, depending on who you ask.

Originally, iMovie was included with only select Mac models, such as the first-generation iMac DV introduced in mid-1999. (That early version of iMovie was eventually updated to iMovie 1.0.2, which was made available for free downloading for compatible Macs until iMovie 2 was released.) In the summer of 2000, Apple introduced the Power Macintosh G4 Cube, which includes iMovie 2, as well as newer Power Macintosh G4 models and iMac DV models that also include the software. Apple also announced at that time that any Mac owner with a compatible Mac model could buy iMovie 2 through the online Apple Store (store.apple.com).

Then, later in 2000, Apple announced the second-generation iBook and iBook SE, which include FireWire ports and iMovie 2. By late 2000, almost every single Mac model that Apple ships includes FireWire ports and iMovie 2, making them all potential movie-editing machines.

iMovie is a simple, easy-to-learn program that gives the consumer an opportunity to learn the basics of DV editing. In fact, you can toss together a project in iMovie 2 in a matter of hours. And iMovie 2 builds on the original iMovie, offering more features and capabilities, including some that have long been reserved for high-end editing applications such as Apple's Final Cut Pro. Plus, iMovie 2 integrates well with Apple's QuickTime technology, making it a fairly simple matter to create video for playing in the QuickTime Player application or even for transmitting over the Internet.

What can you do with DV and iMovie?

So, DV has advantages over VHS or other types of analog video. And iMovie is simple to use. But why do those advantages add up to a killer app? One word: *editing amateur video* (er, *editingamateurvideo*).

After all, for more than twenty years, you've been able to buy a VHS camcorder and take videos on vacation, on the job, or at school. Before that, 8mm cameras had been available for decades, offering families (from the dark ages of the 1950s and later) the opportunity to bore other family members and friends with endless spools of vacation film.

But, unless you were handy with a razor blade and had access to some high-end equipment, it was beyond the average Jane's resources to edit that raw footage into something that might keep Uncle Ralph's attention.

With a DV camcorder, you can get your footage into a FireWire-equipped Mac easily. With iMovie, you can manipulate that footage, edit it, and send it back out to the camera for easy playback. (Heck, you can even control the camera from within iMovie.) It's easy, easy, easy.

Okay, it's easy. But is it powerful? Actually, yes. Even I'm surprised at the sophistication that's possible with the program. (And I don't surprise easily. That time I cried in the haunted house was because I was *startled*, not scared.) Here are a few types of video projects that you can accomplish with a DV camcorder, iMovie, and a compatible Mac:

✔ **Home video.** Shots of the kids, the dog, the car, the boat, the vacation house, the beach, the birds, the moon, the stars, the relaxing ebb and flow of the tide . . . (sorry, I got lost in the moment). Any of that stuff can be dumped into your Mac, edited, transitioned, and titled to make it more entertaining to family and friends.

✔ **Event video.** Shoot the company softball game, a kid's play, or a church function, and then edit it, clean up the sound, and you have it archived for posterity.

✔ **Educational video.** Teachers and students alike can use a video camera and iMovie to document and edit all sorts of projects, from independent research projects to field trips to the zoo or aquarium. Likewise, kids can edit a video for a school-based news channel, teacher or principal announcements, and so forth.

✔ **Training video.** Teachers, trainers, or human resources departments can shoot training videos, informational videos, or videos of company seminars that need to be edited and handed out to new hires or others on a need-to-know basis. Plus, iMovie lets you add still images, animations, and graphics created in other programs, so you can cut between slides and live action for training purposes.

✔ **Organizational or sales video.** Need to sell something, ask for money, or otherwise toot your own organizational horn? A DV camcorder and iMovie are perfect for that sort of thing. Shoot the product enticingly, interview your CEO or director, and show the world what your organization is made of.

✔ **Fiction.** Write something! Make something up! Assemble actors or friends or family and start yelling "Action" and "Cut"!

Even without new footage from a DV camcorder, you can translate other video, photos, or animation into a readable format (external devices for translating VHS tapes, for instance, are available) and edit away using iMovie. In fact, iMovie is a great way to create a standalone, narrated slide show or presentation, even if it doesn't have a lick of video footage.

What It Takes to Make Movies

If you're convinced that you need to make movies to survive *one more minute* on this Earth of ours (or if you're ready to spend thousands of dollars to further justify the purchase of this book), you're ready to assemble the necessary tools to make this all happen. Fortunately, you need only three things: a DV camcorder, a compatible Mac, and iMovie. I talk about the digital camera in the next section; for now, make sure you have iMovie and the right Mac to run it on.

Getting iMovie and supporting software

Obtaining iMovie should be the easy part: If you have an iMac DV of any make or model, you should have at least iMovie 1.0, if not iMovie 2. iMovie 2 has also shipped on any Mac (except the low-end iMac) introduced after

August 2000, including the latest round of Power Macintosh G4 models, the Power Macintosh G4 Cube, the PowerBook G3 (after September 2000), and the iBook (also after September 2000).

If you don't have one of these machines, or if you have iMovie 1.0 and you'd like to upgrade to iMovie 2 (which I recommend), you can order iMovie directly from Apple. In fact, you can not only order iMovie 2, but also download it directly from the Apple Store (store.apple.com) on the Internet.

With iMovie 2, you also need to make sure you have the latest versions of Mac OS 9 (9.0.4 or higher) as well as Apple's FireWire 2.4 or higher. Apple releases occasional updates to iMovie itself, which you can generally find at www.apple.com/imovie/ on Apple's Web site.

Is your Mac DV-compatible?

Macs that can run iMovie include all iMac DV models, all PowerBooks and iBooks that came with FireWire ports, as well as all Power Macintosh G3 and G4 models that came with FireWire ports. (That includes pretty much any Power Macintosh model that isn't beige.)

Along with having one of these computer models, you should also have at least 64MB of RAM (*random access memory,* also called *system memory*) installed on your Mac; more than that (128MB or more) is absolutely recommended for the best results. iMovie requires a lot of system memory because it deals with very large files: DV files. Remember that one second of DV video can be 3.5MB in size, so moving all that video around takes up a lot of system memory.

So how can you tell how much RAM you have? In Mac OS 9 or earlier, select the Apple menu, and then choose About this Computer. (If you don't see the About this Computer command, you need to switch to the Finder first.) Find the Built-in Memory entry in the About this Computer dialog box (see Figure 1-2). If you have 64MB, you're okay for running iMovie. If you have more, all the better.

If you're running Mac OS X, you might need more than 64MB to run iMovie effectively. (iMovie for Mac OS X isn't out at the time of this writing, so check Apple's Web site or iMovie's documentation for help.) 128MB should be a good start for running iMovie and Mac OS X together.

Likewise, you need a large hard disk to work with iMovie, especially if you plan to create movies of more than a few minutes. A completed, 15-minute video, for example, can take up nearly three gigabytes (GB) of storage space. So, you need a large hard drive — a minimum of 10GB — if you plan to use iMovie. Fortunately, most Macs and iMacs that ship with iMovie have at least this much hard disk space. If you're running out, though, you might want to consider upgrading your internal hard disk, especially if you're planning any feature-length productions. (You see how to gauge your exact amount of space in Chapter 3.)

Here's how much RAM you have installed

Figure 1-2:
Determine
the amount
of built-in
memory
installed on
your Mac.

Choosing (and using) a digital camcorder

If you don't have a digital camcorder, you may want to check out this section
and Chapter 18, where I discuss the basics of choosing camera accessories. If
you already have a DV camcorder, you're probably ready to get out and do
some shooting. First, and perhaps most importantly, you need to determine
whether or not your camcorder is compatible with iMovie. Many consumer
DV cameras from Canon, Sony, and Panasonic are compatible with iMovie,
although each brand has its own quirks. (Occasionally, for instance, a camera
may not be fully controllable from within iMovie, forcing you to press buttons
on the camera to make things happen.) Apple maintains and updates a list of
compatible cameras at www.apple.com/imovie/shoot.html.

After you determine that your camera is compatible, you can move directly
to shooting video, as described in Chapter 2. But I wouldn't necessarily
recommend that. As with any consumer item (aspirin, hair-restoration tonic,
garden shears), the more you know about your camcorder, the better the
results will be. So, I look into some of that camcorder technology now.

Understanding DV formats

You'll encounter a few different DV formats when you examine different types
of cameras. Realize that these formats don't have a whole lot to do with DV
itself — all cameras that support the DV format are working with the same
sort of data file. If your camera is compatible with iMovie, the type of DV
format it uses simply refers to the type of tapes (or other storage) you'll be
working with.

In terms of convenience, cost, and compatibility, MiniDV is the recommended
choice. MiniDV cartridges are easy to work with, compact, and the most
common in the business. Proponents of MiniDV also claim that the format
offers better quality than its rivals, although the general feeling is that any
quality difference isn't noticeable. Still, if you have a choice, MiniDV is probably the best one.

Digital8, a Sony technology, allows you to store DV data on standard, analog Hi-8 cassettes. This has the advantage of allowing you to purchase slightly less expensive cassettes (about $10–$15 for a MiniDV cartridge versus $5–$10 for a Hi-8 cartridge). After you use the tape for DV, it won't play back in standard Hi-8 or 8mm cameras. Other than that, the only real problem with Digital8 is that you're locked into a Sony-only technology.

Exposing yourself to CCDs

Camcorders use CCDs, or *charged-coupled devices,* to sense levels of light through the lens and then record that information to form video data. Most inexpensive digital camcorders have one CCD, which means that single CCD is responsible for recording the information for all colors in an image. Higher-end cameras use three CCDs together to record the red, green, and blue information in a given frame of video.

In general, a one-CCD camera offers plenty of quality for any sort of consumer task. In fact, three-CCD cameras don't always offer better image quality than one-CCD cameras. For most shooting, the quality will be almost the same. The three-CCD camera does fare better under low-light conditions or where the light is heavily weighted toward one color or another (such as shooting in a dance club).

Although CCDs are often used as a measure of quality, the true measure of the quality of a camcorder (or any other camera) is the focal capabilities of its lens. The better the lens, the better — and, most likely, pricier — the camcorder. The highest quality camcorders have interchangeable lenses.

Some digital camcorders offer a *progressive CCD*, which is used for still shots (photos) instead of video. If you have reason to believe you'll want to take still photos with your camcorder, you may want to invest in a camera with a progressive CCD, because this nets you the best quality. You may also want to buy a camcorder that stores those still photos on a different storage mechanism, such as a memory stick or memory card, instead of DV tape. That makes the images easier to load on a computer.

You can use most camcorders with progressive CCD technology to shoot in a special mode called *frame mode*, which means the image isn't automatically interlaced for TV playback. The result is a slightly more film-like look that's also good for Web-based videos because frame-mode data translates more directly into QuickTime movie format.

Deciding on digital effects

Part of the fallout of the DV phenomenon is that it allows DV camcorders to perform a number of tricks that analog camcorders can't pull off. These include editing within the camera, digital zoom, and digital stabilization. Having those features is nice, but being able to turn them off is nice too.

The importance of being filtered

Oddly, many camcorders come out of the box without any filter for the lens, even though all digital camcorders I've encountered are capable of accepting them. Filters can be used for quite a few different effects and touches, including changing the tone of shots, helping with glare, and giving the shot a slightly fuzzier, warmer, film-like look. (Suddenly I feel like I'm writing copy for a toy catalog.) Anyway, see Chapter 18 for more on the different types of filters and lens adapters for cameras.

In the meantime, buy and use a UV (ultraviolet light) filter for your camcorder at all times! Install it and forget about it, at least until you go to change the filter. (In fact, you can usually stack other filters on top of the UV filter.) The filter does two things: It protects the optics from damaging UV light, and it offers a barrier from scratches and spills. Plus, if the filter gets dirty or dusty or smudged, it can be cleaned and eventually replaced with a new one. Replacing a damaged lens, on the other hand, can be so pricey that you may opt to replace the camera instead.

For instance, *digital zoom* (the capability of a camera to zoom beyond its lens focal length) is less useful for zooming in on a person and more useful as a special effect when you'd like your video to look like a low-quality surveillance camera. The feature is handy occasionally, but you're better off buying a camera with a longer *optical zoom*, if possible. With optical zoom the lens performs the zoom, resulting in much higher quality.

Similarly, digital stabilization can be a nice effect, especially if you have no choice but to hold the camera while walking around. A better choice, though, is using a tripod or other device to stabilize the camera.

And as far as editing within the camera — that's why you have iMovie! iMovie is far superior to any in-camera editing or effects you can perform while shooting. Instead, if you have a few extra dollars, get a camcorder with a better lens or a longer optical zoom or save the money for investing in camcorder filters, lighting, and sound equipment to help you get better input for your iMovie.

Other things to look for

Digital effects aren't the only considerations when shopping for a camcorder. Here's a short list of some other items to look for in a good camcorder:

- **Analog line-in.** Not all camcorders have analog line-in, which allows you to hook up a VHS player or TV *to* your DV camcorder. (All camcorders let you send the signal *from* the camera, but not all cameras let you send the signal *to* the camera.) Why is this important? With analog-in ports, you can connect your VHS player to your DV camcorder and then record from the analog tape to the digital tape. The result? An instant conversion from analog video to DV, so that you can edit the footage in iMovie.

Without analog-in ports, you must *digitize* VHS footage using expensive add-on cards if you want to edit that footage in iMovie. Of course, if you don't have any analog video you want to edit, analog-in ports aren't all that important. (I talk about it more in Chapter 3, along with another way to get analog video into iMovie.)

✔ **LCD display.** Again, most DV camcorders have LCD displays, but here I'm recommending that you get a camera that has a *good* LCD. If you get a chance to compare them in the store, do it. Why? Unless you hook up an external TV while you're editing in iMovie, the LCD display on your DV camcorder will be the best way to see your video as you're editing it. Of course, you can play back on your Mac's screen, but the LCD display gives a better indication of how the video will look on a TV screen.

✔ **Long battery life.** A DV camcorder's battery can go dead before you've even finished shooting a single tape, especially if you have the LCD viewer on the entire time. After all, it's a complex camera doing a lot of computing. When shopping, look for cameras that offer long battery life and, if you can, pick up additional batteries and chargers. There's nothing fun about a camera that runs out of juice while you're getting great shots in the field.

✔ **Accessory shoe.** An accessory shoe on the top of your camera lets you add a focused light or special microphone that will make your shots look and sound better. Some smaller cameras don't have the shoe, which is fine if portability is the number one priority. But you'll eventually find a reason to want that shoe.

Doing It Like the Pros: Lights! Sound!

All camcorders have two limitations when it comes to making the best movies. First, your camcorder isn't as versatile as your eye and won't always shoot great video under adverse lighting conditions. Second, you can't always put your camcorder's microphone right in the middle of your action because the microphone is probably attached to the camera. For the best video, then, you need to think about how light and sound affect your camcorder. You may opt for additional accessories. Fortunately, a little investment in add-ons can go a long way toward great video.

Lighting up your life

One issue that can affect the look of video you shoot is the lighting. Sometimes you can't compensate for bad lighting (especially in situations where you have no control). But when you can control the lighting, good lighting can make a production look its most professional. If you're shooting corporate or institutional video, good lighting can make a serious difference in the quality of the final product. But even for day-to-day video, having an awareness of your light source (and doing what you can to improve it) will show through on your videos. Chapter 18 covers shopping for lighting kits and lighting accessories for your camcorder.

Key light

For basic shooting, you need to consider your primary and secondary light sources. Your *primary light source,* called your *key light,* should generally be placed above and to the right or left of your camera. If you're outside, your key light is most likely the sun. In that case, try to shoot with the sun behind you so that it's on your subject. (If you're getting video of people, this doesn't mean you have to make them squint into the sun. In bright sun situations, it's okay to shoot people in the shade or in less direct light — just be aware of where the sun is and try to avoid deep shadows on your subject's face.) Inside, your key light is whatever lighting the room has or whatever lights you bring with you.

The goal with most artificial lighting is to give the camera enough light to make the scene vibrant while minimizing distracting shadows. In a studio, you have plenty of options for lighting the set. Working outside (or when you're mobile with the camera) may present more limitations.

One solution is to bring a key light with you, especially if you think you may be shooting in low-light situations. Depending on your camera model and manufacturer, you may be able to get a battery-based light that attaches to the camera itself and casts a powerful beam on your subject — good for person-in-the-street type interviews. (I'd also recommend getting your person-in-the-street to move to the sidewalk.)

The temperature of color

Color has a *temperature,* which is actually measured in degrees Kelvin. (No, not the "six degrees" — that's *Kevin* Bacon.) The temperature of indoor light usually comes in around 3200 degrees, with fluorescent lights offering up about 4000 degrees. Outdoor-rated lights offer about 5600 degrees; the sun itself can have a temperature (color temperature, that is) of 7200 degrees or more.

So, what does all this mean? In general, it means that the best lighting is temperature balanced, so that the shot has a reasonably uniform look to it, without explosions of color or other odd effects happening in parts of the picture.

For instance, you may notice that when you shoot inside a room with sun streaking in through the window, that window can show up as a bluish color, giving the shot a less than ideal look. The solution is to either close the window or put filters on the glass of the window. If other parts of your image seem to have odd, colored tints, unmatched light sources may be the culprit — turn off fluorescent lights, for example, and try to make the light as uniform as possible. (You should also make sure you're properly white-balancing your camera, as discussed in Chapter 2.)

Fill light

Whether your key light is attached to the camera, is held behind you on a light stand (or by an intern), or is the sun, the second issue is to try to diffuse the shadows and glare that the light casts on your subject. This is usually accomplished using a *secondary light source* called a *fill light* (see Figure 1-3).

It isn't always practical to have a fill light along with you, especially if you're shooting on the run. The solution in that case can be a *fill card* or a *reflector* — items that you place close to the subject at about the same angle as a fill light. Light bounces off the reflector and onto the subject, thus filling in some of the shadows.

A reflector can be as simple as a sheet of white posterboard or as specialized as five-foot diameter reflector screens that pop out of small bags. (See Chapter 18 for shopping tips.) So, if you're seeing severe shadows — especially on a person who is sitting or standing still — a reflector of some sort may be in order.

Backlight

The third type of light is something you're not likely to have available for an outdoor or mobile shoot, but it's something you can consider using in a studio or for an interview (for a school project, a documentary, or a hard-hitting investigative report). Called a *backlight,* or *kicker light,* it shines on the back of your subject to separate the subject from the background. (It puts highlights into hair, puts a little light on the back of a person's shirt, and so on. It looks good. Trust me.) This effect gives your image a bit more 3-D appeal.

Although a backlight isn't practical when shooting outside, it can still be nice to have highlights in your subject's hair. The solution is to reverse your key light (the sun) and fill, as shown in Figure 1-4. Put the sun behind your subject (at an angle) and reflect light onto the subject's face with a fill reflector. This is one approach that still photographers use to take full advantage of sunlight.

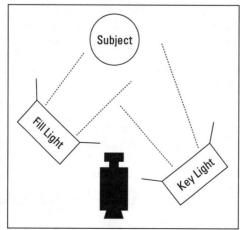

Figure 1-3:
A two-sided approach helps avoid shadows on your subject.

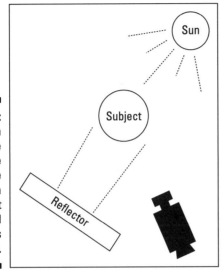

Figure 1-4:
When you're outside, the sun can be both a backlight and reflected as a fill light.

Background light

The last type of light in a standard studio or interview setup is a *background light,* which adds interest to the backdrop behind a guest. This is especially useful for white or beige backgrounds that don't look, in the world of Lawrence Welk, *wunderful, wunderful, wunderful.* A sickly looking wall can look just a bit better with some colorful light playing on it. Usually, you shine a background light up onto the background from a relatively low position.

How does it sound?

Good lighting and acceptable composition (discussed in Chapter 2) are great ways to keep people's attention during your video. But nothing differentiates the amateur from the professional like good sound in your video.

Most DV camcorders actually have good sound capabilities. If you haven't yet bought a camera, buy one that supports 16-bit stereo sound in two channels or 12-bit stereo in four channels. (In most cases, you'll shoot two-channel audio, which is standard stereo.)

The problem with most cameras is that the microphone is stuck right there on the camera. This configuration is useful only when your subject is close to you, the camera isn't moving much, and you're not making a bunch of noise yourself as you fuss with the camera.

A partial solution is a *directional* microphone (often called a *cardioid* mic) that's attached at the top of the camera. This microphone still has the disadvantage of being attached, but it also has the advantage (if the microphone is really good) of being better designed to pick up sound that's *only* in front of the camera, even if it's a good number of feet away. It will probably still hear you (assuming you're the photographer) talking, but if the microphone is detached from the body of the camera, it won't pick up the sound when you press a button and move things around. Just try to remember the "quiet on the set" part. (This type of microphone is usually an add-on purchase available from your camcorder manufacturer.)

An even better solution is to get your microphone away from the camera and closer to your action. This will take some additional investment; you'll need to buy special microphones and other equipment to get the best sound. But I wholeheartedly recommend that you get at least one additional, high-quality microphone to use with your camcorder.

Here are a few of the basic options for getting great sound for video:

- **Handheld microphone.** This can either be a directional microphone that is held off-camera by an intern or assistant or a handheld microphone that your subjects use on-screen. (This is the standard "reporting live from . . ." approach, in which the person you're filming holds the microphone.) If you're using just one microphone, you should be able to wire it directly to your camera. Two types of handheld mics are common: condenser and dynamic. *Dynamic mics* are cheaper and lower quality but don't require internal power. *Condenser mics* offer better sound, but be sure to keep spare batteries around at all times because the microphone won't work if the batteries aren't fresh.

  Need the crunching of helmets while taping your local high-school football game? Well, you can always cheat and add the sound effects later, but the best way is the way they do it on *Monday Night Football* — using a microphone called a *hypercardioid* (or shotgun) mic. It's a special type of microphone that can pick up sounds in one tightly focused direction.

- **Boom microphone.** In this case, a directional microphone is placed on a long *boom* — an extended metal arm that can be held over your subjects but out of the camera's view. This is best for fiction and documentaries, where it shouldn't appear that a microphone is in the scene at all. A boom microphone is also good when you want ambient noise, such as birds, ocean waves, or protestors in the background. Booms are used often in television shows and movies.

- **Lavalier microphone.** A lavalier microphone (or simply a *lav*) is the name for that tiny pinpoint microphone you clip to your shirt collar. This sort of microphone is good when you want your subjects' hands free, want the microphone mostly hidden from view, and don't need a lot of ambient noise. These microphones come in wired and wireless varieties, with wireless more expensive. (If you use a lav, check the sound before recording to make sure the microphone isn't rustling against clothing as your subject moves around.)

In most cases, moving the microphone away from the camera means you need a longer microphone cable. Many cameras are designed to accept mini-plug connectors, and this is okay for three- to six-foot lengths of cable. A longer cable, however, can add noise to your recordings, so when you need more than six feet of cable, try to use *balanced cabling* — the type with 3-prong XLR connectors (see Figure 1-5). Professionals use this type of cable to get better sound for longer cable runs. Unfortunately, only the more expensive cameras come with XLR plugs.

If your camera doesn't come with XLR plugs — or if you'd like to attach more than one microphone — you need an audio adapter. Adapters are available that fit under the camcorder, screwing into the tripod mount; they give you two XLR adapters for microphones. BeachTek (www.beachtek.com) makes one of the most popular adapters, with models that fit a variety of popular DV camcorders.

Figure 1-5:
XLR connections are best for long cable runs.

I also recommend that you get some headphones so you can listen to what the camera is recording. That way, you can make sure everyone is speaking into the microphone correctly and there's no unwanted noise. Most DV camcorders have a built-in mini-plug that can accept a standard set of headphones. Walkman-style headphone are fine, but more expensive *closed-ear* models sound a little better and make you look more professional!

Finally, test your sound before you shoot. Turn on the camera and mics, record a few seconds, and then play it back to make sure everything is working and sounds good. It's no fun to record for thirty minutes and then realize you haven't plugged your microphone in all the way.

Are you shooting outside with handheld or boom microphones? Remember to put *wind guards* on your microphone(s). These are the big, fuzzy (or foamy) slip-on covers that you put over a mic to keep it from making a rustling or booming sound when the wind picks up. Some camcorders have a digital wind guard setting that makes the mic less sensitive; it works okay but is not as good as the real, fuzzy thing.

Chapter 2

And Action! Shooting Your Movie

*T*here's a saying in technical circles that comes from computer programming: *Garbage In, Garbage Out.* It means that if the raw material you put into some process isn't good, that process will not magically make it better.

You can certainly apply this philosophy to editing video in iMovie. If you shoot great footage, you can use iMovie to enhance it — add music, titles, transitions, edits — and make it that much more presentable to others. If your video isn't compelling to begin with, though, your best hope is to use iMovie to make it a well-edited, well-presented, non-compelling video. Hmm.

The good part is, taking good video is easy! In fact, the process takes only a few pages to cover. To start, you find out the basics of handling the camera while you're shooting. Then, later in this chapter, you can dig a little deeper into the operation of a DV camcorder if you like — I recommend doing so because you'll discover some tricks of the trade for getting good shots. With just a few tips under your belt, you'll have great looking video that will work well after you get it into iMovie (which I begin discussing in Chapter 3). And did I mention that the chapter has plenty of pretty pictures?

Rule #1: Lock It Down!

If you have friends or neighbors who own video cameras, you've probably seen some pretty bad amateur home video. The bottom line is that the cameras can only get *so* sophisticated. Eventually, it's up to the carbon-based camera activation unit (you) to make some decisions and get things right.

Here's one way to do it: Watch a little TV. But instead of getting engrossed in the dramatic story line (did he do it? was he framed?) or giggling along with the laugh track, take some time to watch the camera work. (This is especially effective when you're watching the evening news or some other show where a lot of one-camera, hand-held shots are used.) You'll see some of the basic, professional video tricks play out right before your eyes.

The number one rule? Move the camera only when you have to and only when it makes sense for the shot. And when you do decide to move the camera, do it cleanly, deliberately, and with authority. (In this respect, it's sort of like karate, but you can wear jeans.)

Want to instantly make your video doubly-watchable? (Is that a word?) Buy a tripod and put your camera on it. Use the tripod as much as you possibly can.

Most of what seems *amateur* about amateur video is a shaking camera. Although some DV camcorders offer a special image stabilization feature, it won't cover up the fact that you're holding the camera in your hand. In most cases, a digital stabilization feature will help in only limited ways, such as by smoothing out shots in which you use a high level of zoom. But only a good tripod will keep you from moving the camera too abruptly, tilting it slightly or jostling it accidentally.

The tripod doesn't have to be pricey; an inexpensive one ($35 or less) should do fine. Most tripods are easy to adjust, standing to five feet or more but collapsing, even with the camera still attached, to two feet or less. Most tripods will also often help you *pan* (move from side to side) the camera smoothly, and some enable you to tilt the camera up and down smoothly as well.

See tripod.mov in the Chapter 2 folder on the *iMovie 2 For Dummies* CD-ROM for an example of video shot with and without a tripod.

If you're in a situation where you can't use a tripod, you still have a few options. First, you can use some sort of camera stabilization device to help you keep the camera steady; Chapter 18 discusses them in detail. Stabilization systems range from shoulder-mounted *steady-cam* setups to small, weighted balances that you can use for easy, hand-held shots where you need to move the camera. These cost a few hundred dollars and may not be right for home video, but they're perfect for video you're shooting for an organization or business.

Second, you can place the camera on something that will make it as steady as possible, such as a fence post or a car hood. If you can't get the right angle on the shot with the camera on such a platform, you might try putting your elbows on the platform to hold the camera as steady as possible.

If you're forced to hold the camera, try to hold it in two hands, preferably with one hand under the base of the camera. (You may find this convenient also for zooming or manual focusing.) Keep your elbows close to your body and plan your shots so that you can rest between them — you'll get tired of holding the camera like this, and your shots will start to get jittery and uneven.

Composing the Shot

Just like still photographers, videographers worry very much over composing their shots in an interesting way. Even with a simple, automatic DV camcorder and something as basic as a vacation video, good composition can really make your video entertaining and effective.

Composition refers simply to the aesthetic nature of the images as you *frame* them within your camera's viewfinder or LCD display. Although a certain amount of wonderful composition requires artistry and style (something I don't have and, hence, can't give you), some of it also follows basic rules that can help you frame your shots well. The artistry and style are up to you.

Being off-center

One of the most basic rules of video composition is to put your subject matter just slightly off from the center in the viewfinder. Center, after all, is where your news anchor, president, or terrorist goes when he or she has something important to say directly to the camera. When your subject isn't speaking directly to the camera, it makes more sense to the audience if he or she (or it) is somewhere about one-third of the way from the edge of the screen.

Which third? If the subject is a person, the rule is to have that person looking *into* the center of the screen, not toward the edge of the screen. In other words, if the subject is looking to the right, he or she should be on the left side of the frame; if the subject is looking left, he or she should be on the right side of the frame. That way it seems they're always looking toward the center instead of off-camera (see Figure 2-1). Note that if you *need* your subject to be looking off-camera, it makes sense for them to look toward the edge instead of toward the center.

If your subject isn't a close-up of a person, you should still remember that the audience thinks of itself as in the center, so action should take place *across* the center. That means action should go from the left of the frame to the right of the frame or vice-versa to involve the audience. This doesn't mean that the subject can't be walking toward or away from you; it simply means that you should place the camera so that the person walks across the center of the frame, if possible. (For instance, the person starts far away on the left side of the frame and, as he or she approaches, moves across the center of the frame toward the right side.)

Figure 2-1:
In most cases, your subject should be looking toward the center of the frame.

Of course, rules are made to be broken. Occasionally, you see a shot in which all the action occurs only on one side of the frame. This is usually an artistic choice (it occurs a lot in music videos), where the videographer doesn't use the entire frame for the shot. If you see this while channel surfing, note that it's a stylized approach that may be jarring in non-fiction or corporate video but can be fun to use for other types of productions.

Avoiding amputations

When you're shooting a person, avoid cutting off the top of the head and don't frame a person so that he or she is cut off at the neck, waist, knees, or ankles. All of these look disconcerting, as if the person doesn't have a body, legs, calves, or feet, respectively. Instead, shoot just below the neck (so we see a little shirt collar), waist (so we see the top of their jeans), and so on, so that we know the person continues from the end of the frame (see Figure 2-2).

Also, in extreme close-up, cutting off the top of someone's head is acceptable but cutting off the chin is not. Seeing someone's mouth open and close without seeing the chin move is odd and looks like an uncomfortable B-movie horror shot in which a disembodied lump of flesh is talking on its own.

Figure 2-2:
Shoot just
below the
shirt collar
so that the
audience's
mind can fill
in the rest of
the subject's
body.

Watching your background

Shooting with the sun or another light source directly behind the subject can cause problems, as can any oddly shaped, colorful, or busy background. Also, check to make sure that you aren't accidentally composing the shot against a distracting background object, such as shooting so that it appears that a tree is coming up out of your subject's head.

One frequent recommendation is that you shoot with the sun over your shoulder and behind you, with it shining on your subject. This is good advice, unless your subject is squinting into the sun or otherwise made uncomfortable. In that case, a little shade for the subject might be in order, or you can try a slightly different angle with the sun off to one side of both you and the subject. Just try to avoid heavy shadows on the subject's face.

Also note that for most computer-based video playback (CD-ROM, desktop, and Web-based video), the more complex the background, the worse the final video clip will look and compress. When a QuickTime movie is compressed into a final movie file, duplicate material in the background on each frame is discarded to make the file more compact. If you have a lot of movement in the background (such as waving tourists or cars in traffic), all that movement must be rendered in the final QuickTime file. The result is a movie that's hard to watch and takes up a lot of room on your hard disk or CD-ROM. The solution is to put your subjects against a simpler background that doesn't move on its own. For more on QuickTime, see Part IV.

Considering your angles

When composing shots, another important consideration is the angle you use between the camera lens and your subject. Following are a few considerations:

- **Shooting up from low angles.** If you shoot your subject from below, it makes the subject appear bigger and more imposing. In *Citizen Kane,* director Orson Welles had sections of his sound stage floor removed so he could get dramatic camera shots from far below the Kane character, making him appear larger than life. (Orson Welles later took a different, more culinary approach to making himself look larger than life.)

- **Shooting down from high angles.** Stand on a chair or a ladder or use a camera crane and shoot down at your subject or actor and you make him or her appear small and meek. (If you also end up showing his bald spot, you better check his contract to make sure that's allowed.) High angles are good to suggest adults looking at kids; low angles are good for suggesting kids looking at adults.

- **Shooting at crazy angles.** Tilting, or *dutching,* the camera at an angle to the ground (the *MTV* or *Monday Night Football* interview effect) can give a suggestion of hipness, coolness, or mystery to a shot — if used *very* sparingly. Crazy angles can also be used to suggest sloping ground or the "ship is sinking" effect or to show the crazed psycho chasing down the innocent victim in a slasher film. Again, use crazy angles as a confection, not the main course.

Two other rules govern angles. Professionals call the first one the *180-degree* rule, which suggests that you shouldn't change the "right and left" of a scene between cuts. You should try to avoid crossing the line of action: If you start on one side of the action, stay on that side of the action. Otherwise, the audience becomes confused — it's like constantly switching sidelines while watching your kid's soccer game. (The only time this works is in a *Rocky*-esque 360-degree shot, where the camera rolls all the way around the action to establish tension.)

The other rule is the *30-degree* rule, which means that you should change the angle of the camera (relative to your subject) at least 30 degrees if you're cutting between two angles without a transition. Of course, you don't need to employ your protractor and vast knowledge of trigonometry to figure out what equals 30 degrees; the idea is simply to make sure you're changing the angle of the camera between two shots that will be edited together. If you cut between two clips that don't have a dramatic enough difference in angles, it just looks like you bumped the camera or made a mistake in iMovie.

Positioning the camera

Remember that having people walk toward or away from the camera is okay — and often effective. You can use this to involve your audience intimately in the action. For example, think of the coverage of a NASCAR race. You have many shots that follow the cars, but some of the most effective footage is when a car zooms right past a stationary camera (or, as the case may be, slams into the wall right in front of said camera).

As a person nears the camera, he or she comes closer into view and you get a good look at facial expressions and body language. The angle of the camera as the person passes can also be suggestive — if the camera is at waist level, for instance, the subject is more imposing, purposeful, and directed. (A low angle makes your kids look cute if the camera is at their level as they approach.) Even in vacation videos, you should mix up shots of people walking past the camera with shots of them from the side.

And don't be afraid to have people walk into and out of the frame instead of always moving the camera to follow them. When your subjects walk off camera, that's the perfect moment for a cut to a new angle. It's an effective technique that keeps your audience interested while you avoid moving (and shaking) the camera too much.

The Fine Art of Zooming

Zoom is the process of changing the focal length of a lens. If you've ever had a fixed-length camera (one that didn't have a zoom lens), you know that to change the perceived distance to a particular object, you have to move the camera. With a zoom lens, you can change the focal length without changing the location of the camera.

Another calling card of amateur video is a zealous use of the zoom buttons. Something happens to people when they get behind a camcorder with a zoom feature. They zoom in, they zoom out. Zoom in on the baby, zoom out from the baby. Zoom in on grandma, zoom out from grandma. Zoom in on the plush interior of your new car. . . .

Spend a little time doing some research (that is, watching TV), and you'll see that a professional rarely zooms in and out during a single shot. (It happens sometimes in news footage and during newscasts but not much in interviews, informational shows, and fictional shows.) That doesn't mean the zoom feature is useless. It just means that changing the focal length *between* shots instead of *during* shots is generally more effective.

Zoom technique and the three shots

Professional videographers, rather than zooming and moving the camera to follow the action, often use a series of shots taken from different angles and using different focal lengths. To get better looking pictures for your own video, you should consider using this tactic. The common shots follow:

- ✔ **An establishing shot.** An establishing shot gives your audience a sense of location. Using a wide-angle focal length (zoom set to 0 or, on some cameras, W for *wide*), you shoot an entire scene without necessarily showing your main action or showing it as only a small part of the scene. In establishing shots, showing some zoom, especially to suggest the direction of the action, is common. For instance, if you're showing New York's Times Square in wide angle and you want to make it clear that you're going into the heart of it, you might smoothly zoom in a bit to convey that action.

- ✔ **A medium shot.** A medium shot keeps your subject in full frame, giving the audience the sense of what action is taking place and who or what is the main subject. A lot of your footage will likely be shown in medium shots. Rarely will you want any zooming to go on during a medium shot because it simply distracts from the action.

- ✔ **A close-up.** A close-up shows something particular that continues to tell the story, such as a small object or a person's reaction during dialog. The number of close-ups you use will vary depending on the meaning you're trying to convey. You can sometimes zoom while in close-up, but usually only to emphasize an action. For example, you might zoom in slightly on a sweating interview subject as he makes the fatal admission or zoom away from your on-air narrator as the story is ending. Otherwise, keep the focal length locked up and just shoot the action with a steady hand (or better yet, a tripod).

See shots.mov in the Chapter 2 folder on the *iMovie 2 For Dummies* CD-ROM for examples of the different types of shots.

The point, then, is to avoid zooming too much *during* each individual shot. Instead, shoot your establishing shot and hold steady for a while. Then change the focal length (zoom in) to a medium shot and hold that one. Now, zoom in on a close-up and hold it. Zoom back to a medium shot and hold that.

In most cases, you also want to move the camera to change angles on your subject so that your establishing, medium, and close-up shots all have a slightly different look at your subject. For instance, you could start with a wide, establishing shot from behind your family walking into Times Square. Then get a medium shot from the side of them as they walk past stores. Finally, end with a straight-on close-up from in front of your daughter as she spots something interesting at a sidewalk vendor's stall.

How would you get all these shots? Ideally, you would get one shot, pause the camera, move it, change the focal length, get the next shot, pause the camera, move it, and so on. In practice, this can be tough to do if you're shooting vacation footage. In that case, you should simply make sure you're holding each shot — establishing, medium, and close-up — long enough before you begin zooming and finding a new angle. Then, in iMovie, you can edit out all the zooms and movements while having enough steady footage of each shot to build your edited video nicely.

Performing the zoom

Get to know your camera's zoom controls intimately. How you use them can make the difference between effective zooms and those that aren't as effective, especially if you want your zoom to end up in the final, edited video. (If you're zooming just to get to a different focal length, don't worry about how smoothly you press the buttons, as long as you have enough steady footage for each different shot between zooms.)

Zoom smoothly. Avoid zooming too quickly (unless you're making a music video or following a flying saucer through the sky) and try not to jostle or tilt the camera while zooming. Watching stories on a news program such as *20/20* or the evening national news will give you a good idea of how quickly you should zoom the camera in different circumstances. Most likely, smooth zooming simply means getting used to the controls of your camera. Remember that the more you zoom, the more a small movement of the camera will look like an earthquake to the viewer. If you have some serious zoom action going, put your camcorder on a tripod.

Second, plan your zoom shots before you record them. Sometimes, as you're zooming, you realize that you don't have the subject framed correctly. When you move the camera to correct this oversight, the jagged movement doesn't look great in the final product. Here's a simple trick: If you can, zoom in to the subject (or some landmark) *first,* before you record, and then zoom back out. Now you know that you can press Record and zoom in with the shot well composed.

Many cameras include a wireless remote controller that may, at first glance, seem completely useless. But it can be helpful for smooth zooming, especially if you're working with the camera on a tripod. Using the remote, you can zoom the camera without touching it, ensuring that the zoom movement is as smooth as possible. That means you can even zoom in and out if you're filming yourself!

One more bit of advice: Avoid zooming the camera out to frame your subject, especially if you're in a close-up. Such a corrective zoom is like holding up a sign saying, "Whoops, I made a mistake here!" After you've zoomed in close, a smooth tilt or pan of the camera to get the person properly in frame will almost always look better than "searching" with a zoom movement.

Finally, if your camera has a digital zoom feature, I recommend that you turn it off. Digital zoom uses computer algorithms to go beyond the lens' physical capabilities for zoom. The numbers can be impressive — 320x, for instance, as opposed to 10x or 16x optical zoom — but the results aren't impressive. Most digital zooms look like spy camera footage at best. Unless you're trying to make the footage look like a shaking picture taken from the scope of an assassin's rifle, avoid using digital zoom. If you turn it off by default, you won't accidentally spill over into digital mode when you're pressing the zoom button.

Panning and Tilting

Obviously, you're going to need to move the camera sometimes. When you do, it should be a deliberate movement with a specific purpose. You may be surprised at how deliberate that purpose can be.

Getting the pan

Panning the camera means moving it left and right in a single plane. You can most easily accomplish this with a tripod, although you can also use two steady hands for a smooth pan. A pan is generally used for one of two reasons: to take a panoramic shot of a landscape or to follow action moving from one side of the camera's frame to another.

If you're holding the camera (instead of having it on a tripod), the trick to getting a good pan is to avoid moving your feet. How? Start with your feet planted in the middle of your shot, and turn your waist to the left or the right until you reach the starting position of your pan. Now, begin recording and hold a few seconds. If you're shooting a landscape, begin to smoothly pan across it. When you reach the end of the pan, wait a few seconds before pausing the camera.

To follow action with a pan, you perform it the same way but do your best to keep the subject framed at about the same point within the viewfinder. For instance, if the subject is walking from your right to your left, keep him or her framed in the right one-third of the shot (see Figure 2-3). Then follow the action until you reach the other limit of your ability to pan, and hold the shot. If your subject walks off the other side of the frame, that's fine — it will work well for your next angle.

While panning, avoid doing other things with the camera, such as tilting it or zooming in and out. If you'd like a zoom to be part of the shot, wait until you've stopped the pan and then begin the zoom movement. Two movements at once may distract your audience, but flowing nicely from one movement to the next will have them hiring you to shoot their kids' little league games.

Figure 2-3:
During an action pan, follow the action with your subject in about the same place in the frame.

Knowing when to tilt

Tilting the camera (moving it up and down relative to your subject) is another movement you'll do less than you may think. After you have the camera placed correctly for a medium shot, for instance, moving the camera up and down is rarely useful. One instance where it can be used to good effect is to show extreme size — for instance, to tilt up from a low angle to show how huge a professional wrestler, a politician, or a city building is. (Tilting is also used frequently for shooting models in beer commercials or on fashion runways.) If you decide to tilt, use a smooth motion and keep the subject nicely framed. When you reach the end of the tilt, hold the shot for a few seconds before performing any zoom or other movements.

When Good Footage Goes Bad

It sounds like a bad Fox TV special, but "When Good Footage Goes Bad" is actually something to watch out for when you're out there in the real world, shooting with your DV camcorder. After you've become familiar with using your camera for better composition, you'll also want to keep in mind some tips that will help you when you move your video footage to iMovie. Nothing is more frustrating than getting a well-composed shot, only to find out that you cut the scene too early, talked over important dialog, or otherwise messed things up. (Okay, maybe it would be more frustrating if you accidentally fell over the huge waterfall while backing up, trying to get that perfect vacation shot.)

Here are some tips to help avoid getting bad footage from good composition. Note that most of the tips follow right along with the classic commands barked by a director on a Hollywood movie set (or even the set of a cheesy cable TV show, as I can personally attest). Anyone can use Quiet! Action! and Cut!, even if you're only thinking them to yourself:

✔ **Avoid extra noise.** When you're getting ready to shoot your video, let people around you know that they need to be quiet, if appropriate. How? Yell "Quiet on the set," of course! (You might not tell your family to pipe down during vacation footage, but if you're on a set for a commercial or fiction project, you're the director, so you're in charge.) "Quiet on the set" also means "quiet behind the camcorder" — think about how you breathe, talk, and mutter and how carefully you handle the camera while shooting to avoid making unnecessary noise.

Using extension cables and external microphones, as discussed in Chapter 1, places the audio recording closer to your subjects, leaving you free to make a little more noise back near the camera.

✔ **Start recording early.** If you're filming with actors or directing your subjects, calling "Action" tells them to begin performing. However, you should actually start recording a few seconds *before* the action starts. This is called getting an *in handle,* which gives you a little extra footage on the tape to play with when you're editing later in iMovie. Then, everyone in the scene should count to three (silently) after hearing "Action" before doing anything because it makes it easier to edit out the "Action!" statement when the video clip gets into iMovie. (You can also point to your actors or count down with your fingers to silently tell your actors when to start acting. On the set of my TV show, the control-room director would start the tape, and then a floor director would say "5, 4, 3, 2, 1" and point at us to signal "Action!")

✔ **Stop recording late.** You should wait a few seconds after the action in a scene has taken place to yell, "Cut!" More importantly (especially if it's not the right time or place to yell, such as during a wedding) you should wait a few seconds before pressing the Pause button on your camcorder. This gives you an *out handle,* which makes it easier, once again, to edit in iMovie. If you press Pause immediately after the action stops, you may find that you didn't quite get enough footage for a clean transition when you're editing in iMovie.

In general, the goal is to get a little more material than you'll need in the final movie (sometimes called "shooting fat"). With in handles and out handles, you'll be freer to make cut and transition decisions in iMovie because you'll have a little extra footage to work with.

Professionals also tend to record a few minutes worth of extra footage at every filming location, just pointing the camera around, getting slow pans of the area, extra establishing or cutaway shots, and whatever else makes sense. You can then use this footage and sound to edit into other scenes, to replace unwanted noises (such as a low-flying plane), or anything else that may detract from an otherwise good scene. Having that extra filler material can help make the editing process easier.

Going Manual with Your Camcorder

You probably want me to regurgitate your camera's manual about as much as I'd like to write such rabble. We all know that such things are no fun to read; if they were fun, you'd probably know how to watch one channel on cable while another channel was taping on the VCR. None of us know how to do this. (Or, at least, the number of people who do know is statistically insignificant enough that I can get the word *none* past our legal department.)

Instead, I focus on some of the basic operations that every camera features. Then you can check out your camera's manual on your own to see how you perform these steps with your camcorder.

Automatic versus manual mode

Any DV camcorder has an automatic mode that handles the essentials while you're shooting. The camera takes care of focus, aperture size, shutter speed, and color correction. One of the first things to know about your camcorder, especially if you won't always be shooting under optimal conditions, is how to turn automatic mode on and off.

Automatic mode is best for two different scenarios: when you're taking typical tourist video under very good conditions (outdoor lighting) and when you're shooting action that changes very quickly — so quickly that you can't keep up with it manually. Otherwise, you may find it useful to work in either full manual mode or with at least some elements of your camera operation, such as focus and aperture settings, in a manual mode. After you conquer a few of these manual modes, you may not want to go back to automatic settings.

Putting things in focus

One of the first settings you should consider using in manual mode is your camcorder's focus. Like any automatic focus, the focus built into camcorders is good but not great. If you're running along with the camera or shooting action that's beyond your control, auto focus can be good enough to get the shots. But if you'd like the best results possible, you should switch your camera to a manual mode and focus images yourself. That way, you'll avoid the "focus hunt" that happens with some camcorders, especially when conditions are dark or overcast or you're far away from the subject.

Focus on your subject

Manual focus enables you to determine which elements will be the focal point of your composition, even if the subject isn't centered in the frame. Because a camcorder's auto focus generally seeks something in the center of the frame to focus on, manual focus can be important for keeping a frame in focus even if your subject isn't in the center of the screen. One way to quickly get that focus is to aim at your subject, auto focus on him or her, and then switch to manual. Now the camera won't seek other distances or try to focus on closer or more distant objects while you're moving the camera.

You can use manual focus for a few other techniques as well. For example, one problem you may encounter is a camcorder that "hunts" for focus when you're zooming in on a subject. There's a trick to correcting this: Begin by zooming all the way in on the subject and manually focusing the camera. Now, turn off auto focus to "lock in" that focal point and back the zoom out to wide angle. Your subject should still be in focus (or in some cases, a touch fuzzy, but that could add to the effect). When you begin recording, slowly zoom back in on the subject. When you reach the end of your zoom, you're in perfect focus with no "hunting."

The zoomfocus.mov QuickTime movie in the Chapter 2 folder on the CD shows this zoom-and-focus technique in action.

Depth of field

One of the main reasons for using manual focus is to create a sense of *depth of field,* or a situation in which objects at different distances are in different states of focus. One of the differentiators (to the human eye) between film and video is the fact that video tends to have a large (or wide) depth of field, meaning a wide range of distances can be in focus at once. If you use a wide-angle zoom setting (the least amount of zoom possible) and shoot a large area, you'll notice that most of the picture is in focus.

Sit down and watch a rented movie, however, and you'll see that film has a relatively shallow depth of field — when the subject is in focus, items that appear in the foreground or background are out of focus. This is used often in the visual storytelling of a film, with the shallow depth of field useful for making the audience's eyes zoom in on the subject that you want them to pay attention to.

If you *happen* to have access to a TV, turn it on and look for an episode of any of the three most recent *Star Trek* series. (I choose *Star Trek* because most likely at least one episode is on at any given moment in any part of the world.) Wait for a scene that occurs on the bridge of the ship. Note how the focus of the camera is used to move your attention from one character to another. That's a shallow depth of field.

A combination of zooming and manual focus can make some of those same effects happen with video. Mount your camera on a tripod and move it farther away from your subject than you would for a standard shot. This is true whether it's a medium shot or a close-up (although close-ups work better). Next, zoom in to frame the picture. (You can also open the lens aperture a bit, as discussed in the next section.) Focus on the subject using manual focus — this looks particularly good if you've composed the shot using the "off-center" rule. You'll see a difference in your depth of field, as shown in Figures 2-4 and 2-5.

Figure 2-4:
This shot has a wide depth of field — elements at various distances are in focus.

Figure 2-5:
With a shallow depth of field, background elements are fuzzier.

Although depth of field sounds cool, but you shouldn't obsess over it, especially for non-fiction video. Often it's more important to get the camera close to your subject (for good audio recording) than it is to worry about all these settings. But, it's a fun effect to play with..

Setting the exposure

Another manual setting you can dig into is *aperture size,* or iris setting, which enables you to determine how much light enters the lens. Like your eye, a camera lens is designed with an iris or aperture that you can open or shut to allow in more or less light, respectively. The amount of light you let in depends on the lighting conditions you're working in: The less light there is, the more light you should let in through the iris. Coupled with shutter speed, aperture size determines the *exposure* of your shot.

Many DV camcorders have two levels of automation for exposure: an automatic setting and a sort of semi-automatic setting. At automatic, the camera is completely free to determine the exposure for the shot. At semi-automatic settings, you generally give the camera a vague indication of the conditions — such as Sports, Low Light, Sand & Snow — allowing the camera a range of automatic settings but giving it a better idea of problem areas.

Finally, a fully manual exposure setting allows you to choose an *f-stop* number from 16 (sometimes 11) to 1.6 (varies according to the camera). The larger number is a small aperture (iris is almost completely closed), and the smaller number is a large aperture (iris is completely open). Choosing your own aperture setting takes some practice, but might be useful if you're shooting in oddly lit conditions, against a very bright background, or very active or very still scenes. Also, opening the iris (setting a small f-stop number) can contribute to a shallow depth of field.

Check your camcorder for a *zebra* feature, which you can use to determine which parts of the framed shot are currently overexposed. (They show up in the viewfinder with a zebra-stripe pattern.) If you see the zebra effect, you should choose a smaller aperture setting, or a faster shutter speed setting, or both to correct the overexposure.

Setting white-balance

White-balancing is the process of telling the camera what color to use as a reference for pure white. Set white-balance any time you change the lighting in which the camera is operating; the process gives the camera a color reference for the current lighting.

Camcorders can do an adequate job of white-balancing automatically, but automatic white-balancing is best in situations where the lighting will change — when you're moving from inside to outside, for instance. If you have the camera fixed in one spot for filming (such as for an interview in the subject's office), you should set up your lights for the shot and then manually white-balance the camera.

To white-balance manually, you hold up a white card or piece of paper and then zoom the camera in so that the white object fills the frame. Then set the manual white-balance control on the camera. Zoom back out and your camera is balanced to a pure white under the current lighting conditions, meaning you'll get good color for filming.

Choosing a shutter speed

Your final manual setting is the shutter speed. Like a still camera, *shutter speed* for a camcorder is measured in fractions, suggesting what percentage of a second each frame is exposed. A video camera's shutter speed can affect the perception of motion for your audience.

Standard shutter speed is 1/60, which means each frame is exposed for one sixtieth of a second. Under normal, good light conditions, this is the right setting. If you'll be shooting fast motion, you may want to increase the shutter speed slightly (1/250 or so) to keep the action from blurring. In lower light situations or when you want to blur fast motion (for a streaking effect that's great for filming a lighted highway at night), select a lower shutter speed if your camera supports it.

Chapter 3

Starting iMovie and Creating a Project

In This Chapter

▶ Finding and starting iMovie

▶ Working with iMovie

▶ Connecting a camera, monitor, or VCR for external monitoring

*R*eady to edit? After you have shot some good footage with your camera (as discussed in Chapter 2), you're ready to start iMovie, get that footage into the program, and begin the process of piecing together your masterpiece.

In this chapter, you take a look at starting iMovie and find out how to name and save your project. You also take an up-front look at iMovie, including a quick glance at the interface and some of iMovie's housekeeping commands. Then, you see how to hook up your camera to your Mac as well as how to use iMovie with an external TV monitor and how to connect your camera to a VHS deck for recording your edited movies to tape.

Getting Started with iMovie

The first step in working with iMovie is to find it. If iMovie was pre-installed on your Mac, you'll likely find it in the Applications folder on your hard disk, inside the iMovie folder. If you don't see the iMovie folder, you may have installed it elsewhere on your hard disk. Look on the main level of your hard disk for the iMovie folder or use the Sherlock application to search for iMovie.

Locating iMovie and checking the version

After you've located and opened the iMovie folder, you see the iMovie icon, which you can double-click to launch the application. Actually, what you're seeing is an *alias* that launches the actual iMovie application, which is located in the iMovie subfolder (see Figure 3-1). An alias isn't the application itself, but sort of an empty icon that simply points to the actual application. Still, double-clicking the alias is the same as double-clicking the application's icon.

iMovie alias

Figure 3-1:
Double-click
the iMovie
icon to
launch the
program.

Actual iMovie application is in this folder

Before you double-click the application, you may want to ensure that you have the latest version. So far, Apple has had two major versions (iMovie 1.0 and iMovie 2), along with some minor revisions (for example, iMovie 1.0.2 and iMovie 2.0.1). To see which version of iMovie you have, you need to dig into that iMovie subfolder (shown back in Figure 3-1) and locate the original iMovie application icon. (It is labeled iMovie, without the *italics*.) Now:

1. **Click the iMovie application icon once to select it.**

2. **Choose File⇨Get Info⇨General Information.**

   A window appears that looks similar to Figure 3-2.

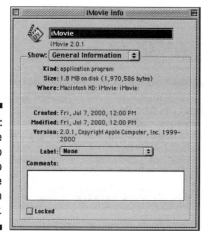

Figure 3-2:
Check the
iMovie Info
window to
find the
version
number.

3. Look toward the top of the window for the version number.

Toward the top of the window, you should see small print that says something like *iMovie 2.0.1*. This indicates the version number of iMovie that you have. If you see iMovie 1.0 or iMovie 1.0.2, you don't have iMovie 2 (or iMovie 2 is installed elsewhere on your Mac). If you don't have iMovie 2, you may need to buy it; see the "Upgrading to iMovie 2" section later in this chapter.

Checking for newer versions

If you do have iMovie 2, you may still need to update it to get the latest features and fixes. The quickest way to find out whether you need to update the program is to note your current version number (for example, iMovie 2.0.1) and then launch your Web browser and visit the site www.apple.com/imovie/. Look closely on the page for indications of a newer version of iMovie. If one is available, click that link to download the newer version's updater and follow the on-screen instructions.

Upgrading to iMovie 2

If you don't already have iMovie 2, you may need to buy it from Apple. As of this writing, iMovie 2 is available for downloading only from Apple's Web site. You can head to the Apple Store at store.apple.com and follow the links that allow you to download iMovie. Remember, you have to pay about $50 and then download a file that's more than 14MB; with a typical 56 Kbps modem, downloading can take an hour or longer.

After you download iMovie 2, you'll see an icon called iMovie.smi, which is a special kind of file called a *disk image*. When you double-click the file, it places a new icon on the desktop, which looks like a disk and is also called iMovie (see Figure 3-3). Double-click that icon and a new window appears that shows you the contents of the mounted disk image. There, you'll see the Install iMovie icon. Double-click that and you launch the iMovie installer.

Figure 3-3:
The
mounted
disk icon
(above) and
iMovie.smi
disk image
file (below).

Now that you've launched the iMovie 2 installer, here's the process for finishing the installation:

1. **On the welcome screen showing the iMovie logo, click the Continue button to move on to the installer.**

   The license agreement appears.

2. **Read the license agreement (especially that line in Paragraph 10 that says Steve Jobs can personally confiscate your favorite pet at any moment) and then click the Accept button.**

   If you click Decline, the installer quits; you can also use the pop-up menu in the lower-left corner to change languages if you're not comfortable with the current one or if you just want to practice your reading skills.

   Assuming you've accepted the licensing agreement, you see the Read Me file. This file includes late-breaking information about iMovie, including its system requirements, compatibility issues, and other interesting tidbits.

3. **Read the Read Me file, beginning to end, and then click Continue.**

   Finally, you're ready to install.

4. **If you prefer to install iMovie in a different location than the default location — which is the main level of your hard disk in a folder called, creatively enough, iMovie — do the following:**

   a. **Select the Install Location menu and then choose Select Folder from that menu.**

      An Open dialog box appears, enabling you to choose the folder where you want iMovie installed (see Figure 3-4).

   b. **Open that folder and click the Select button.**

      Now you're back at the Installer window, where you can click Install to begin the installation process.

5. **Click the Install button to begin the installation process.**

Figure 3-4: Select a folder where you'd like to install the iMovie folder.

Launching iMovie

After you have iMovie located, installed, or updated, you're ready to launch the application. Well, you're almost ready. Before you work with iMovie, you may want to change your Mac's *screen resolution*. The higher the resolution, the easier it is to work with iMovie.

Most iMacs and iBooks and many desktop Macs run at about 800x600 resolution, which is comfortable for day-to-day viewing. iMovie, however, runs more effectively at 1024x768 resolution (or higher, if your monitor supports higher resolutions comfortably), which makes everything on the screen appear a bit smaller but allows more information (and more clips) on the screen at once.

If you'd like to change your screen resolution, choose Apple menu➪ Control Panels➪Monitors. In the Monitors control panel, select 1024x768 from the Resolution menu. (If you don't see this option, your Mac doesn't support 1024x768 resolution, as is the case with iBook models.) Your screen should change immediately to the higher resolution.

Note that iMovie 2 does okay at 800x600 resolution because it offers a scrolling Shelf where clips are stored. So, if you don't like 1024x768 resolution, you don't have to use it; set your Mac back to 800x600 and compute away. If you do use the higher resolution, you'll have a longer Timeline and be able to see more clips at once in the Shelf (see Figures 3-5 and 3-6).

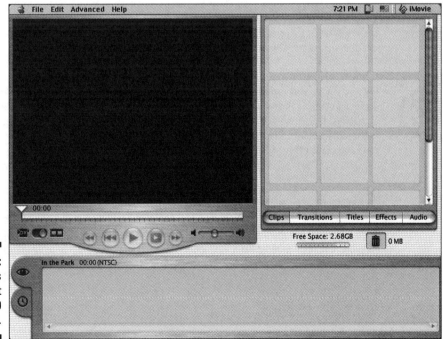

Figure 3-5:
Here's
iMovie 2 at
800x600
resolution.

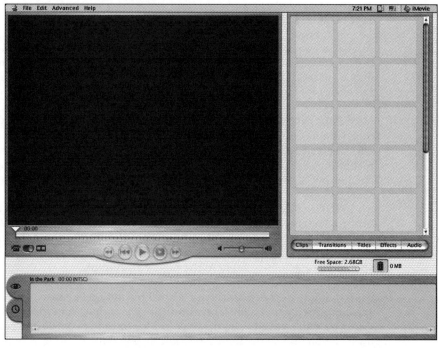

Figure 3-6:
At 1024x768
resolution,
iMovie 2
can display
more clips
and a longer
Timeline.

After you decide on the resolution, you're ready to launch iMovie. Double-click the iMovie icon, and iMovie starts, with the iMovie interface in the background. If you've opened iMovie before and are editing a project, the most recent project appears. Otherwise, you see a dialog box that enables you to create a new project or open an existing one.

Want to automatically change screen resolutions? Simply leave your resolution the way it is and launch iMovie. iMovie asks whether you'd like it to change the screen resolution for you. If you would, click Change Resolution. This changes your resolution to 1024x768 and the launching process finishes. After using iMovie, however, you need to switch back to 800x600 manually, if desired. You can also switch resolutions while iMovie is running; it resizes itself accordingly.

Starting a project

If you've launched iMovie and weren't previously working on a project, you see the Project dialog box, complete with the cutesy little animated iMovie slate and three buttons: New Project, Open Project, and Quit.

If you've previously been working in a project that you'd like to return to, click Open Project. An Open dialog box appears, enabling you to load an existing project (see Figure 3-7). Double-click the folder for the project you'd like to open; you see the project file and a Media folder. Select the project file (by clicking it once) and then click Open to begin editing it. (You can also double-click the project file to open it more quickly.)

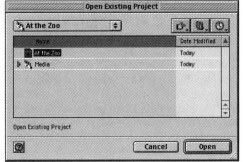

Figure 3-7:
Select an existing project and click Open.

If you'd like to start a new project, click the New Project button. This opens the Create New Project window, where you give your project a name and select the location on your hard disk where you want to store it. This works like most Save dialog boxes on the Mac — just find the location where you want to store the new project (in your Documents folder, for instance) and then click once in the Name entry box and type a name for the project. Now, click Create (see Figure 3-8).

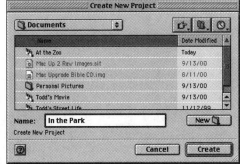

Figure 3-8:
Creating a project.

After you've clicked Create, you are presented with a blank iMovie interface, ready for you to connect your camera and start importing clips.

Getting to Know iMovie

After you have iMovie up and running, it's a good time to get acquainted with the elements of the interface, learn how to work with iMovie help, and figure out a few basic housekeeping commands.

Checking out iMovie's interface

The iMovie interface is fairly straightforward but also deceptively powerful. When you first launch iMovie, you're greeted with a single, large window that scales automatically to the size of your Mac's screen, obscuring everything else behind it. The first thing you may notice is that you're not working in a document window such as those in, say, a word processing or spreadsheet program. Instead, iMovie takes over the whole screen with one large window, which is divided into different sections, or *panes* (to keep the window metaphor rolling). In each pane, you accomplish different tasks, such as viewing and editing parts of your movie, adding special effects, and arranging the parts of your movie. Figure 3-9 shows the interface in detail.

Monitor: Watch and edit clips   Shelf: Store clips and perform effects

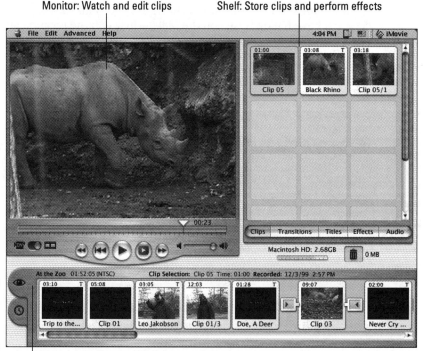

Figure 3-9:
The iMovie
interface.

Clip Viewer: Arrange clips to build a movie

If you'd like a quick start with iMovie (that is, you don't feel like reading any more and you just want to play), check out the following first to see the purpose of each pane:

- ✔ **The Monitor.** The Monitor is where you view clips or the entire movie. You also edit clips in the Monitor, selecting the portions you want to remove from the clip using the controls beneath the monitor screen. You can also switch the Monitor Camera mode and use it to import video from the camcorder, send video to the camcorder, and otherwise control it for playback, fast forward, reverse, and so on.

- ✔ **The Shelf.** When you're importing clips from your camcorder, each individual clip shows up on the Shelf, where you can keep the clips until you're ready to edit them in the Monitor and then transfer them to the Clip Viewer and position them in your movie. The Shelf is amorphous; buttons at the bottom of the pane change the Shelf to show controls for creating transitions, titles, effects, and audio editing tools.

- ✔ **The Clip Viewer.** Down at the bottom of the screen is a filmstrip-like interface where you piece together the clips in your movie, adding transitions and effects between them. The Clip Viewer is the most obvious cut-and-paste pane in iMovie and also where a lot of the power lies. You can change the Clip Viewer to the Timeline by clicking the tab with a Clock icon on it. You use the Timeline to view all portions of your movie, including video, audio, narration, and music (see Figure 3-10).

Figure 3-10:
Use the
Timeline to
edit
individual
sounds,
music, and
narration.

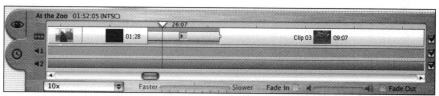

Checking hard drive space

Before you get too busy connecting your camera and bringing in clips to edit, you should take a look at the Free Space gauge on the iMovie screen. This gauge tells you how much hard disk space you have available for movie clips (see Figure 3-11). According to Apple, you need at least 200MB of storage space available to launch and work with iMovie, but I recommend you have a minimum of 1GB of storage space. Remember, five minutes of DV video takes up 1GB of space. The more space you have, the more clips you can import and the longer your final movie can be.

Figure 3-11:
The Free
Space
gauge tells
you whether
you have
enough
space for
editing.

What do you do if you don't have enough space? You may need to return to the Finder and delete unwanted documents, folders, or applications that are taking up space on your hard disk. (If you're deleting documents, don't forget to back them up to a removable disk if you think you may want them later.) You may also need to clean up your iMovie projects' trash files, if they have any. (See Chapter 5 for details on managing an individual project's trash files.)

Getting help

iMovie comes with some good, useful help files that you can use to walk through the basics of using the program. You may find two different levels of help useful:

✔ **Help⇨Show Balloons.** Turn on this command and iMovie tells you the name and function of different parts of the interface as you point at them with the mouse. Unlike some Mac applications, iMovie has a full set of balloon help entries, which is great when you can't figure out what some interface thingy does.

✔ **Help⇨iMovie Help.** This command displays the iMovie Help interface, where you can read different topical discussions of iMovie's features and capabilities (see Figure 3-12). iMovie Help is similar to a Web browser — click an underlined topic to read a document about that topic. To return to the main menu, click the Back button or any Table of Contents link.

Saving a project

As you work on your movie, you should invoke the Save command frequently to save any changes you've made. Essentially, you're guarding against iMovie (or the Mac OS) *crashing*, or encountering an error that causes the application to quit or your Mac to freeze. You can access the save command at File⇨Save. Or press ⌘+S to quickly save your project without using the File menu.

Back button

Figure 3-12:
Using
iMovie Help
is similar to
using a Web
browser.

Quitting iMovie

Quitting iMovie is easy, with no preparation to go through if you'd like to shut down iMovie and work with other applications. You could instead switch to a different application using the Finder's Application menu, if you like, but remember that iMovie requires a lot of RAM while running. If you only have 64MB of RAM, you may find it impossible to open any other application without first quitting iMovie.

To quit iMovie, choose File⇨Quit from the menu or press ⌘+Q. If you have any unsaved changes in your project, you are asked whether you'd like to save those changes. If you would, click Save; if you don't need to save the changes, click Don't Save. (Clicking Cancel returns you to iMovie without quitting.)

Making Connections

After you have iMovie up and running, the next step is to connect your camcorder to your Mac so that iMovie can communicate with it. Then you can optionally connect the camera to an external TV set for monitoring iMovie, to a VCR for recording the finish project from the camera, or to both a TV and a VCR.

Connecting the camera

The first step is a fairly easy one: connecting the camcorder to your Mac. All you need is a FireWire cable and an open FireWire port on both the Mac and the camcorder.

Actually, the cable can be a *little* tricky. For connecting a camcorder, you need a 4-pin connector, which isn't what the typical FireWire peripheral (such as a scanner or an external hard disk) uses. Instead, you need a special 4-pin-to-6-pin FireWire cable used specifically for connecting camcorders to computers. In most cases, this cable comes with your camera.

Whenever you are connecting your camcorder to your Mac, you should probably also connect the camcorder to its AC adapter and plug the adapter into a power socket. That way, you won't drain the battery while you're working with your camcorder and iMovie.

To connect your camera to the Mac:

1. **Connect the 4-pin (square-shaped) cable connector to the DV, FireWire, IEEE-1394, or iLink port on the camcorder.**

   Depending on the manufacturer, the port could have any of those names as its label.

2. **Plug the 6-pin (wider and flatter) connector into the Mac's FireWire port (see Figure 3-13).**

3. **Turn on the camcorder, preferably to a VCR, VTR, or Playback mode instead of to a filming mode.**

   Most camcorders have a power switch on the back that lets you set the mode to one of several types of shooting modes or the Playback (sometimes called VCR or VTR) mode.

4. **On the iMovie screen, locate the small slider control underneath the Monitor (labeled in Figure 3-9).**

   You use the slider to put the Monitor window in Camera mode or Edit mode — you use Camera mode to control the camcorder.

5. **Drag the Camera/Edit Mode switch so that it's pointing to the Camera mode (DV) icon.**

   The Monitor window turns blue and you should see the *Camera Connected* message.

6. **If you don't see this message, do the following:**

   a. **Check your FireWire connections and make sure the camera is turned on to Playback mode.**

   Some camcorders turn themselves off after a few minutes, so make sure that hasn't happened.

b. **If the connection still isn't working, check your FireWire software implementation on the Mac (fire up your Web browser and visit** www.apple.com/firewire/ **to make sure you've installed the latest FireWire software).**

c. **If the problem isn't with the FireWire software, it could be the camera. Head to** www.apple.com/imovie/ **and look up the compatible cameras to make sure yours in on the approved list.**

Connecting an external TV monitor

With your camera hooked up, you may want to complete the connection by hooking up a TV monitor to your camcorder. Using iMovie 2, you can actually preview your movies on your camcorder as you're editing them. But it gets even better. With a TV connected to the camcorder, you can preview the video on the TV. This makes it *much* easier to see what your final movie will look like.

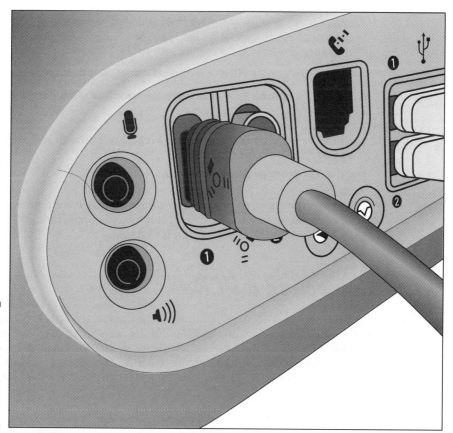

Figure 3-13:
The 6-pin connector plugged into the FireWire port on an iMac DV.

To connect your camcorder to your TV without complicated adapters, you need a TV with *composite* (RCA-style shielded plug) connectors for both the video-in and audio-in connections. Most DV camcorders have a special AV adapter cable that has one plug on the camcorder side, and three composite connectors (red and white for audio and yellow for video) on the other side of the cable. If your TV supports those composite connectors, you'll have no problems.

For *best* results, though, the TV should have an *S-video connector* for video in. You still use the special AV adapter, but you ignore the yellow composite connector. Instead, you use an S-video cable between the camcorder and TV and then use just the red and white composite connectors for the audio connection. (TVs with S-video are a bit more rare than those that offer composite connectors.)

To connect the TV to your camcorder, follow these steps:

1. **Using the camcorder's AV-out port(s), connect the camcorder to the TV's composite-in (red and white for audio and yellow for video) connectors.**

   If your TV has an S-video input, connect an S-video cable between the camcorder's S-video-out port and the TV's S-video-in port. Then connect the camcorder's special AV cable to the camera's AV port. Now, connect the red and white audio connectors to the TV's audio-in ports.

2. **Tune the TV to its video monitor channel, if it has one.**

3. **In iMovie, choose Edit⇨Preferences and then click the Advanced tab.**

   The iMovie Preferences dialog box appears.

4. **Click the check box next to the Video Play Through to Camera option to turn that option on.**

5. **Click OK to dismiss the dialog box.**

Now, whenever you play back a clip in iMovie, you'll see it on the LCD display of your camcorder and on the TV monitor you've connected. This is a great way to get a fairly professional setup for editing.

Connecting a VCR

You can connect a VCR to your camcorder for taping the final version of your edited iMovie, or you can connect the VCR for monitoring playback in iMovie while the editing is in progress. I describe the first one in Chapter 14, which discusses outputting your final iMovie to a VCR. The second option, though, can be useful at any time. While you're editing, you can play back the raw, edited footage and record it using a VCR, if you like. That's great in organizational or corporate settings, where you need to show a quick draft of your project to get committee approval, for instance. (Although I'd hate to think of a movie edited by committee. Yikes.)

If you're an AV-savvy type, you may have already guessed that hooking up a VCR in this instance is pretty much the same as hooking up a TV:

1. **Using the camcorder's AV-out port(s), connect the camcorder to the VCR's RCA-style composite-in connectors.**

   If your camcorder has an S-video-out port and your VCR has an S-video-in port, connect those two ports with an S-video cable. The quality of the connection will be higher. Then connect the camcorder's special AV cable to the camcorder's AV port and connect the red and white RCA-style connectors to the audio-in ports on the VCR.

2. **Tune the VCR to its video monitor channel, if it has one.**

3. **In iMovie, choose Edit⇨Preferences and then click the Advanced tab.**

4. **Click the Video Play Through to Camera option to turn it on.**

5. **Click OK.**

   Now video is played through to your VCR.

If you like, you can record your work-in-progress to VHS tape. Also, if you hook up a TV monitor to your VCR, you can still play through and see the video full-screen on the TV (see Figure 3-14).

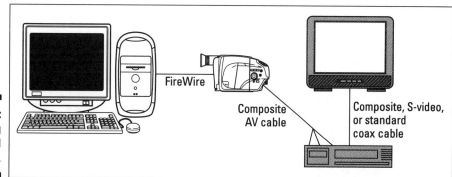

Figure 3-14:
Connecting
a VCR and
the TV.

FireWire

Composite
AV cable

Composite, S-video,
or standard
coax cable

Chapter 4

Importing Video

- -

In This Chapter

▶ Controlling your camcorder in iMovie

▶ Importing video automatically

▶ Importing video manually

▶ Managing your clips on the shelf

▶ Importing non-DV video files

- -

*A*fter you have your camcorder connected to your Mac and have launched iMovie, you're ready to start controlling the camera with iMovie and importing your video. You accomplish most of this using the comfortable, familiar controls found as part of iMovie's Monitor. Then, with a few clips in iMovie, you move over to the Shelf, where you can name the clips, move them, delete them, import them, and get prepped for editing.

In this chapter, we focus on getting video from your camcorder (and other sources) into iMovie and then working with the clips on the Shelf. In Part II, you work those clips from raw footage into dramatic art.

Controlling Your Camera

With your camcorder connected to your Mac (as discussed in Chapter 3), you can actually control the camera from iMovie. First, set the Monitor to Camera mode by clicking the left side of the Camera/Edit Mode switch or by dragging the little switch circle from the right to the left. Then, you can play back your taped video using the controls at the bottom of the Monitor window, as shown in Figure 4-1.

Figure 4-1:
Use the
VCR-like
controls at
the bottom
of the
Monitor
window to
control your
camcorder.

Rewind   Play Stop

Camera/Edit mode Pause   Fast Forward

If you've used a VCR in the past, these controls should be straightforward. (Note that the Stop button is actually redundant; you can simply click the Play button again to stop video that's playing or click the Fast Forward button again to stop video that's fast-forwarding.) These controls enable you to use the mouse to shuttle the camera to sections of your tape that you'd like to view or import. Consider the alternative: using a pinky finger's nail on the micro-controls for playing and stopping the video that a lot of these camcorders have. You'll find working with the mouse is a nice option.

You can, however, play, fast forward, pause, and stop using the camcorder's controls or even its remote control if you have one (and actually have fresh batteries for it). The exception is the Import button, which you must activate from within iMovie.

Importing Video

You can approach importing video from your camcorder into iMovie in two different ways, depending on how you've shot your video. The first way is to set iMovie to begin importing and then leave, get a coffee, play with the dog, and then return. The second way is to slave over the keyboard, importing each clip individually, turning the Import feature on and off as your video scrolls by.

Actually, that second option may not sound like as much fun, but it can be useful and is the more professional approach. You see why after this word from our local station.

As you're importing video, regardless of the method you're using, you should keep an eye on the Free Disk Space indicator. If you get close to empty on disk space, you may not be able to import any more video. And, if you use all your available disk space, it will affect your ability to work within iMovie and can cause problems with other applications. Also note that current versions of iMovie are limited to just under 2GB per clip file, so if you're importing a clip that's longer than about ten minutes, it will be split automatically into a new clip when it reaches 1.9GB.

One-button importing

One-button importing is no doubt the easiest way to import video into your project, and may be especially appropriate if you're bringing in a single, continuous clip that's only a few seconds or minutes long. Performing such an import is simple: Just position the tape at the point where you'd like to start importing video and then click the Import button. iMovie starts your camera and begins the Import process, creating a new clip in the Shelf and noting on that clip's icon the amount of time that's being stored in the clip (see Figure 4-2).

New clip shows amount of time being imported

Figure 4-2: Importing a single continuous clip.

As this process unfolds, you'll also notice that the amount of available hard disk space in the Free Space indicator begins diminishing rapidly. Remember, you only get about five minutes of video per gigabyte of storage space.

If you have a clip that's longer than a minute or two at most, you'll likely want to break it up into different clips. This is especially true if you have different scenes in your movie that you're going to piece together with transitions, titles, and effects. You may notice that iMovie is already dividing the clips for you.

While it's importing a continuous stream of video, iMovie can tell where, on the tape, you've switched from Record mode to Standby or Pause mode on your camera. With the correct preference set, iMovie creates a new clip every time it encounters a switch from Standby to Record mode. So, each time that you stopped filming and started again becomes a new clip.

iMovie works this way by default, so if your importing is being broken out by scene, you don't have to change the setting. If your clips *aren't* being broken out by scene, here's how to change that:

1. **Choose Edit⇨Preferences.**

   The Preferences dialog box appears.

2. **Select the Import tab if it isn't already selected.**

3. **Click the check box next to the option "Automatically start new clip at scene break."**

4. **Click OK at the bottom of the Preferences dialog box.**

Now as video is imported, every new scene you created while filming is placed in the Shelf as a new clip.

Importing manually

In professional videography — especially in fiction, news reporting, or even sometimes in documentary films — you'll often shoot the same scene more than once or shoot a lot more video than you plan to use. If you know this ahead of time, you can import less of it into iMovie at the outset, thus saving space on the Shelf as well as keeping the amount of hard disk space you use at a minimum.

Under such circumstances, it makes sense to import manually. Actually, this isn't *that* manual of a process (you won't have to break open the tape and sketch the images by hand), but you will make more active decisions about the location of the *in* and *out* points of each clip. And you'll do that with one of the most powerful tools ever attached to a computer: the spacebar.

Here's how it works:

1. **Rewind your video to a point that's a little before the segments you want to import.**

   This can be anywhere: Just make sure you give yourself a few seconds of lead time.

2. **In the Monitor, click the Play button.**

   The tape starts rolling.

3. **When you see the video that you want to begin importing into a clip, press the spacebar.**

   The Import button lights up, a new clip appears in the Shelf, and the time code for that clip begins to count up.

4. **When you reach the end of the desired clip, press the spacebar again.**

   The Import button darkens and iMovie stops importing video into the clip, but the video continues playing in the Monitor.

5. **Rinse and repeat.**

   Head back up to Step 3 for each subsequent clip that you want to capture. All you have to do is press the spacebar once to begin a new clip and then press it again to end that clip.

There are a couple of things to note about this process. First, it can get a little screwy if the "Automatically start new clip at scene break" option, discussed in the preceding section, is turned on. You should turn it off so that extra clips aren't created as you're importing.

Second, while you're getting your clips like this, you should endeavor to import handles on either side of the video that you actually want to use. *Handles,* which are a few extra seconds of video that you do away with in the editing process, act as a buffer to make sure you're getting *all* the video you need for a particular clip. Otherwise, if your clip starts too late or ends too early, you have to re-import it before you can add it to your iMovie.

So here's a sticky problem. If you're using the manual method, have you noticed that you *miss* the clips a lot? There you are with your finger hovering over the spacebar and then — bam-o — the scene starts and you're already too late to get a good handle. In fact, you've cut off the first part of your scene. Isn't that annoying? Can't you do anything about that? Why the heck did you pay good money for this book, anyway?

Calm down, calm down. The solution is simple, but you have to be willing to work for it. The trick is to know the time code.

Knowing time code and blackstriping

As you record, your camcorder usually keeps an accurate measure of where, on the tape, a particular scene was filmed. This is the *time code,* which is measured in hours, minutes, seconds, and frames, in the form 0:00:00:00. So, 0:01:55:26 (or 01:55:26) is 1 minute, 55 seconds, and 26 frames. (If you're editing NTSC video, 30 frames tick by for every second of video; for PAL video, it's 25 frames every second.)

This code is stored on the tape itself, so it's a lot more accurate than the little manual counter you may remember from the days spent endlessly dubbing songs from the radio to a cassette.

With a time code, you can do like the pros do and keep track of the time while you're filming. Professionals tend to keep a log of each clip they take, noting the *in* and *out* time for each segment that they shoot. (For instance, I know that I took a great shot of a polar bear that started at 00:55:26 and ended at 01:24:06. How do I know? I wrote it down when I took it.)

Now, manual importing is easy. Just keep a log of the in and out times for each clip you want and use the log to move to parts of the video that you'd like to import. The Monitor window shows the time code while the camera is stopped, fast forwarding, or rewinding (see Figure 4-3). And, if you have iMovie set up so that video plays through to your camcorder (or to a TV monitor, if one is connected), you'll see the time code on your LCD or TV monitor as well. (See Chapter 3 for more on hooking up external monitors.)

Figure 4-3:
The time code appears in the top-right corner of the Monitor window.

Unfortunately, there can be one teensy little problem with the time code: It isn't always right. In fact, it can be wrong a lot of the time, especially if you've stopped and started the camera often or recorded a segment, stopped the camera, fast forwarded slightly, and then recorded again. When something like this happens, the camera can't keep an accurate time code and may even start over at 0:00:00:00 every once in a while. This is called *broken* time code.

How do you deal with broken time code? The best way is to avoid it by *black-striping* your tapes ahead of time. You do this by sticking the tape in the camera, pressing Record, and forgetting about the camera for 30 minutes, an hour, or however long the tape is. You can even leave the lens cap on. (Record black or some other solid color for blackstriping, so that when you record over the tape, you won't be confused by two different images.) By blackstriping, you're having the camera write time code to every last bit of the tape inside the camera. It's almost like formatting a floppy disk before your computer can use it. Now, when you rewind the tape and record to it, you'll have a solid, unbroken time code for the entire tape.

If you've already recorded to the tape without blackstriping, the second option is to use the one-button import feature in iMovie with the "Automatically start new clip at scene break" option turned on in iMovie's Preferences dialog box (see the "One-button importing" section). Although the time code is broken, iMovie can import each scene into a separate clip.

Using the one-button approach may mean that you end up with a lot of clips you don't want. So, the third option is to correct the time code. You can do that one of two ways:

- ✔ You can import all the video from the tape into iMovie with the "Automatically start new clip at scene break" option turned off and then blackstripe the tape, arrange all the clips in the Clip Viewer in iMovie, and export the video right back to the tape continuously.

- ✔ You can connect two DV camcorders and *clone* one tape to another. (Connect a 4-pin-to-4-pin FireWire cable between the two cameras and push Play on one and Record on the other.) This is the easiest way to correct broken time code, but it requires two DV devices, which you may not have.

Now you can use the spacebar method for getting into and out of your best clips, as long as you know the code. Then you can move quickly to the next task, which is managing your clips within iMovie.

Managing Your Clips

After you have your clips imported, you're left with an unsightly mess of clips — just sitting there — on the Shelf. What's a director to do? First, you can do a few housekeeping chores.

Selecting clips

Select a clip on the Shelf and iMovie is automatically switched to Edit mode, which enables you to view the clip (instead of viewing your camera's tape) in the Monitor. The selected clip becomes highlighted on the Shelf (it turns yellow), which lets you know that it's now active. When you work the controls in the Monitor — Play, Rewind, Fast Forward — you are performing those commands on the clip. To select another clip, just click on it once on the Shelf.

You can select more than one clip by holding down the Shift key as you click each clip. Each, in turn, turns yellow, indicating that it's selected. Now you can drag the whole group around to different parts of the Shelf, to the Trash, or down into the Timeline.

Renaming clips

Although nothing could be more fun than watching the clips you've just imported (which is a good idea, just to make sure you did get all the footage you were planning to get), the first pragmatic thing you might consider doing is naming your clips. This will help immensely as you're editing because, unfortunately, the *poster frame,* or the first frame of the clip that appears as part of the clip icon, isn't always representative. Often, the poster frame is just a black image that doesn't tell you anything about the clip.

Renaming is easy:

1. **Click once on the *name* of the clip you want to rename and then leave the mouse pointer pointing at the name.**

   After less than a second, the name becomes highlighted.

2. **Click the mouse again.**

   An insertion point (cursor) appears.

3. **Delete the name "Clip 1" or whatever it is and type the name you'd like to give the clip (see Figure 4-4).**

4. **Press Return.**

   The new name is assigned to the clip.

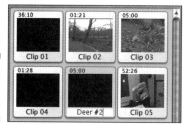

Figure 4-4:
Renaming
a clip.

Deleting clips

If you already know that you don't want a clip you've imported, you can simply drag it off the Shelf to the Trash icon. (You can also drag more than one clip to the Trash if you've selected more than one, as noted in the preceding section.) When you do, the clip is placed in the Trash, and the amount of space that clip takes up is noted next to the Trash icon. As you continue adding clips to the Trash, you see the amount of disk space continue to mount. This space hasn't been cleared off the hard disk yet, however, because you need to *empty* the Trash before that space is available again for importing more clips or for storage by other applications on your Mac.

First, though, I should note that you can't really dig into the Trash (like you can in the Finder) and retrieve a clip. The only way to get back a clip that you've trashed is to use the Edit⇨Undo command. iMovie supports multiple Undo commands (up to 99), so you'll be able to get the clip back on the Shelf even if you did something since dragging it to the Trash. Unfortunately, you also have to undo any tasks that took place *between* the time you dragged the clip to the Trash and the time you want it back, so this can be a mixed blessing. The bottom line: Drag a clip to the Trash only if you really mean to get rid of it.

Emptying the Trash

Note that emptying the Trash makes it impossible for you to use the Undo command and recover any other edits or changes you made up to this point.

Ready to empty the Trash? Choose File⇨Empty Trash from the menu. You see the Confirm dialog box, which asks whether you're sure you want to empty the trash. If you're willing, click OK. If not, click Cancel.

Because the Trash is an important part of recovering clips and portions of clips that you've edited (you start doing that in Chapter 5), think carefully before emptying it. Consider emptying the Trash only when you've reached major milestones and know that you won't need to recover changes. If you have enough disk space, you might consider not emptying the Trash until you're finished with your project completely.

Getting info on clips

iMovie has another command you can use with clips, although you'll probably use it only in specialized situations. Select a clip and choose File⇨Get Clip Info from the menu. The Clip Info window appears, as shown in Figure 4-5.

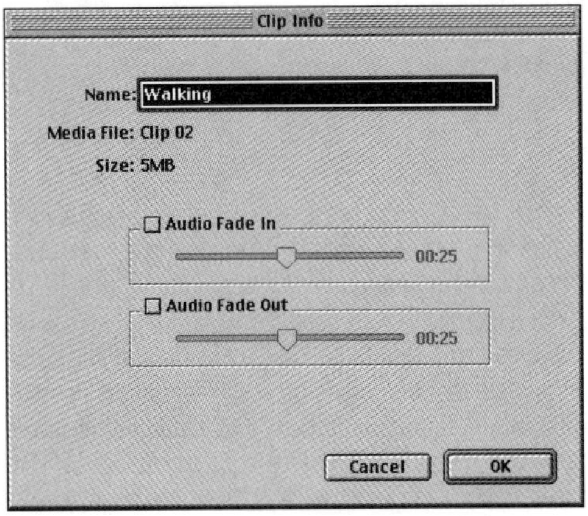

Figure 4-5:
The Clip Info
dialog box.

The Clip Info window tells you a few things about the file, including its current name, the actual name of the associated media file (which is stored on the hard disk), and the size of the clip in megabytes. As a bonus, you can use the Name entry box to quickly rename the clip. Just click once in the box, delete the current name, and type your new one. Press Return and the clip is renamed.

The Clip Info window is also useful for one other task: setting audio fade in and fade out for the clip. I cover this in detail in Chapter 8, but for now you may be interested to know that the Clip Info dialog box is the only way to set the length of time for a fade in or fade out.

Importing non-DV video

iMovie is designed to deal primarily with DV video, which is an actual file format, akin to the .DOC file format used for Microsoft Word documents or the .TIFF format used for graphics files. Although DV is great for dealing with direct-from-camcorder and direct-to-camcorder transactions, it's not as commonly used for other types of video, such as the video files you view on a Macintosh desktop using QuickTime Player. If you have that sort of video and want to get it into iMovie, you have to jump through some additional hoops.

The main hoop is getting a program that allows you to make the translations. Fortunately, Apple provides one pretty cheaply — QuickTime Pro. Using the same QuickTime software that's likely already installed on your Mac, you simply pay $29.95 (as of this writing) and enter a registration code in the QuickTime Settings control panel, as shown in Figure 4-6. You can access the QuickTime Settings control panel by opening the Apple menu and selecting Control Panels⇨QuickTime Settings in Mac OS 9.*x* and earlier or through the System Preferences application in Mac OS X.

Registering QuickTime Pro activates some of the high-end functions in QuickTime, including the capability to take a non-DV-formatted movie and translate it to a DV Stream, thus enabling you to use it in iMovie. You can find information and online ordering of the QuickTime Pro update at www.apple. com/quicktime/ or the Apple Store at www.apple.com/store/.

Figure 4-6:
Enter a
registration
code to
activate
QuickTime
Pro.

Knowing the format

Before you delve too deeply into the types of desktop movie formats, understanding a bit more about QuickTime would be helpful. QuickTime is a number of things, but at its most basic, it's simply a technology. When you install QuickTime on your Mac, QuickTime augments the Mac OS with the low-level capability to deal with time-based data, whether that data is a series of images, a series of digital sound samples, or a combination of the two.

Take a series of images and show them quickly enough and you have a digital movie. Take a series of sound samples and play them one right after another and you have an audio track. Add some sophisticated math and programming that no mere human could possibly understand and you have a technology that allows you to play back and translate these types of files.

After you install QuickTime (version 4.x or higher), you can pretty much forget about it — it's there as an extension to the Mac OS (in Mac OS 9 and earlier) or as a built-in part of the OS (in Mac OS X and later). What you're more interested in is QuickTime Player, which is the manifestation of QuickTime on your desktop.

QuickTime Player is more than a player, which also means it's poorly named. (Sorry . . . just stating the obvious.) QuickTime Player can not only play desktop movie files and audio files of varying formats, but also translate between them, especially if you've upgraded to QuickTime Pro.

After you have QuickTime Pro up and running, you'll be ready to translate from a number of desktop movie file formats to the DV Stream format, which you can then import to iMovie. Here's a quick look at the formats QuickTime Pro can work with:

- ✔ **QuickTime Movie.** This is the basic format that QuickTime is designed to deal with. These files are sometimes called Moov or QT files, mostly because they take a .Mov, .Moov, or .Qt filename extension when used on other computing platforms. (Mac OS 9.x doesn't really require these "dot something" filename extensions, but applications in Unix, Mac OS X, and Windows operating systems often do.) A QuickTime movie file doesn't have to contain images — it can contain just sound — but it's still called a movie.

- ✔ **MPEG.** The MPEG format (which, very uninterestingly, stands for Motion Pictures Experts Group) is another common format used particularly for Web-based and CD-ROM movies. If you come across an MPEG 1 movie, it can be loaded and viewed in QuickTime Player just as easily as a regular QuickTime file. You can then, just as easily, translate the file to DV Stream. (Note, however, that some types of MPEG 1 files enable you to import only the video portion.)

- ✔ **AVI.** AVI, which stands for Audio Video Interleave, is a common format for Microsoft Windows video applications, so you'll see it often on the Web and on CDs or other media that include video clips. Again, you can load it right into QuickTime and play it as if it were a QuickTime movie.

You'll find that movie files in any of these formats can be opened in QuickTime Player either by dragging and dropping the file onto the player or by launching QuickTime Player and choosing File⊃Open from the menu. If this doesn't work, you may need to choose File⊃Import and then select the file in the Import dialog box. Once selected, QuickTime translates the file into QuickTime format for playback.

What movies import well?

Although any of the previously mentioned files (QuickTime, MPEG 1, AVI) can be exported to DV Stream and then imported into iMovie, only high-quality files are going to be worth the effort. After all, a movie that has been saved for presentation on the Web is probably not full-screen, may be highly compressed (along with a significant loss in quality), and can have other problems, such as a less-than-ideal frame rate. (*Frame rate* is the number of frames per second that make up the video. The ideal rate for use in iMovie is 30 frames per second if you'll be exporting your movie to NTSC equipment and 25 frames per second if you'll be exporting to PAL equipment.)

So, you need to know these things about the video file that you plan to translate. The basics are simple:

- ✔ **640x480.** The video should be smooth and clear running at 640x480 resolution, which is the approximate resolution of clips used in iMovie and displayed on TV. If the clips are considerably smaller (320x240 or 160x120 — both common for Web video), they will be very chunky and blurry when used with other video within iMovie.

- ✔ **30 fps.** Again, video for the Web or CD-ROMs is often saved at something less than full motion, which is 30 frames per second, or fps. (Actually, the number is 29.97 frames per second for NTSC-format television and 25 fps for PAL-format TV.) If you export to DV Stream a movie that has been rendered at something less than 30 fps (or 25 fps for PAL), the quality will suffer and the video may appear staggered after you import it into iMovie.

- ✔ **Low compression.** A highly compressed movie (one that has a compression rate of more than approximately 4:1) will not look very good after it is translated to DV Stream and imported into iMovie. If you notice that the video is pixelated or jerky when you're watching it in QuickTime Player, be assured that it won't look much better in iMovie.

So, now that I've ruled out pretty much any video that you'll download from the Web, transfer in e-mail, and so forth, what movies *would* look good in iMovie? For the most part, they must be movie files you've created specifically for the task of editing in iMovie. For instance, if you have analog video that you've digitized using a PCI adapter card and software, you could translate that to DV Stream and use it in iMovie. Similarly, some companies offer USB video-in hardware that you can use with an analog VCR or camcorder to digitize video. If the hardware works at 640x480, 30 fps with low compression, it should create QuickTime movies of high-enough quality that you can translate those movies to DV Stream and import them to iMovie.

Translating to DV Stream

If you can successfully view a movie file in QuickTime Player, you can successfully translate it to DV Stream. (The one exception is that some MPEG 1 movies allow only the video portion to be translated to DV Stream, unless you use a third-party program.) After it's in the DV Stream format, bringing it into iMovie as a clip is easy. Here's how to translate to DV Stream:

1. **In QuickTime Pro Player, open the movie you want to translate.**

2. **Choose File⇨Export.**

   The Export dialog box appears.

3. **Select a folder where you'd like the DV file to be stored and then enter a name in the Save exported file as entry box.**

4. **From the Export pull-down menu, select Movie to DV Stream (see Figure 4-7).**

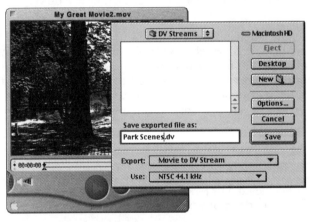

Figure 4-7: Name the file you want to create and select DV Stream as the type of file you'll be exporting to.

5. **To make additional modifications, pull down the Use menu and choose among the various options.**

   Select a format and audio setting if you don't want to use your default setting. If you have video equipment from North America and want high-quality sound, choose NTSC 44.1 kHz. If your equipment is European or Asian (that is, PAL format), choose PAL 44.1 kHz. You can also choose from the 32 kHz options if you'd like a smaller file with slightly lower-quality audio.

6. **Click Save.**

   The export process begins.

Exporting to DV Stream takes a long time. Under informal testing conditions (my watch has a second hand), it took me about three minutes to export a 5MB QuickTime clip that comprised only a few seconds of video. And what's worse, you can't really do anything else with your Mac until the export process is over. (At least, you can't if you're using Mac OS 9.*x* or earlier. If you're using Mac OS X, you can switch to other tasks, although you may not want to because doing so lengthens the time necessary for the conversion.) After the Exporting Movie dialog box disappears, however, you should have a DV file ready for use in iMovie.

Because exporting to DV takes a long time, I recommend that you edit the clip down to the bare minimum using QuickTime Pro Player and its editing tools. The tools are similar to those in iMovie; if you have trouble figuring them out, online help documents in the QuickTime Player's Help menu can get you started.

Importing DV Stream to iMovie

After you have your DV file exported, you're ready to import it into iMovie. This is the easy part:

1. **With iMovie active, choose File⇨Import.**

   The Import File dialog box appears.

2. **Select the DV file that you want to import.**

3. **Click the Import button (see Figure 4-8).**

   iMovie begins the process of importing the clip, which can take a while to accomplish.

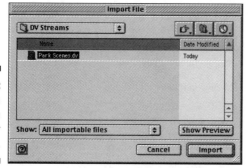

Figure 4-8: Selecting a DV Stream file for importing.

When iMovie has finished, you'll have the new clip on the Shelf, just like any other clip. Now the clip is ready to be viewed, renamed, or (drum roll please) edited.

Part II
In the Editing Bay

The 5th Wave   By Rich Tennant

"Do you think the 'Hidden Rhino' clip should come before or after the 'Waving Hello' video clip?"

In this part . . .

Now we're getting serious. In Part II, you explore the editing tools on iMovie. You start with the basics of moving clips around and cutting them down to size. Then it's on to adding transitions, titles, and credits. From there, you explore the nuts and bolts of iMovie 2's hidden talent — editing audio. This is where you can really make your edited movie shine. (In fact, I recommend that you read Chapter 8 as soon as you get a chance, just so you know how to plan correctly for editing your audio.) This part ends with a driving beat, showing you how to add narration and a soundtrack to your movie.

Chapter 5

Making Edits and Placing Your Clips

. . . .

. . . .

*T*hey say that most of writing is rewriting (at least, that's what my book editors always seem to be saying) and most of moviemaking is editing. Well, here's your chance, as editor, to leave one of your major actors (preferably the one that gave you the most trouble over the type of food served and the size of his or her trailer) on the proverbial cutting-room floor. And it will, in fact, be *proverbial* because iMovie is your cutting room (as well as your screening room, your sound booth, and your effects house).

After you import clips into iMovie (Chapter 4), you're ready to dig into the Monitor and edit those clips. You begin by trimming the edges of your clips, cropping down to, roughly, the portions you'd like to have in your video presentation. You also see a few other things that you can do with clips, such as reversing the direction of the clip, splitting a clip in two, or creating a still clip from a moving one.

Then, with some rough edits made, you can place the clips in the Clip Viewer, organize your movie, and play it back to see how things are coming along.

In this chapter, you get up close and personal with the Monitor, finding out how to cut your clips down to size and get them ready for the Clip Viewer. Then, you progress to the Clip Viewer, where you place clips and move them around to begin building your story. Finally, you view the video full screen to see what's going on so far in your movie.

Editing in the Monitor

When you click a clip on the Shelf, the Monitor switches automatically to Edit mode and shows that clip's *poster frame* (the first frame in the clip) in the Monitor window. If you've imported video (as discussed in Chapter 4), you know that the VCR-like controls are used to control your camcorder when in Camera mode. In Edit mode, however, the controls are used to control the selected clip. Using those controls you can (respectively) rewind, move immediately to the beginning of the clip, play the clip, play the clip full screen, or fast-forward through the clip (see Figure 5-1).

Figure 5-1:
In Edit mode, the Monitor becomes control-central for viewing and editing your clips.

Rewind/Review | Play | Volume slider

Home (back to start of clip) | Fast Forward

Play Full Screen

Most of these buttons are self-explanatory, with a few things worth noting:

✔ The Play button now has the double duty of both Play and Stop. Click it, while playing, to stop the playback of the clip. You can still use the spacebar to toggle Play on and off.

✔ The Play Full Screen button is a new control, unique to Edit mode, which plays the clip full screen. (The iMovie interface disappears and your Mac's entire screen is filled with the clip.)

✔ None of the buttons — including Fast Forward and Rewind — requires that you click and hold down the mouse button. Instead, just click the button once to turn it on and then click it again to stop what action is taking place.

✔ The volume slider is for your benefit during playback; it doesn't affect the volume levels within the clip itself. You can use the up and down arrow keys to change the volume during playback.

Each time you select a clip in the Shelf, the Monitor changes to display that clip and enables you to control it. You should realize, though, that you can view only one clip at a time in the Monitor while the clips are on the shelf. If you want to see one clip after another, you have to move the clips to the Clip Viewer first.

Using the Scrubber bar

Aside from the buttons at the bottom of the Monitor, Edit mode introduces another new tool: the Scrubber bar. This is the solid blue bar with small time marks that appears just above the controls. You use it to get a sense of whether you are at the beginning, middle, or end of the clip. You can get an *exact* sense of where you are with a combination of the playhead and the small clock that appears next to the playhead (see Figure 5-2).

Figure 5-2:
The
Scrubber
bar shows
you where
you are in
the clip.

Playhead   Clock

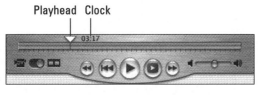

By using the Scrubber bar and the playhead, you have a few ways to move around and view different portions of your clip:

✔ **Scrubbing.** The Scrubber bar lets you scrub back and forth to different parts of your clip using the playhead. (*Scrubbing* means that you can see what you're moving toward as you move toward it.) With a clip selected on the Shelf, point to the playhead with the mouse and then click and hold the mouse button. Now, drag the playhead back and forth along the Scrubber bar to move to a different part of the clip.

✔ **One-clicking.** You can move directly to a point of time in the clip by aiming the mouse pointer at a portion of the Scrubber bar and clicking the mouse button once. The playhead will move immediately to that spot in the clip.

> ✔ **Pressing arrow keys.** For precise movements, you can use the arrow keys on the keyboard. Press the left arrow once and you move the playhead back in your clip by one frame; press the right arrow once and you move forward one frame. If you'd like a slightly faster pace, hold down either of the arrow keys to slowly crawl up or down the Scrubber bar, frame by frame. (If you hold down the Shift key when you press an arrow key, the playhead jumps ten frames in the direction you press.)

Using crop markers

So now you're moving around on the Scrubber bar, but let's face it, that's only *so* exciting. The next step is to select portions of the clip so you can trim to the parts of the clip you want to keep. You do that using the crop markers.

As you see in the next few sections, the footage in clips can be cropped, cleared, cut, copied, or pasted. Before you can accomplish any of these tasks, however, you must select the portion of the clip you want to act upon.

You do that with the crop markers, which appear below the Scrubber bar when you select a portion of your video. With a clip in the Monitor, hold down the Shift key and click right below the playhead. You see the two crop markers appear.

You can place the crop markers more exactly, too, if you'd like. Start by placing the playhead at the point in the clip where you'd like one of the crop markers to appear. Now, point the mouse at the point on the Scrubber bar where you'd like the other crop marker to appear. Hold down the Shift key and click. Now you see the crop markers appear with the section of footage selected and highlighted in yellow (see Figure 5-3).

Figure 5-3:
The crop markers show the portion of the clip you've selected for editing.

Crop markers

Now you can get more precise with your selection by dragging the crop markers. Point at one of the markers, click and hold down the mouse button, and then move the mouse to the left or right.

You can also use the keyboard arrow keys to move the marker more precisely. Click once on a crop marker and then press the left or right arrow key. This moves the crop marker exactly one frame in the direction of the arrow you press. To move ten frames in either direction, hold down the Shift key while pressing an arrow key.

What should you do if you've set crop markers but then don't want to use them or you'd like an opportunity to reset them without having to drag them all over the screen? The easy solution is to click the clip's icon on the Shelf, which quickly clears the crop markers and lets you start over in the Monitor without them.

Clearing part of a clip

Often, you want to take a little off the beginning or the end of a clip. (If you want to do both, you should crop the clip, as described in the next section.)

To begin, I show you how to select and delete a portion from the beginning of the clip, perhaps to get rid of a handle that you imported or that rousing, emotional shot of removing the lens cap before the real action begins. Here's how:

1. **Start by placing the playhead at the *end* of the portion of video that you want to remove.**

2. **Hold down the Shift key and click the very beginning of the Scrubber bar.**

   That part of the Scrubber bar turns yellow and the crop markers pop up.

3. **Move the crop markers to the exact point(s) in the clip that you want to select.**

   Because you're deleting from the beginning of the clip, make sure the leftmost crop marker is all the way to the beginning of the Scrubber bar. (The bar should indicate 00:00.) Then move the right crop marker to the exact point in the clip where you want the new beginning to the clip.

4. **Choose Edit⇨Clear.**

   This deletes the selected portion of the clip. If you'd like it back, choose the Edit⇨Undo command.

Now the clip on the Shelf is a bit shorter; note that the amount of time indicated on its icon has changed. You're ready to work with the shorter clip.

If you want to delete a portion from the end of the clip, move the right crop marker all the way to the end of the Scrubber bar and then use the left crop marker to select the point on the clip where you'd like the new ending. Choose Edit➪Clear.

Did a second clip appear on the Shelf? This happens when you accidentally leave a little bit of the clip unselected on both sides and therefore have actually deleted from the middle of a clip. (This still deletes the selected footage but also splits the clip into two clips — one clip with everything on the left side of the deleted portion and one clip with everything on the right side of the deleted portion.) Choose Edit➪Undo and then go back into the Monitor and make sure that one of your crop markers is at the very beginning or very end of the Scrubber bar. Then choose Edit➪Clear again.

Cropping a clip

You don't have to be a farmer or a barber to know a little something about cropping. *Cropping* is the opposite of the clearing that took place in the last section. With cropping, you keep the portion you selected while deleting portions (in this case, from either side of the clip) that you didn't select. Although clearing is best when you want to delete from only one end of a clip, cropping is best when you want to keep a middle portion of a clip but trim both ends. (In that respect, cropping is also the opposite of liposuction.) Here's how to crop:

1. **Place the playhead on the Scrubber bar where you'd like the cropped clip to begin.**

   This will likely be a little distance in from the left side of the Scrubber bar.

2. **Hold down the Shift key and click the position on the Scrubber bar where you'd like the clip to end (see Figure 5-4).**

Figure 5-4:
I've selected the portion of the clip that I want to keep so I can crop the rest of it.

3. **Use the mouse and keyboard arrow keys to more precisely place the crop markers.**

   Again, you can drag the crop markers using the mouse, or you can click a crop marker once (to select it) and then use the left and right arrow keys to move it precisely.

4. **Choose Edit⇨Crop from the menu or press ⌘+K.**

   The portions of the clip that fall outside the crop markers on either side are deleted (put in the Trash) and the clip is now a bit more svelte. Note that the Scrubber bar resets to reflect the newly sized clip.

Before you start clearing and cropping away, there's something else to consider. Do you want the *audio* from a clip you're cropping, even if you don't want the video? If that's the case, you may want to use some sound editing commands. See Chapter 8 for details on editing sound and the steps for pasting over (instead of cropping and clearing) the video portions of your clips while keeping the sound intact

Cutting and copying parts of a clip

Along with clearing or cropping your clip, you can use the Copy and Cut commands in the Edit menu to place a portion of a clip on the Mac's clipboard. The *clipboard* is the Mac's repository for any sort of data — text, images, even video — that can be cut from one portion of a document and pasted into another portion of a document. If you've used Cut, Copy, and Paste commands in a word processor, for instance, you've used the Mac OS clipboard.

If you highlight a portion of a clip (using the crop markers) and choose Edit⇨Copy, a copy of that clip segment is placed on the clipboard, but the original clip is unaffected. If you highlight a portion of the clip and choose Edit⇨Cut, a copy of that clip segment is placed on the clipboard and simultaneously cleared from the currently selected clip, just as if you'd chosen Edit⇨Clear.

So what do you do with the video segment that's on the clipboard? If you choose Edit⇨Paste, that video appears in the Shelf as a new clip (see Figure 5-5). Pasting is a convenient way to duplicate portions of existing clips or to crop a clip without losing the original. As long as you have enough hard disk space available, this may be a convenient way to create smaller, cropped clips while still being able to head back to the original clip if necessary.

In the version I'm using at the time of writing (iMovie 2.0.1), clips that are larger than three seconds sometimes show up as two clips on the Shelf when pasted. One way around this is to click the Shelf before invoking the Paste command. (The other solution is to Cut or Copy only clips less than three seconds long!)

Figure 5-5:
After using
Edit➪Cut
and
Edit➪Paste,
I have a
new,
smaller clip
that's made
up of only a
selected
portion of
the original
clip.

Splitting a clip

For a variety of reasons (some of which will be more apparent when you're creating transitions and effects for your movie), you may find it useful to split a single clip into two or more clips as you're editing. This happens to be a good editing technique for storytelling. For instance, suppose you're putting together a documentary (or school project or news feature) on the endangered Black Rhino and you'd like to show footage you shot of the rhino at the zoo. Viewers would likely be bored by a full minute of that footage, even if you have entertaining music or an interesting voiceover.

The solution? Split the clip into two or three separate clips. Now you'll be able to put other clips between them. You could, for instance, interview a zoologist or a professor or a politician and intersperse the video of that person with the video of the rhino. (As you can see in Chapter 6, putting images of one thing over audio from another is easy, so you could simply have the interview with the professor continue in audio while you're showing clips of the rhino in video.)

Splitting clips is easy:

1. **Select the clip you want to split.**

   It can be on the Shelf — or in the Clip Viewer or Timeline, for that matter.

2. **Place the playhead at the point on the Scrubber bar where you'd like the clip to be split.**

3. **Choose Edit➪Split Video Clip at Playhead.**

Now you have two clips — one with the original clip's name and a second one probably called *Name*/1, where *Name* is whatever you had named the first clip. (For that matter, it could be Clip 5/1, if you never named the clip yourself.) See Figure 5-6.

Figure 5-6:
Splitting a
clip results
in —
drum roll
please! —
two clips.

Creating a still clip

Here's another quick little clip edit that you may find useful. You can take an existing clip and use it to create a *still clip* — a single image that can appear on the screen for a certain amount of time (five seconds by default). What is this good for? Other than for certain MTV-type effects (for instance, having someone frozen in mid-air while the screeching of a guitar continues in the background), a still clip is great for when you'd like the audience to focus on a particular item or read something on-screen.

For instance, suppose you've shot a sign you'd like the audience to read, but the camera was shaking a bit. Instead of leaving in the shaky footage, create a still image and leave it on-screen for a few seconds. Then, with an advanced audio cut (discussed in Chapter 6), your audio or narration can continue while the still image is on the screen.

Again, creating a still clip is easy:

1. **Select the clip from which you'll be creating the still.**

   Select and drag the playhead on the Scrubber bar to locate the exact frame of the clip that you want to use for the still clip.

2. **With that frame selected, choose Edit⇨Create Still Clip (or press ⌘+Shift+S).**

   The new clip is created and, if it's your first still clip, named Still 01.

Be default, still clips are five seconds in length. You can change the length of each individual still clip later, using the Timeline, as discussed in Chapter 6. If you'd prefer a different default amount of time:

1. **Choose Edit⇨Preferences.**

2. **Make sure the Import tab is selected.**

    Note the entry that reads Still clips are 5 seconds by default.

3. **Simply type a new number (such as 10) to change that default (see Figure 5-7).**

    If the entry box isn't selected, you may need to double-click it to highlight the current number for entry.

4. **Click OK to set the preference.**

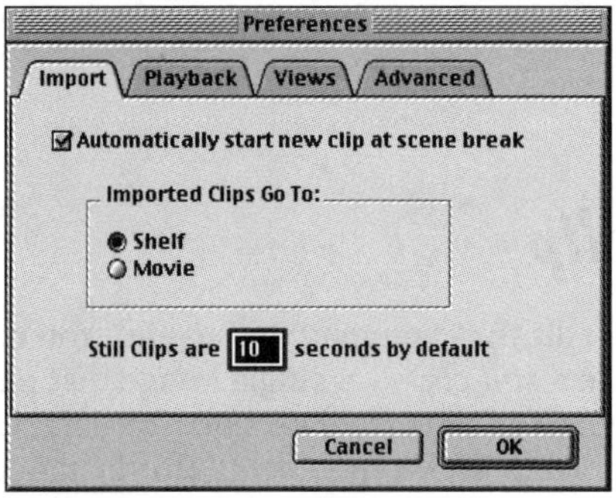

Figure 5-7:
Setting the default amount of time for still clips.

Reversing a clip

Reversing the direction of a clip may seem like a high-end special effect appropriate for a more advanced chapter, but it's so simple that I squeeze it in here. In essence, a single command makes it possible for you to run a clip backwards.

Your head is probably brimming over with possibilities for this one. You could show your kid, the cross-country runner, running from the finish line to the start. You could show your kid, the cross-country biker, riding from the finish line backward to the start. You could show your kid, the Niagara Falls barrel rider, traveling up the falls instead of down. (Seriously, don't do this one.)

If it's not clear from the sarcasm of my commentary, the one important suggestion for this effect is to use it *sparingly.* If you're talking about a family gathering of folks who aren't that computer-savvy and will be really wowed by this one, okay. But use this effect too much and it will become as annoying as Hollywood's tendency to drop commercial messages right into feature films. (I can hear *Awnuld* now: "Aw'll be back . . . right after I *sooper size* my *Mikey Deluxe* burger for only forthy-nine *cents!*")

Here's how you reverse a clip:

1. **Select the clip.**

   The clip can be in the Shelf, in the Clip Viewer, or even in the Timeline (discussed in more detail in Chapter 8).

2. **Choose Advanced⇨Reverse Clip Direction from the menu.**

   The clip is now reversed.

3. **Play the clip back in the Monitor, and let the hilarity ensue.**

Oh — the audio is also reversed, so be ready for that. (Got any Beatles concert footage?) If you don't want the audio reversed, you must first extract the audio and then reverse the clip. Extracting audio is discussed briefly in Chapter 6 and in detail in Chapter 8.

Restoring a clip

Did you make some edits to a clip that you didn't mean to make? Sometimes you can get well into editing multiple clips before you return to a previous edit and realize you cut the wrong things — or too much of the right thing — from an existing clip. If you just made the change, you can use the Edit⇨Undo command to restore the lost footage. But if you changed some other things in the meantime, you have to undo all of *those* changes, too, to get your footage back for this edited clip. That wouldn't be fun, especially if you're happy with the other edits you made.

Fortunately, as long as you haven't emptied the Trash, you can return to a particular clip and restore the media you cut from it:

1. **Select the clip (whether it's on the Shelf or elsewhere, such as in the Clip Viewer).**

2. **Choose Advanced⇨Restore Clip Media.**

   A dialog box appears, detailing the gruesome details (see Figure 5-8).

3. **If all is agreeable with you, click OK.**

   The clip's trimmings are restored, and you can reevaluate your editing decisions.

Figure 5-8:
If you
choose to
restore clip
media,
iMovie tells
you exactly
how much it
has in the
Trash.

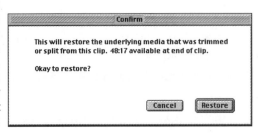

Working with Clips in the Clip Viewer

After you've cleaned up your clips in the Monitor, you're ready to place them in the Clip Viewer. The Clip Viewer is where you lay out the sequence of your video, literally dragging and dropping the clips to put them in the order in which you'd like them to appear. The power of iMovie is that you can change that order pretty much at any time, making it possible to completely change the way you tell your story simply by rearranging clips.

(If life were like this, you could, for instance, rearrange things so that you bought Apple stock *before* the introduction of the iMac or got the job with PlasticCo *before* you told your boss off at RubberInc.)

Dragging clips into the Clip Viewer

Getting your clips into the Clip Viewer is pretty simple. All you have to do is make sure the Clip Viewer is active (click the tab that has an icon that looks like a human eye) and drag the clips from the Shelf to the Clip Viewer. You can drag each clip individually or select multiple clips (hold down the Shift key as you click them, or click the Shelf once and press ⌘+A) and drag them all at once to the Clip Viewer. In either case, your clips in the Clip Viewer will look suspiciously like one of those government-funded filmstrips (Please advance the frame. Beep!") shown in high school (see Figure 5-9).

After you have your clips in the Clip Viewer, some subtle artistry is involved in moving around within it. First, you may notice that when you select a clip in the Clip Viewer, the clip becomes highlighted and the Monitor changes to show that one clip. Now you have another opportunity to edit the clip as discussed in the previous section "Editing in the Monitor."

Figure 5-9:
Clips have
been
dragged and
dropped on
the Clip
Viewer.

If one or some of the clips are highlighted (yellow), you may want to deselect them. You can do that by clicking the top title portion of the Clip Viewer — the portion that lists the clip selection, recorded date, and other information about the clip. You can click any gray area within the Clip Viewer, including beyond the last clip or even the eye icon. When you click one of these areas, the yellow highlights go away — now, no particular clip is selected. You also see another change: The Monitor now shows the first frame of your first clip in the Clip Viewer. What's more, the Scrubber bar now represents the entire length of your video as arranged in the Clip Viewer, complete with vertical lines representing the breaks between clips (see Figure 5-10). If you click the Play button at this point, the Monitor will display all your clips, in the order in which they're arranged in the Clip Viewer.

Figure 5-10:
With no
clips
selected in
the Clip
Viewer, the
Scrubber
bar shows
the entire
video,
complete
with small
lines
representing
each new
clip.

Moving clips

The next step, after you have your clips in the Clip Viewer, is to move them around. This is just a drag-and-drop process. Move the mouse pointer to the clip you want to move and then click and hold the mouse button. Now, drag the clip to the portion of the video where you'd like it to appear. As you drag past clips, note that a space opens up between them (see Figure 5-11). When you get to the opening where you'd like the clip to be, release the mouse button.

Figure 5-11:
As you pass
by each clip,
a space
opens up to
let you know
where you
can drop the
clip.

You can also select multiple clips and move them at once, as long as they're contiguous. Unlike the Shelf, the Clip Viewer won't allow you to use the Shift+click method to select clips that aren't right next to one another. You can, however, use Shift+click to select two or more clips that are side-by-side. Then drag and drop those clips to a new area on the Clip Viewer.

And, of course, you can drag clips to the Trash or back up to the Shelf, if you like. To get a clip back from the Trash, you must invoke the Edit⇨Undo command. Put a clip on the Shelf, though, and it's there for safekeeping until you decide to drag it back into the Clip Viewer.

Looking more closely at the Clip Viewer

The Clip Viewer and the clips within it offer some interesting information if you take a close look. A readout at the top of the Clip Viewer contains quite a bit of information, including the name of the movie and the total amount of time of the movie, in minutes, seconds, and frames (see Figure 5-12).

Name of the movie (as much as can be shown)

Name and length of selected clip

Total time for the movie

When the clip was recorded

Figure 5-12:
The Clip
Viewer
reveals
interesting
information
about your
movie.

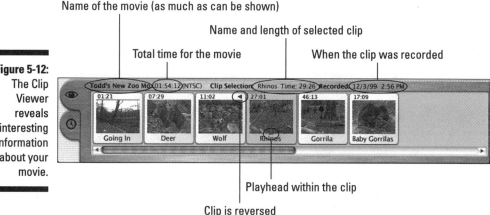

Playhead within the clip

Clip is reversed

You also see the name of the currently selected clip (if one is highlighted) and its running length, along with the date and time when it was recorded. If multiple clips are selected, the name of the clip is replaced with <Multiple>, but their total running time is still shown.

Within the clips themselves, you get two or three bits of information. In the top-left corner of each clip's icon is the total running time for that clip. If the clip happens to be in the Monitor, though, you also see a small red indicator that shows you where the playhead is currently located in the clip.

The third bit of information appears if you've reversed the direction of a clip. (See the "Reversing a clip" section previously in this chapter.) A small triangle appears in the top-right corner of the clip icon, showing you that the clip is currently set to play reversed.

Playing Back Your Movie

One thing you'll definitely be doing a lot with your movie is watching it — over and over again — to see whether it's cleanly edited and sounds right. That means you'll get to know the controls for playing it. But there are a few scenarios to look at, depending on how you want to play it back, along with how much you want to play back. (If you're questioning whether or not you should play it back, maybe it's time to take a break.)

If you're ready to sit back and enjoy the splendor of your entire video, playback is easy:

1. **With either the Timeline or Clip Viewer active, click the top little information bar that includes the name of your movie and its running time.**

   This, as you may remember, is how you clear any selections. The Monitor now displays each small clip segment in the Scrubber bar, which means the Monitor is ready to play all your clips in their current sequence.

2. **To watch the video in your Monitor window, click the Play button.**

   If you've set iMovie to playback through your camcorder (and you have your camcorder connected to a TV monitor), you can watch the video unfold on the external view screen or monitor.

Chapter 3 discusses connecting an external TV monitor for viewing your movie-in-progress.

You can move to any point in the video by dragging the playhead along the Scrubber bar and then releasing it. But what if you want to view only certain clips from start to finish? Easy. Just select the clips you want to play back in either the Clip Viewer or the Timeline — remember that you can hold down the Shift key while clicking clips to add them to the sequence. (You can't select clips out of sequence; they must be in a continuous row.) After those clips are selected, you're ready to rumble. Just click the Play button in the Monitor and only those scenes will be shown.

Finally, there's the granddaddy of view options: full screen. iMovie enables you to preview your movie by displaying it full screen on the Mac or iMac's monitor. Frankly, this option is less useful than it may seem because iMovies tend to be of slightly lower quality when played back full screen on your computer versus playing them back full screen on a TV monitor. If you don't have a TV monitor handy, though, a full-screen computer display will have to do.

And it's easy to do. Make your deselection (click the title portion of the Clip Viewer or Timeline) to view the entire iMovie, or Shift-click multiple clips that you want to see. Then, click the Play Full Screen button, just to the right of the Play button in the Monitor. Voila! You see the iMovie full screen.

See what I mean about lower quality? Depending on the speed of your Mac or iMac, you might see playback that looks more like a flip-card animation than a full-speed video or movie. That's part of the slings-and-arrows of full-screen playback. It takes a lot of processor power to display an iMovie smoothly and clearly on a computer screen, even though the iMovie will look much better after you export it back to your camcorder or display the finished product on a TV screen.

 You do have one recourse, however, if you don't like the way your movie looks:

1. **Choose Edit⇨Preferences from the menu.**

2. **In the Preferences dialog box, click the Playback tab (see Figure 5-13).**

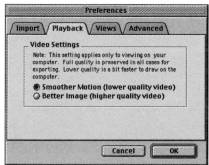

Figure 5-13: iMovie's Preferences include a choice of better quality video or smoother motion.

3. **Make your selection.**

   You have two options that enable you to make a basic trade-off: Do you want to see better quality video or smoother video motion? The smoother motion option means the images will seem a bit more out of focus, but you'll see more frames displayed more quickly, making it a little less painful to watch.

4. **Click OK.**

Now you're ready to try the full-screen display again.

Chapter 6

Building Transitions between Clips

. . . .

In This Chapter

▶ Discovering the difference between cuts and transitions

▶ Adding and tweaking transitions

▶ Looking at the different transitions included with iMovie

. . . .

*W*hat gives a video presentation that professional flair? Clearly it's a combination of elements, such as good, smart camera work, interesting special effects, and a rocking soundtrack. Those are, indeed, very important, as is having an A-list million-dollar actor as your star. Oh — and a good agent. Not to mention great producers and some wonderful mentors along the way.

But one of the factors that can separate amateur and professional-level video is the quality of edits and transitions. iMovie offers some strong tools for creating transitions between your scenes, and the results can look very professional. But another part of professional editing is knowing whether a transition or a *straight cut* — a transition without any special effects — will be better for your storytelling.

In this chapter, you look at the difference between cuts and transitions as well as some tips on when to use each. Then you see how to add transitions in iMovie under various circumstances. At the end of the chapter, you read about the transitions included in iMovie and advice on when to use each one.

Understanding Cuts and Transitions

Chapter 5 focuses on cutting your clips down to size and placing them in the Clip Viewer to determine the order in which they'll be presented. That's a good starting place to begin thinking about the final presentation of your movie — how will the story be told, and how do the clips relate to one another? The reason for this is simple: After you know the relationship between two clips, you know how you will transition between them — or if you need to transition at all.

What's a transition? What's a cut?

A *transition,* in the context of iMovie, is a visual effect that creates a bridge between one clip and the next. iMovie comes with a number of these transitions built in, including basic fades (fade in and fade out), *cross dissolves* (in which one clip dissolves into another clip), and various *wipes* or *pushes,* in which the first clip is moved from the screen and the second clip takes over.

A *cut,* on the other hand, is simply a transition from one clip to another without an effect. You move from the end of one clip to the beginning of the next. No fades, no wipes — one second you're watching one clip and then the next second you're watching the next clip. In iMovie, that simply means you don't do anything special to the clips. If they've been placed in the Clip Viewer, iMovie plays one clip right after the other. If there's no transition effect between the two clips, there's simply a cut.

Which should I use — and when?

When many people first get their hands on iMovie, they become transition freaks. Transition from one kid to the other kid. Transition between the shot of Mt. St. Helens from five miles out and the shot of Mt. St. Helens from three miles out. Lions (transition), tigers (transition), bears (transition). You get the idea. But the truth is, the best videos and movies have far fewer transitions than you think.

This is another great time to sit and watch a little TV or another movie. (Isn't this book doing wonders for your free time?) What you'll notice is something very basic and very interesting. Unless you're watching a live sports presentation or a Saturday-morning kids-style news show, you'll see fewer transitions on television (or in a feature film) than you may have expected.

Transitions are generally used for one reason: to smoothly move a video presentation from *one idea* to the *next idea*. With transition effects, such as a wipe or a fade, you can tell your audience that you want them to stop thinking of one topic and start thinking about another topic. Depending on how you implement the transition, you may even be able to communicate to your audience how abrupt that change in thought should be, that is, how different the next topic is. How much of a shift in their chair should the audience make? Where are they going next?

In a vacation video, you might transition between the different days of the week. Fade out on a particularly beautiful sunset on Monday and then fade in on the kids singing campfire songs in the backseat of the station wagon on Tuesday. (Okay, maybe that's less like your family vacation and more like an episode of the *Brady Bunch.*)

In a fiction piece, you might transition between the chewing out in the captain's office and the hero showing up at the docks to take on the bad guys. In a documentary, you might transition between different subjects of your story, or you might add a transition when you've moving from one idea, such as "crime is high," to the next idea, such as "big business is at fault."

In general, though, you use a transition when you want to suggest that something is changing: time has passed, you're moving to a new topic, you're moving to a different part of the story.

So, you may be asking, what do you do when the idea isn't changing from clip to clip? Don't transition.

Straight cuts between two clips — in which one clip butts right up to the next one — can be effective and easy for your audience to watch, even if the cuts seem too jagged or abrupt while you're editing. After your movie comes together — perhaps with audio, narration, and music — those cuts won't seem nearly as abrupt as you thought. Instead, the cuts between numerous, reasonably short clips will make your video more interesting, while a few well-placed transitions will help your audience understand when you're moving from topic to topic.

And even when you think a straight cut between two clips is *still* too abrupt, you should consider something else. What would happen to the two clips if you had a continuous clip of audio beneath them? Think about a newscast: You see the anchor woman, then you see a clip of the story, then you see her again, and then you see footage of another story. Most likely, you don't see visual fades or wipes between all those clips — just straight cuts from clip to clip to clip to clip. What *is* continuous is the audio, possibly the anchor or reporter talking the entire time. The abrupt cutting works because the audio continues.

Fortunately, these types of audio edits are easy. I discuss them in detail in Chapter 8. In the meantime, all you have to do in preparation for Chapter 8 is decide which clips continue the same idea, time frame, or issue. Gather those clips together in the Clip Viewer and leave the straight cuts between them. (You can always add transitions later.) Now, for your major idea changes, you can build transitions.

Adding Transitions

You have two different twists on adding transitions in iMovie, one using the Clip Viewer and the other using the Timeline. I cover both here, although the Timeline interface is a bit more complicated. (You can spend some time getting to know the Timeline in Chapter 8.)

iMovie makes it almost painfully, laughably easy to add a transition within the Clip Viewer. It's basically just a drag-and-drop procedure. The only real fact to remember is that there are two type of transitions. One type (for instance, a fade in or wash out) acts on a single clip — either the beginning or end of that clip. The other type (such as a cross dissolve or an overlap) acts on two clips, transitioning between them. So, depending on the type of transition, you drag it to the beginning of a clip, the end of a clip, or between two existing clips. You can't place a transition in the middle of a clip, although there's a way to get around that, as discussed a little later.

A one-clip transition doesn't add any time to your movie; the entire transition occurs within the space of the selected clip. So, for instance, if your first clip is one minute long and you apply a fade in transition to it, the clip is still one minute long (and thus the length of the movie doesn't change) even though it's fading in. The first few frames of the clip are black, with each subsequent frame becoming a little more transparent until the clip is fully bright and viewable.

Some transitions, however, can subtract time from your movie. A transition that acts on two clips, such as a cross dissolve, remove a little time from the original overall length of the two clips. (For instance, if the two clips together were 05:00, adding a one-second transition between them cuts the overall length to 04:00 because the final second of the first clip is overlapping the first second of the second clip.) Note that when you overlap transitions, you overlap also the audio between the two clips. (You can extract and edit that audio later, as detailed in Chapter 8.)

The fact that a transition alters the clip (or clips) means something else that's important to you as the editor: You can't alter (cut, clear, crop) the portion of the clip that has a transition attached to it unless you first delete the transition. If you have a fade in on one of your clips, those few seconds at the beginning of the clip can't be cut or cleared unless you delete the transition. So, before adding transitions, it's best to cut or crop your clips (as discussed in Chapter 5) exactly as you want them.

Oh — you also can't transition a transition, just in case you were thinking of trying. A transition affects one side of at least one clip — either the beginning of the clip or the end of it. After you add a transition to the beginning of a clip, you can't add another one to the beginning (although you could add one to the end and vice-versa). In other words, one transition at a time.

Using the Transitions panel

To begin working with transitions, click the Transitions button at the bottom of the Shelf. This causes the Transitions panel to appear. The panel replaces the Shelf, as shown in Figure 6-1.

Choose the direction

Choose the speed

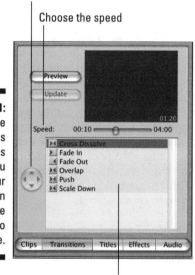

Figure 6-1:
The Transitions panel is where you prep your transition before adding it to your movie.

Select a transition

With the Transitions panel open, you see a list of possible transitions, including their names and a small green icon. The icon may look meaningless, but it's telling you how many clips the transition will act on and when. Here's a quick guide:

 ✔ With only one arrow, this transition acts on only a single clip. Because the arrow is at the beginning facing right, it suggests that the transition will occur at the beginning of the clip. (This icon represents an In transition, such as Fade In or Wash In.) If you drag-and-drop this transition into the Clip Viewer, drag it to the front of a clip.

 ✔ Again, one arrow means the transition acts on a single clip. In this case, the transition will occur at the end of the clip. (This icon represents an Out transition, such as Fade Out or Wash Out.) When you drag-and-drop this transition into the Clip Viewer, drag it to the end of the clip.

✔ With two arrows, this icon indicates that the transition occurs between two clips, acting on the ending portion of the first clip and the beginning portion of the second clip. When you drag-and-drop this clip, drag it between two clips.

Aside from the list of transitions and their icons, you see some other controls: a Speed slider, a transitions preview area, a direction control, a Preview button, and an Update button.

Selecting and previewing a transition

The little transition icons discussed in the preceding section are convenient because the arrows show you where to drag the transition when you're adding it to a clip. What these arrows *don't* tell you, though, is how to select your clips in the Clip Viewer so that you can properly *preview* the transition. (iMovie has a capability called previewing, in which it can show you how a transition will look without forcing you to sit through the process of creating the final transition.) Note that you don't have to preview transitions if you don't want to; you can just drag and drop a transition into the Clip Viewer (or, as you'll see, into the Timeline) and begin rendering the transition immediately. It's usually advisable, however, to preview first.

If you want to preview a one-clip transition (one with only one arrow, regardless of the direction it's facing), simply select the clip in the Clip Viewer that you want to preview. For a two-clip transition, select the *second* clip of the two to see an accurate preview.

If you've gone ahead of me and are working in the Timeline, selecting a clip in order to preview it works the same way. Select the target clip for a one-clip transition, or select the second clip of the two for a two-clip transition.

After you've selected your target clip(s) in the Clip Viewer, you can click the name of a transition in the Transitions panel. Note what happens — the transition preview area lights up with a small representation of the transition. Immediately, you have some idea of what will happen with this transition (see Figure 6-2).

One oddity of the current version of iMovie (version 2.0.1 at the time of writing) is that the transition preview area doesn't always seem to work correctly for a one-clip transition. Sometimes you select a clip and select a transition, but a *different* clip (usually the clip before or after the selected clip) appears in the transition preview area. This seems to be a bug that may be fixed in a later version. For now, use the following workaround. If you're previewing a transition that's meant to begin the clip (an In transition), make sure that the playhead (in the Monitor) is placed within the first half of the selected clip. For an Out clip, make sure that the playhead is placed in the second half of the clip. Now, when you select a transition in the Transitions panel, the preview area displays the correct clip.

Figure 6-2: When you select a transition, a small preview appears in the transition preview area.

If you like, you can click the same transition again to view it again, or you can click other transitions to see how they'll look. You can also, at this point, customize the transition a bit to make it a better fit:

- ✔ **Speed.** Using the Speed slider bar, you can change the speed of the transition. This bar is used to determine exactly how long the transition will last. As you drag the selector along the bar, you see the exact time of the transition in the transition preview area. When you release the mouse button, the preview replays in the transition preview area, showing you the new length. Generally, a transition takes only one or two seconds, and iMovie generally limits you to four seconds. Be warned, though, that the slower (and hence longer) you make the transition, the more time iMovie requires to render the transition (perform all the mathematically computations to alter the clip or clips) when you finally drag it into the Clip Viewer or Timeline.

- ✔ **Direction.** If you select a transition that has the capability to move in different directions, the direction indicator (the four-way circle) lights, enabling you to click up, down, left, or right. (Of the default transitions included with iMovie 2, only Push has a direction option.) Click the direction in which you'd like the transition to move, and the transition preview area lights up, showing how the transition will look.

Now, with these selections made, you can do one of two things. You can either cut straight to the chase and place the transition in your movie, or you can use the "official" Preview function to preview the transition in the Monitor.

If you want to preview the transition, click the Preview button. The Monitor window begins to show a (somewhat jagged) version of the transition. This preview isn't *exactly* how the final transition will look, because the computer still hasn't performed all the computations necessary for a smooth transition. But it does give you a filmstrip-esque presentation of the transition to give you a better idea.

Placing a transition in the Clip Viewer

Now that you have the transition just the way you want it, it's time to add it to your movie. And, wouldn't you know it, doing so is as easy as drag-and-drop. All you have to decide is whether you want to add the transition using the Clip Viewer or the Timeline.

Here's how to add a transition using the Clip Viewer:

1. **Make sure the Clip Viewer is active.**

   If necessary, click its tab — the one with the eye icon.

2. **From the Transitions panel, drag the icon for the transition you want to use down to the Clip Viewer.**

3. **In the Clip Viewer, drag the transition to the appropriate spot relative to the clip(s) you're going to transition.**

   This is the tricky part. If the transition will affect the beginning of a clip (such as a fade in), drag it to the left side of that clip's icon. If the transition will affect the end of that clip (such as a fade out), drag it to the right of the clip. If the transition is between two clips, drag it between those two clips in the Clip Viewer. As noted previously, you can't add a transition where a transition already exists, so a spot won't open up where a transition already exists.

4. **When the appropriate opening appears between clips, release the mouse button.**

   The Clip Viewer shows you where a transition will appear by opening a small space in front of, behind, or between two clips (see Figure 6-3). When you have the transition in the right place, releasing the mouse button drops it into the Clip Viewer.

Figure 6-3:
As you drag the transition, small spaces open up between clips.

After you place the transition, it begins to render immediately. During this process, iMovie is rendering: performing all the math, physics, or . . . er . . . something that it needs to do to figure out how to make that transition appear as smooth as possible. A small indicator bar appears under the transition icon to show you the progress of the transition.

 While the rendering is taking place, you can still view and edit other portions of the movie, but you can't view the transition. You may notice some jaggedness while you're working with other portions of the movie — the program is thinking hard about the rendering, so it can give less attention to your mouse clicks and commands. If you're offended by this poor responsiveness, the best plan is to pointedly ignore your Mac until the rendering is completed. (Then, all can be forgiven.)

Placing a transition in the Timeline

If you elect to place your transition in the Timeline rather than the Clip Viewer, you won't see much difference, except everything is a bit smaller and slightly less friendly and cartoony. The basics are still the same: drag and drop to the beginning or end of a clip.

 You may need to change the zoom factor in the Timeline to see all your clips at once. The zoom factor is controlled with the Zoom pop-up menu, which appears in the lower-left corner of the Timeline. Open the menu and select 1x to view all your clips in a single span of the Timeline.

Here's how to add a transition using the Timeline:

1. **Make sure the Timeline is active.**

   If necessary, click the Timeline's tab — the one with the clock icon.

2. **From the Transitions panel, drag the icon for the transition you want to use down to the Timeline.**

3. **In the Timeline, drag the transition to the appropriate spot relative to the clip(s) you're going to transition.**

If the transition will affect the beginning of a clip (such as a fade in), drag it to the left side of that clip. If the transition will affect the end of that clip (such as a fade out), drag it to the right of the clip. If the transition is between two clips, drag it between those two clips in the Timeline.

4. **When the appropriate highlight appears between clips, release the mouse button.**

In the Timeline, a space doesn't open up as it does in the Clip Viewer; instead, you see a faint blue line appear at the point where the transition will be placed (see Figure 6-4). When you are at the right point and the blue line appears, release the mouse button to drop the transition.

Figure 6-4:
As you drag the transition, a blue line appears between clips.

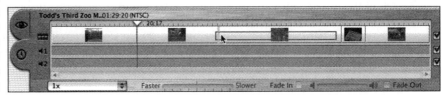

As in the Clip Viewer, placing a transition in the Timeline causes the transition to render immediately. When the rendering is finished, a small transition indicator appears on the Timeline.

Playing back a transition

After you have the transition placed and rendered, you'd like to watch it, right? That's easy. The best plan is to click the first clip in the transition (for a two-clip transition), hold down the Shift key, and then click the second clip in the transition. Or, if it's a one-clip transition, click the transition itself, hold down the Shift key, and click the clip that's being transitioned. You can even select the transition on its own: Just click it once in the Clip Viewer or Timeline.

Now, click Play in the Monitor and you'll see the rendered transition played back. If you have an external TV monitor or playback through your camcorder, you should see the transition on that external screen. In fact, transitions look much better — like the final product — on an external display.

Updating a transition

Want to tweak a transition a bit? Select the transition in the Clip Viewer or the Timeline, and the Transitions panel redisplays its settings. (If the Transitions panel isn't currently active, click the Transitions button to make it active.) Now you can use the panel to change those settings: Change the speed, click a different direction, or select a new transition from the list. Click the Update button to begin the process of re-rendering the transition. When the rendering is finished, the new settings replace the old ones.

Undoing or deleting a transition

If you've just completed a transition that you'd like to get rid of, you can use the Edit⇨Undo Add Transition command or press ⌘+Z. If you've performed other editing tasks since completing the transition, you can simply select the transition's icon (click it once in the Clip Viewer or Timeline) and choose Edit⇨Clear or press the Delete key on the keyboard. That deletes the transition, enabling you to add a different transition or move on to other editing tasks.

And don't worry about the video that was part of that transition. iMovie automatically adds it back to its original clip, safe from harm.

Transitioning in the middle

Do you have a transition that you'd like to put in the middle of one of your clips? This isn't often recommended because a transition should be used to tell the audience that you're changing ideas or points of view. Still, you may have a good reason to do it. (For instance, a series of fade out transitions on the same walking footage through the woods could suggest the passage of time, making it seem like the trek is taking longer than it is.)

The solution is to simply split the clip. There's no other way to add a transition in the middle of a clip. But even when you split the clip, the scene will appear to continue unhindered. This is a computer, after all, so it's not as if the film splice will get caught in the projector and start burning (although that's a feature slated for iMovie 3).

Here's how to add your transition in the middle of a clip:

1. **Select the clip in the Clip Viewer or Timeline.**

2. **In the Monitor window, place the playhead where you'd like the split (and, hence, the transition) to occur.**

3. **Choose Edit⇨Split Video Clip at Playhead.**

   The original clip splits into two.

4. **Head up to the Transitions panel and drag the transition from the panel to the point between the newly split clips.**

5. **Release the mouse button when a spot opens up between the two clips (in the Clip Viewer) or when the blue line appears between the two clips (in the Timeline).**

   The transition icon appears and the progress bar indicates that the clip is rendering.

If you split a single clip and then use a two-clip transition between the two newly created clips, the audio overlaps (just like the video does) during the two-clip transition. If that audio is someone talking, the audio that's part of the transition is useless because you have two bits of audio overlapping. That doesn't make the effect useless: It's a nice effect for a music video (or some other project in which the underlying audio isn't important), and you can correct the audio problems, as discussed in Chapter 13.

Transitioning over titles

Before you go on a tear with your transitions, note that you can't place a title on a portion of a clip that's part of a transition. For instance, if you have a fade in that happens during the first two seconds of a clip, you can't add a title during those two seconds.

Fortunately, you'll almost never do this anyway, because it's bad editing. A title is an effect and a transition is an effect, and having them both happen at the same time is not going to work. Instead, it's best to split the clip into a portion long enough for the transition and then another clip that can begin with the title overlay. You see how to do this in Chapter 7.

If, for some reason, you do want a title to be part of a clip that's in transition, first add the title to the clip and allow it to fully render. The title becomes part of the clip. Now, add the transition.

Exploring the Transitions

Now that you've seen how to add your transition to your movie, it's time to explore the built-in transitions that are at your disposal. Although you're free to experiment with all the transitions (especially with that handy little Preview button in the Transitions panel), I also toss my two cents into the discussion, describing those that I think are useful or, frankly, cheesy.

In Chapter 12, I discuss some other transitions you can add to iMovie by downloading and installing the iMovie Plug-in Pack 2 from Apple.

iMovie offers a few basic transitions that you can use to give certain scenes in your movie that sense of a new idea, time, or point of view. The fact that iMovie offers reasonably few transitions may seem odd at first, but I suggest that it's a good thing. After all, the best movies have relatively few transitions, and simple transitions are often the best.

Indeed, transitions are a little like fonts in newsletters and presentations. It seems cool to be able to add all sorts of fancy fonts to your newsletter, but the best newsletter designs generally use two fonts, which are often Helvetica and Times. Similarly, the best movies generally have very few transitions, and those transitions are almost always *not* of the high-thrill-factor variety.

Here's a quick look at the basic transitions included with iMovie 2:

- **Cross dissolve.** Used between two clips, the cross dissolve causes the first clip to appear to dissolve away, leaving the second clip running behind it. The cross dissolve is especially good for slight changes in point of view or time, or as a transition from one person to another within the same space (from a teacher to students, for instance). It's also good for a dream sequence quality.

- **Fade in.** You use this transition at the beginning of a single clip, fading from black up to the full color and brightness of the clip. Fade ins are good for starting stories or portions of stories and are especially effective during voiceovers and narrations, where you hear sounds before you see the images. (More on those sorts of edits in Chapter 8.)

✔ **Fade out.** Used at the end of a single clip, a fade out can suggest the end of a story or your entire iMovie. Fade outs are especially good for poignant endings. Incidentally, avoid following a fade out with a fade in. An abrupt cut or a two-clip transition such as a dissolve or a push that follows a fade in can be effective.

✔ **Overlap.** Used between two clips, an overlap is similar to a cross dissolve. In a cross dissolve, however, the first clip disappears, and in an overlap, the second clip appears on top of the first. This transition tends to suggest "this story continues at a different location." It's a great transition for news stories, projects, and anything with audio narration.

✔ **Push.** A push is used between two clips. The first clip's last few frames of video seems to be shoved aside (or down or up) by the next clip's frame. Although the push is a little gimmicky, you can use it to change locations and stories — to move to the next reporter at the trade show, for instance, or to end a scene on a wacky or punchy note.

✔ **Scale down.** The scale down is used between two clips as well. In this one, the first clip becomes a smaller and smaller box, disappearing in front of your eyes, while the second clip plays behind it until, lo and behold, it's the only video left on the screen. This is another gimmick, one you see on lighthearted magazine-style TV shows. The scale down is most useful when you're ending a particular story or idea, especially when the second clip is something familiar to the viewer, such as the host of your show or a special graphic you've designed. This transition sort of suggests "this segment is over, now back to Roger and Diane at the news desk."

Chapter 7

Giving Credit: Adding Titles and Text

· ·

In This Chapter

▶ Adding basic titles to your movie

▶ Adding subtitles

▶ Setting margins

▶ Splitting a clip before you add titles

▶ Creating closing credits

· ·

Good-looking titles, credits, and subtitles are among the many ways that iMovie can turn your production into something that makes people corner you in the hallway and ask, pointedly, "How did you do that?" Even the most basic home or vacation videos will look that much better with a fancy title sequence or scrolling credits at the end.

And subtitles don't have to be in French, either. *Subtitles* are also what we call the graphics you put on the screen to show someone's name and title, such as Betty Schmooze, VP of Marketing. Add those subtitles to your organizational or corporate video and watch the jaws drop. Who knew you were so good? Maybe they should make digital video your full-time job!

In this chapter, you see iMovie's interface for adding titles, subtitles, and credits to your movie. Then you dive into the nitty-gritty of putting the titles on the screen, including a few hints on what to do and what not to do. The fact is, with the right music, you could do a movie of nothing but titles and subtitles. It wouldn't be a good movie, but there you go.

Adding Titles to Your Movie

If you read through Chapter 6, you may be ready for some of what's coming in this section. After all, you use that same area in the top-right corner to select your titles as you do to select your transitions; you just switch it to the Titles panel. And you use the same drag-and-drop technique to choose where your titles will appear in the Clip Viewer or Timeline. The only thing that has really changed at all is everything else. We focus on those parts here.

One of the major differences between titles and transitions is that titles are generally added so that they become part of the clip that you choose to title. (A transition, by contrast, is added before or after a clip but remains sort of separate.)

You can create two basic types of titles: titles over existing footage and over-black titles. If you want the title of your movie to appear over the images that play in your first clip, you can do that. It looks cool, especially if your first clip is a wide shot from a helicopter of, say, New York, L.A., or Tokyo. When you add a title to a clip, iMovie goes through a rendering process in which it draws the title on the individual frames of the clip.

Alternatively, you can choose a special Over Black option that creates a black background for your title, which in effect creates a new title clip that you can move around in the Clip Viewer.

You can't add a title to a transition, however. iMovie won't let you do it. This is probably a good thing, because having two effects happening on the screen at once can be a little like having two lead singers in a heavy metal rock band — too much of a good thing.

The only way around this is to first create a title on a clip and then add a transition to the titled clip. A better way to deal with this, however, is probably to split the clip to create the title. I discuss the advantage of doing that later, in the "Splitting a Clip before Titling" section.

One on one with the Title panel

To begin adding titles to your movie, you need to display the Title panel. Click the Title button at the bottom of the Shelf area (on the right side of the iMovie interface). That displays the Title panel, which is a little busy (see Figure 7-1).

With the Title panel open, you see a list of title types to choose from, including their names and a small blue-green (aqua? turquoise?) icon. Unlike the icons for transitions, this one doesn't tell you anything other than *T* for *title*. Each icon's main purpose is to serve as something you can drag into the Timeline or Clip Viewer. Next to the list is the direction controller, which you can click when you're implementing a scrolling or moving title. Some titles fly in from one direction or another, and you can select that direction with this control.

Choose the speed and amount of pause

Title preview area

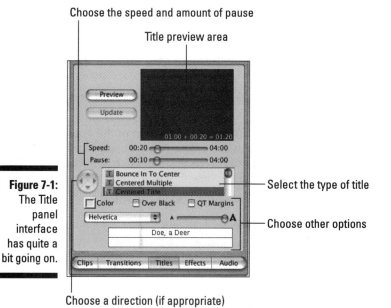

Figure 7-1:
The Title
panel
interface
has quite a
bit going on.

Select the type of title

Choose other options

Choose a direction (if appropriate)

Above the list are two slider controls, one for the speed of the title and one for pausing. The speed is the overall amount of time in seconds and fractions of a second that the title effect will take to complete. The pause is an extra bit of time you can select to leave a *motion* title on the screen after it has worked its magic. The title might fly in from one side of the frame or another, but if you want it to stay on-screen a little while longer, you choose that time with the Pause slider.

Up above those sliders is the preview area, where you see titles previewed the moment you select them. You can also click the Preview button to see the title in the Monitor window (rendered on the fly, so the quality is lower) or click the Update button to alter a title that has been added to a clip.

At the bottom of the Title panel are a number of options for customizing the text, such as Color, a fonts menu, a font size slider bar, and two special options: Over Black and QT Margins, discussed a bit later. Below that is the text area, where you type the text that will be used to create the title.

Creating a basic title

With the preliminaries out of the way, you can move on to adding a basic title. In my definition, a *basic title* is one with no action that appears over video within one of your clips. This is a common way to give your movie its beginning title or to title sections of your video.

Here's how to quickly add a basic title to a clip in your movie:

1. **Select the clip you want to title in the Clip Viewer or Timeline.**

   Note my annoying habit of using the word *title* as a verb. It's one of those wannabe-Hollywood traits.

2. **In the Title panel, select Centered Title from the list of possible titles.**

   You see a quick preview of the title in the title preview area. If you don't have any text in the text area down at the bottom of the Title panel, this preview will probably be worthless. (You won't see any words!) Note, though, that throughout the next steps you can click the Centered Title item again at any time to see a preview of your title-in-progress.

3. **At the bottom of the screen, type the text of the title.**

4. **Use the font menu to select the font for the title.**

5. **Use the font slider to select the size of the font.**

6. **Click the Centered Title list item again to see a mini-preview in the title preview area (see Figure 7-2).**

   This should give you a good sense of how the title is shaping up.

7. **Head back to Steps 4 and 5 to tweak the look of the title text as necessary.**

8. **Choose a speed for the title using the Speed slider control.**

   For Centered Title, you're limited to four seconds for the title to appear and disappear (not including the amount of time it pauses, as discussed next.)

Figure 7-2:
Click a title
name in the
title list to
see how
it looks.

9. **Select an amount of time for the title to pause on the screen using the Pause slider.**

   The minimum is ten frames (about ⅙ second for NTSC video), but you can make the title remain on the screen for up to four seconds before it starts to fade out again. Notice that, in the title preview area, the amount of time required for the entire title is calculated for you — 02:00 + 00:1400.50 = 02:14, for instance, suggests that the two-second speed plus the fourteen-frame pause will take about two and a half seconds, or 2:14 in time code notation. That's handy to know because you probably have a certain amount of time in which you'd like your title to fit so that it looks good overlaying a clip.

   Your title doesn't *have* to fit within the selected clip. If you make a title that's longer than the first clip that's selected, the title simply continues to the next clip. In fact, it can continue over a transition, if you like.

   Now that you've set the options for your title, the next step is to preview it in the Monitor.

10. **Click the Preview button in the Title panel.**

   You see a frame-by-frame view of the newly titled video in the Monitor. Why frame by frame? Because the title hasn't been rendered yet, so iMovie must still do some math and processing before it can play back the title smoothly.

Adding (or removing) the title with the Clip Viewer

If you're happy with the preview, you're ready to add the title to a clip in the Clip Viewer. It's easy enough — just drag the title's icon (it's a Centered Title in my example) from the list of titles down to the beginning of the clip you'll be adding the title to. This opens a small gap in the Clip Viewer, which tells you that iMovie is ready to accept the title. Release the mouse button and the title begins to render. A small red bar at the bottom of the clip shows the progress of the rendering process (see Figure 7-3).

As the rendering process is complete, there's often a little bit of fallout. If the title portion of the clip takes up less time than the actual clip itself (for instance, the clip is eight seconds but the title took only four seconds), iMovie splits the clip into two — the one that has the title and the one that doesn't. The first clip is named based on the title; the second has the clip's original name (See Figure 7-4).

Figure 7-3:
Drag a title icon to the Clip Viewer and a gap opens up; once dropped, you see the render bar progress until the title is completed.

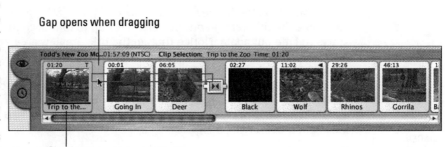

Gap opens when dragging

Here's a title already rendering

Figure 7-4:
After adding a title to the Going In clip, it was split in two; the first one is the title clip.

Here's the *T*

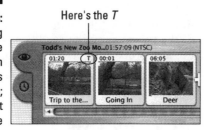

Title clips are distinguished in the Clip Viewer by the small *T* that appears in the top-right corner of the clip's slide icon. This is convenient, but watch out for two things. First, if you move the titled clip, any non-titled clip that was created during the rendering process does not necessarily come along for the ride, so you might be accidentally messing up the order of your movie. Second, if you delete the title clip, the video that's part of the title clip is added *back to* the non-titled clip (if one was created). In other words, if I delete Trip To The . . . in Figure 7-4, all of that video is added back to the Going In clip, which was the original before the titling process split it into two clips. When you delete a title clip, you simply undo the title rendering itself.

Adding the title using the Timeline

If the Timeline is active, using it to add a title is about as easy as using the Clip Viewer — it's just not quite as animated. C'mon, admit it. Using the Clip Viewer is *fun*.

Drag the Title's icon from the Title Panel down to the Timeline. Move to the beginning of the clip where you'd like the title to be added, and a small blue line appears. When you see the line, release the mouse button. The title is added to the clip. Now, a small red line appears at the bottom of the clip to indicate that the title is being rendered. When the line has progressed across the clip, the rendering is finished. (See Figure 7-5.)

Figure 7-5:
A title is already rendering on the first clip; now I'm adding a title to the second clip.

The Thin Blue Line

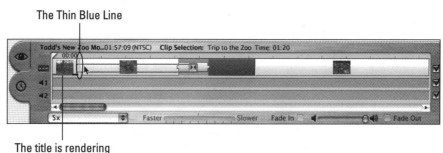

The title is rendering

You can't really remove a title using the Timeline. Instead, you must switch back to the Clip Viewer and delete the title clip to restore the video to the original clip sans title text.

But, that's okay. There's stuff that the Clip Viewer can't do that the Timeline can. Nanner, nanner, bo, bo.

Oomph it up: Action titles

You've seen how to add a basic, boring title. You're probably thinking to yourself, how about all those other ones? There's, like, a whole list of titles we haven't covered yet. What the heck is wrong with this author?

Plenty. But let's try to focus on the titles, here. Action titles are so defined because they do more than just sit there: They fly onto the screen, bounce, and scroll, oblivious to the havoc they wreak in their wake. And for the most part, they're about as easy to add as a basic title.

 The only real difference is that action titles often have a direction in which they're moving, which means the Direction control comes into play. You'll also find that action titles tend to require a little more tweaking in the Speed and Pause categories because more is going on, making the timing more crucial.

So which ones are the action titles? Here's a quick look:

- **Bounce In To Center.** In this one, your entire title comes in from the top or the bottom of the screen and then pauses. After the pause, the title disappears. The effect adds a light or happy feel to the credit.

- **Drifting.** Similar to the basic Centered Title, the main difference is that Drifting causes the title to move slightly to one side before it fades out. This is a great effect for something that's supposed to be sinister or scary. Ooooh.

- **Flying Letters.** Each letter of your title flies in from the top or the bottom of the screen. It's a good effect, forcing your audience to feel the impact of each letter as they read. Effective for "Death by Fire!" or something equally expressive and action-y.

- **Flying Words.** This is a good effect for surprising your audience. The entire title flies in from the top or the bottom of the screen, landing in the middle. Add some zzzzzzzzzz-bong! type music behind this title and it's an effective sequence for either an action flick or one of those cheesy entertainment news shows.

- **Scroll with Pause.** With this one, your entire title scrolls up (or down or left or right), stops in the middle for the length you choose to Pause, and then completes its journey off the other side of the screen. What's it good for? I like it for a quirky, comic title, perhaps one that's between two sequences. It reminds me a little of mice scurrying across the screen; it's cute and grabs your attention (especially if you're a cat). Something as simple as "Then . . . on Tuesday . . ." could be made a bit funnier with this effect.

Select one of the titles and then go through all the motions: Type in some text, choose a font and font size, and then choose your Speed and Pause time settings. (You'll probably want to experiment with the time settings to see which ones look exactly right. Each time you change the Speed or Pause setting, the preview plays again.) Now, use the direction control to click the direction in which you'd like the title to move. I suggest trying them all at least once to get a sense of which looks best.

When all the options are set, you're ready to drag the title to the Clip Viewer or Timeline. Do so as discussed in one of the "Adding the title . . ." sections, presented previously in this chapter.

A brief mention of title color

So far, I've gone through most of this discussion while skipping a completely decent and wholesome looking button right there on the Title Panel interface — the color control. What am I thinking?

I'm thinking that when you create titles that go over video, rarely does any color but the default look good. The default title text has a black drop shadow behind it, so using black-colored text, which would seem to make sense in some cases, ends up looking odd. But if you're putting a title over a very light, very bright video image, you may want to experiment with a darker gray or black color for the title text.

To change the color, click the color button. A small palette of colors appears (see Figure 7-6). If you click a color once, it's previewed in the title preview area. If you double-click a color, it's selected and the palette disappears.

Figure 7-6:
Choosing
a color
for your
title text.

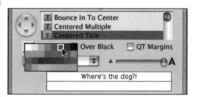

If you absolutely want to use a color for your credits, go ahead and do so. I can't stop you. I'm not your daddy. (None of you. Forget the rumors.) But just for the record, it's not often done. White-on-dark images or black-on-light images are the most readable on a TV screen.

Creating an over-black title

So far, all the titles you've seen have been rendered over the video as it runs. If your opening sequence shows your family walking into Disneyland, the title appears over your kids tripping through the glorious archway, into the tunnel under the train, and on to Main Street. (Did you know that the second floors of the buildings are built at somewhere near three-fifths scale to give the appearance that they're taller than they really are?)

But what if you'd like a simple black background for your title? This is an effective way to start a video or break up a presentation with titles, drawing your audience directly to the words and — for all practical purposes — peeling back their eyelids and making them read. It's also really, really easy to do.

Here's how to make an over-black title: Turn on the Over Black option. Regardless of the type of title you're creating, you'll always see the Over Black option on the Title panel. Click the box next to Over Black to put a checkmark in it. When you do so, a preview in the title preview area shows you — lo and behold — the title over a black background. Looks good, doesn't it?

When you create an over-black title, dragging it to the Clip Viewer or Timeline doesn't cause the title to black out any portion of the clip. Instead, it creates a new black clip that lasts the duration of the title sequence (see Figure 7-7). In other words, its adds time to your movie. If you have a five-second title sequence (that is, if the Speed and Pause times you set add up to five seconds), you add five seconds to your overall movie. This shouldn't be a problem, but it can be an issue if you've already timed your music or audio carefully. (This is one reason why you generally edit audio toward the end of the editing process.)

Figure 7-7:
Creating an over-black title adds to the total time of your movie.

Giving People Names: Subtitles

In case you tuned in late, the subtitles I talk about in this section aren't necessarily those that you see in the films they show at the Academy Awards that only people who've gone to special MPAAS screenings can vote on. Subtitles are pretty much anything you want to put on the bottom of the screen as a type of overlay for the video. In other words, they don't have to be in another language. In fact, the only real distinction in iMovie is the fact that subtitles show up on a different part of the screen.

iMovie has three built-in title options that you can use as subtitles: Stripe Subtitle, Music Video, and Typewriter. Stripe Subtitle is a good-looking option that's perfect for overlays in documentaries, project videos, or corporate video when you need to identify someone or something (see Figure 7-8).

The Music Video subtitle works a little differently, enabling you to add more text in the bottom-left corner of the screen, much like MTV does for the title, artist, and label of its music videos. (You can use the Direction controller to select the right side of the screen, if you like.)

The Music Video subtitle looks good not only for videos, but also whenever you need additional information on the screen. Just remember to set the Speed slider so that you give your audience enough time to read the text. Figure 7-9 shows the Music Video title in action; note the extra entry space iMovie gives you in the Title panel for typing an entire block of text.

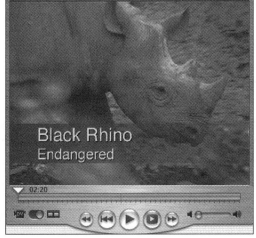

Figure 7-8:
Identifying
something
on-screen
with a
subtitle.

Block of text

Figure 7-9:
The Music
Video
subtitle
enables you
to put a full
block of text
in the
bottom
corner of
the screen.

The third type of subtitle, Typewriter, is perfect for the *X-Files* aficionados among us. With this one, each character appears on the screen as if typed from left to right. This is standard for titles that establish the time or location of a scene, such as "10 A.M., FBI Headquarters," popular on *X-Files* and their ilk. It's a nice effect for any subtitle, as long as you don't overuse it.

For a true "typewriter" look, choose Courier or Monaco as the font for this subtitle.

Selecting QuickTime Margins

The subtitles discussed in the preceding section offer one example of an interesting issue in iMovie. At first glance, you may notice that some subtitle text seems a bit far from the edges of the screen. There's a good reason for this.

A television, unlike a computer monitor, operates in what's called overscan mode, meaning there's more of the TV picture than is displayed on the standard TV screen. Whereas the image on your computer monitor has a small black border around the edges (unless you're using an LCD display), most TV screens are slightly rounded at the edges, with the TV's housing covering the very edges of the screen.

What this means to iMovie is simple: It's important to keep titles and text in the *safe area* of an edited video image. Although you can see text at the very edge of the video clip in iMovie, you can't be sure of seeing that text on all TV screens — unless the text is placed in the safe area. By default, that's exactly what iMovie does, which is why the text appears padded from the border of the screen.

 For the most part, the safe area is a good thing. But if you're editing your movie for distribution through QuickTime — that is, as a video that will be played only on a computer screen — you don't need to worry about the safe area because QuickTime displays the entire, rectangular video clip. So, if you'd like your titles and subtitles a bit closer to the edges, just select the QT Margins option before you drag the title icon to its clip.

Splitting a Clip before Titling

One problem with the current approach to subtitles is that you have to start them at the beginning of a clip. It's often useful to place a subtitle — especially one with a name or additional information about the subject that's on-screen — at some point in the middle of a clip. The solution? Split the clip.

Remember that splitting a clip into two doesn't affect the way the clip looks when it's played back — there are no jumps or frayed edges to worry about. But splitting a clip does allow you to add a subtitle effect (or even a regular title effect) at a point that *appears* to be in the middle of the clip to your audience. Here's how:

1. **Select the clip in the Clip Viewer.**

2. **Make sure the subtitle options are set.**

3. **Using the Monitor, place the playhead at the point in the clip where you want to put the subtitle.**

4. **Choose Edit⇨Split Video Clip at Playhead.**

5. **In the Title panel, set your subtitle options and text as outlined in the "Giving People Names: Subtitles" section, and then drag the title icon to the beginning of the *second* clip that was created by the split.**

   A gap opens up, enabling you to drop the title icon.

6. **Drag the title icon to the beginning of the *second* clip that was created by the split.**

   A gap opens up, enabling you to drop the title icon.

7. **Drop the title icon.**

   The title begins to render.

Now, play back both parts of the split clip and the subtitle seems to appear in the middle of the clip, as planned.

The QuickTime Movie SplitClipSubtitle.mov in the Chapter 7 folder on the *iMovie 2 For Dummies* CD-ROM shows this effect.

Adding Credits to Your Movie

You'll find out very quickly that the credits are the most important part of a movie — at least, they are for everyone involved in your movie. The stars, the producers, the caterer, the dog — anyone and everyone who has something to do with your movie deserves some credit, and they'll probably go storming off in a huff if you forget them or, heaven forbid, misspell their names.

iMovie has a number of different credit sequences, some of which are appropriate for opening credits, some for closing credits, and some you can use wherever you want. The basic difference between a credit title and the titles you've seen before is simply that credit effects generally allow you to plug in a lot of text at once.

Adding opening credits

The title effect that looks most like an opening credits sequence is the Centered Multiple title, which is similar to the Centered Title option, except that it allows you to enter more than one name. With the Centered Multiple title sequence, you enter up to two lines of text for each screen. The first two lines are displayed and then fade out, then the next lines fade in, pause, and fade out, and so forth. That's perfect for giving the title of your movie, then the star, then the writer, then the producer, then the director . . . just like you see in the movies.

Select the Centered Multiple option in the Title panel, and the text area at the bottom of the panel changes slightly. What you're seeing are the controls that allow you to add more than the basic two lines of text (called a *Title Pair*) that Centered Title supports (see Figure 7-10).

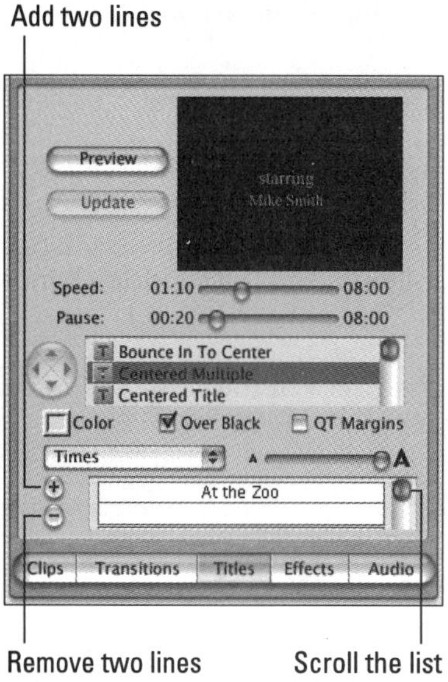

Add two lines

Figure 7-10:
Centered
Multiple has
plus and
minus
buttons for
adding and
removing
extra lines
of text.

Remove two lines   Scroll the list

When you click the Add Title Pair (+) button, another box appears in the text area, complete with two more lines for typing text. Each pair has a top line and a bottom line, although you don't have to use both. The top line creates text that's slightly larger than the bottom line. If you want to enter just a one-line title ("Trip to the Zoo," for example), you might put it on the top line and leave the bottom line blank. For the next Title Pair, you might put "Starring" on the first line and "John Doe" on the second line.

To add another two lines, click the Add Title Pair (+) button; the two lines appear in a new box at the *bottom* of the list, so you may need to scroll down to see the pair. You can also drag a Title Pair box around in the list if, for instance, you need to put a credit *before* another that's already in the list. Just point the mouse at a Title Pair, hold down the mouse button, and drag the pair to another part of the list. You can delete a pair by selecting it with the mouse (click once and the box around the pair becomes highlighted) and then clicking the Remove Title Pair (-) button.

When you click the Add Title Pair button, it adds a pair immediately after the currently selected Title Pair. So, if you need to add a title pair between two that already exist, select the first one (so that the box that surrounds the pair is darkened) and then click the Add Title Pair button. The new blank pair appears between the two.

When you've finished entering Title Pairs, you can click Centered Multiple again to see a small preview in the title preview area. Then, adjust the Speed and Pause (the amount of time each Title Pair appears on the screen). Finally, drag the icon next to Centered Multiple down to the Clip Viewer and place it at the beginning of the clip you'd like it to overlay. Or, if you're using the Over Black option, drag the icon to the point in the iMovie where you'd like the Over Black title to be created. The rendering process will begin. When it's finished, you have credits!

Adding closing credits

The interface for closing credits is similar to that for opening credits using Centered Multiple, but the result is a little different. For closing credits, you'll likely want a scrolling list with two sides: a left side that gives the name of the character or the position on the crew and a right side that gives the associated individual's name. You can accomplish this effect using the Rolling Credits or Rolling Centered Credits title. Figure 7-11 is using the Over Black option.

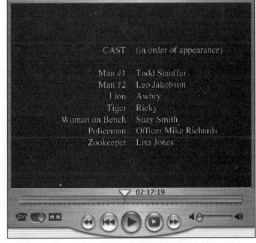

Figure 7-11: The Rolling Centered Credits option looks a little more modern than the Rolling Credits effect.

Being Woody: Over Black and Centered Multiple

Are you a Woody Allen fan? Even if you aren't, if you've seen two different Woody Allen movies, you may have noticed that there's a certain *something* to the way he does his titles and opening credits. They're always the same, and they have a particular look that can make a movie instantly look sort of artsy.

Using Centered Multiple and the Over Black option, you can instantly create a Woody Allen-esque opening credits sequence that I like to call "Just Add Gershwin." You'll see what I mean.

Choose Centered Multiple as the title type, and type your title into the text box area. Now, choose Times or Times New Roman from the font menu and make the font size about ¾ on the slider. Next, click the Over Black option. Choose a Speed that's somewhere around 2 seconds for each credit (for instance, 10 seconds for five screens of titles) and about 2 seconds of Pause for each.

That's all it takes. After you finish typing all the credit text, drag the Centered Multiple icon down to the beginning of your movie. Next, move on to Chapter 9 to add a Gershwin (or Gershwin-like) soundtrack. You might also want to check out Chapter 10, where you can add a sepia-tone old-style effect, too. (As a bonus, Appendix Z discusses how to snub the Academy if you ever win an Oscar.)

Select either Rolling Credits or Rolling Centered Credits in the Title panel and then enter as many Title Pairs as necessary in the text area at the bottom, using the Add Title Pair (+) button to add additional two-line entry boxes. In this case, the top line is for the left side of the credit roll (where you usually put the character name or one of those job name's that no one understands, such as Gaffer or Best Boy). The bottom line is for the right side of the credit roll, where you generally put the person's (or entity's) name.

It can take awhile to enter all your credits, but at least it's cheaper than paying salaries. After they're entered, select an appropriate Speed using the slider control; check the title preview area to see whether the credit roll is too fast.

Now you're ready to render the credits. Drag the icon next to Rolling Credits or Rolling Centered Credits to the Clip Viewer and place it before the clip over which you'd like the credits to scroll. If you've chosen Over Black (as you likely will for more credit rolls), you can drag the title icon to the very end of your movie and drop it there. The rendering takes place and, after a few moments, your credit roll is ready.

Actually, both Rolling Credits and Rolling Centered Credits give you the option of scrolling down the screen, instead of just up the screen, by selecting the down arrow in the Direction controller. I don't know why you'd want to do that, but thought I should let you know that the option exists to avoid getting angry letters from any members of People for Additional Credit Roll Alternative Techniques (PACRATs) out there.

Scrolling blocks

So you know how to add cast and crew credit rolls, but what about adding those all-important text blocks containing copyright lines or dedications or "No animals were harmed in the making of this motion picture." You use the Scrolling Block title.

Select Scrolling Block from the title list and then enter a paragraph of text in the text area. You can press Return while typing to create another paragraph of text; you can even press Return twice to add additional space.

After you've entered the text, use the Speed slider bar to determine how quickly the scroll will take place and then drag the Scrolling Block title icon down to the Clip Viewer to place it and begin the rendering process. (If you've chosen Over Black, you can drag the title icon to the very end of your movie; otherwise, you need to drag the icon to the beginning of the clip over which this scrolling block will appear.)

You may find that Scrolling Block is the easiest way to add all sorts of credits, as long as you're willing to put up with the fact that every word in the block must be the same font, color, and point size.

Putting titles together for credits

Here's one you may have thought of already: You can get some really cool effects by using multiple *title* sequences to create your credits. For instance, using the Drifting title, you can create a title line that drifts slightly in one direction or another. But you can use that for credits, too. Create a title for the movie and have it drift in one direction. Then create another Drifting title, this time with the name of your actor or director, and have it drift in a different direction.

The only trick to this is that each title must be dragged to the Clip Viewer before the next one can be set up in the Title Area. Each is rendered individually. If you're using the Over Black option, you can simply keep dragging the titles down to the Clip Viewer and adding them after the previous effects (see Figure 7-12).

Figure 7-12:
You can drag title clips one after another to the Clip Viewer to put together some creative credits.

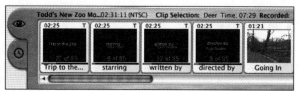

If you're not using Over Black, you must wait for each title to completely render before you can add the next title. After the first title is rendered, the clip is split into titled and untitled portions. Now you can drag the next title effect to the untitled portion. And don't forget that if you're overlaying multiple titles over a single video clip, the clip must be long enough to accommodate all those titles.

The movie CoolCredits.mov in the Chapter 7 folder on the CD-ROM shows title effects used as credits.

Chapter 8

Editing Your Audio

● ●

In This Chapter

▶ Taking another look at the Timeline

▶ Extracting, deleting, copying, and pasting audio

▶ Splitting, locking, and unlocking clips

▶ Altering a clip's volume and effects

● ●

*W*hat gives a movie that professional flair? Clearly it's a combination of things, such as good, smart camera work, interesting special effects, and a rockin' soundtrack. Those are all, indeed, very important.

One of the most important editing touches, however, is attention to audio. Audio is incredibly important to the quality of your movie, as well as an important component during the editing process. Close attention to the audio in your movie will really make the difference if you want a professional feel to your editing. In fact, audio is the cornerstone of some important editing techniques that go a little beyond drag-and-drop.

In this chapter, you take a look at the heart of iMovie's advanced editing capabilities — the Timeline. The Timeline is, in fact, primarily there to help you edit audio in your movie, including both the audio tracks (which I define as audio that you've recorded using your camcorder) as well as narration and music tracks, which I discuss in Chapter 9. Once you get to know the Timeline a little more intimately, you're ready to break out your audio, cut and edit it up, and even add in sound effects and other imported sounds.

Introducing the Timeline . . . Again

If you've read some of the previous chapters, you know that I touch on the Timeline only briefly. That's partly because it's a more sophisticated tool for piecing together movies, but mostly because the Timeline is really best suited for editing your audio and video together. The Clip Viewer is perfect for arranging clips, building transitions, and adding titles. The next step, though, is to dig into the Timeline to edit your audio.

The Timeline in theory

Start by taking a closer look at the Timeline. (That's right . . . scrunch in tight to your monitor.) To view the Timeline, click the Timeline tab that appears beneath the Clip Viewer tab. (The Timeline tab has as round-faced clock icon.) Now what you see is a linear representation of the video you've built so far, much as you see in the Clip Viewer. The difference is that the Timeline shows the different *tracks* of your movie, including a video track (the top one) and two audio tracks (see Figure 8-1).

Video track   Audio track #1   Audio track #2

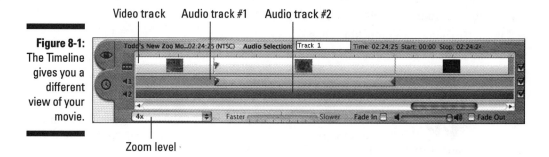

Figure 8-1:
The Timeline
gives you a
different
view of your
movie.

Zoom level

Allow me to digress into a little theory. The Timeline is different from the Clip Viewer because it shows you a linear, time-based representation of your entire iMovie. The focus with the Timeline isn't individual clips that can be shuffled back and forth however you like — that's what the Clip Viewer is for. The Timeline, instead, is about managing your movie at any given time.

For example, viewing the iMovie with the Clip Viewer, it's actually reasonably difficult to tell what, exactly, is happening at four minutes, three seconds into the entire movie. You have to do some math, which I am wholeheartedly against. But with the Timeline, you know exactly what is happening at that time.

Why is this significant? Well, first of all, the Timeline isn't about dragging and dropping clips to arrange them — it won't even let you do that. Instead, once you switch to the Timeline, it's assumed that the overall linear progressions of your scenes, transitions, and titles are set (for the most part). Second, the Timeline is really about tweaking — you can cut and paste, adding in a few things here and there, clean up the audio, and work with narration and some background music.

Third, the Timeline is about managing multiple *tracks* within your movie, and bringing them together as a cohesive whole. If you've ever taken music-reading lessons, you'll notice that the Timeline is a little like sheet music — the clefs, in this case, are tracks, which all make up a distinct portion of your movie. For the movie to be good, all three have to be in harmony.

The Timeline in fact

Whew! So much for stretched musical metaphors. Let's jump back into the pragmatic. The Timeline offers a few features worth pointing out, which I do here, in pretty much random order.

First, note that each clip is laid out on the video track, the top track of the Timeline, complete with a playhead indicator that shows you where the playhead is in relation to the clips in your movie.

You can individually select each clip in the Timeline by pointing to the clip with the mouse pointer and clicking. (No news there.) When a clip is selected, it becomes highlighted in yellow. You can select multiple clips by holding down the Shift key while clicking them, but the clips must be contiguous (they have to be touching one another). If you hold down the Shift key and select a clip that's not touching the currently selected clip, all clips between the two are also selected.

At the bottom of the Timeline are some special controls: menus, sliders, and check boxes. The menu at the bottom left is the Zoom menu (Apple calls it the Timeline zoom pop-up), where you can select the zoom level for viewing this Timeline. What does this mean? If you select 1x, which means *no* zoom, you see the clips for your entire movie in one width of the Timeline. This can be useful in some cases, but the longer your movie, the shorter each individual clip appears in the Timeline. (After all, all of them have to squeeze in there.) With a long enough movie, that may make some of your clips difficult to select and work with (see Figure 8-2).

Figure 8-2:
At 1x zoom, some shorter clips will be tough to differentiate from others.

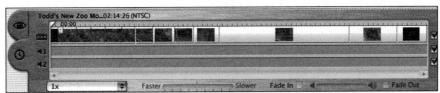

As this chapter progresses, you see that it's important to be able to perform precise mouse movements when you're working in the Timeline, so iMovie makes it possible for you to zoom in, effectively seeing only part of the movie at one time. Using the menu, you can select 2x, 3x, 5x, and so on up to 50x, which shows you only a few seconds worth of your clip. If you're the sort of person who doesn't make decisions well, try the Auto option, which attempts to automatically show you clips in such a way that they're easy to work with.

(In reality, as with most such settings in modern computer applications, it simply automatically annoys you with the sheer cluelessness of most of its choices.)

Other controls along the bottom of the Timeline include the Clip Speed slider, which you can use to speed up or slow down the action in a clip. (It's for slow-motion and fast-motion effects, which I discuss in Chapter 12.) You also see the Fade In and Fade Out buttons, which you can use on individual clips to slowly bring the sound level up at the start of the clip (Fade In) or to slowly bring the sound level down at the end of a clip (Fade Out). Along with those is a Clip Volume slider, which enables you to select the volume for a given clip (or series of clips if you've selected more than one). You take a closer look at those in the "Fading a clip in and out" section.

Finally, out of a desire for diligence and a nagging sense of duty, I point out that there are three small check boxes located at the far right of the Timeline. You use them to turn on and off the video, audio #1, and audio #2 tracks, respectively. After you get into editing your audio and sound tracks separately from your video, you might find it useful to turn off one or more of the tracks to preview only one of them. Or you might even want to export your video with only certain tracks selected. At this point, though, it's kind of academic because unless you've recorded any sounds or broken out your video — which you do in the next section — you have only video to turn on or off.

Want to see more detail about your clips while looking at the Timeline? Open the iMovie preferences (choose Edit➪Preferences) and click the Views tab. Now, turn on the Show More Details option. You can also play with the other options here if you'd like to change the look and feel of the Timeline further.

Editing Audio Clips

You may notice an undercurrent of enthusiasm in this chapter. That's because you're about to do something that makes iMovie a powerful program. So far, most of the edits have been sophisticated and easy to accomplish, but they've also been edits you can perform fairly easily with older technologies, such as a VHS camcorder and a few thousand dollars worth of accessories from Radio Hut or Video Shack or whatever.

iMovie, however, enables you to actually *separate* the audio and the video that you've recorded using your camcorder. That means a few different things, not the least of which is the fact that you can get rid of audio that you don't find useful and replace it with something else. For instance, if you have some good video of your child's fifth birthday party, but feel it was ruined by, say, all the kids yelling and screaming in the background, then you could break out that audio and delete it. Then, record some Chopin or Mozart (see Chapter 9) or an old Keystone Cops soundtrack and you have (to my ear) a much improved video presentation.

But beyond removing the audio from a given clip, you can break out the audio and then edit it separately from the video. What this means, in a nutshell, is that the audio playing through the speakers can be different than the video on the screen. Because audio from one clip can play under the video of another clip, you can perform specialized audio edits that will go a long way toward a professional-quality movie.

Again, I ask, beg, and cajole you to watch a little more TV. (I know it's a sacrifice, but it's for the Cause.) How often do you hear one thing while you're watching something else? All the time, especially during those news magazine shows such as *20/20* and *60 Minutes.* As the reporter talks, you cut to video of what she's talking about and then back to her and then back to more video, all the while hearing a continuous audio track.

But audio edits aren't just about narration. Watch even more TV and you'll hear audio of actors who are off-camera, experts testifying about cars exploding while cars are exploding on the screen, and so on. For the type of video you're likely creating — home, organization, business, or educational video — adding a few special audio edits in which the visuals are dynamic while the audio remains the same is just darned cool. That's why this chapter thrills me.

Oh — and I'm a geek.

Extracting your audio

All of this audio editing starts with a fairly simple command: Extract Audio. What this does is removes the audio from the selected clip — where it was previously part of the video track — and places the audio on the audio #1 track. After the audio is broken out, you can edit it, cut it, or move it around in your movie.

After you extract audio, it's difficult to cut or crop the video clip without messing up the synchronization of the audio clip. So make sure that the video clip is well cropped or cut, as detailed in Chapter 5 before you extract audio.

To extract audio, select a clip in the Timeline and choose Advanced⇨Extract Audio. The result is a small alert box telling you that audio is being extracted from the clip. When it's finished, a new audio clip appears on the audio #1 track, as shown in Figure 8-3.

The extracted audio appears on the audio #1 track in a pale orange line, which should run the length of the video clip because it was just extracted from it. (Even if the sound wasn't very good, your camcorder was likely recording something, so nearly all video clips initially have an audio component that can be extracted.)

Locked icons

Figure 8-3:
An
extracted
audio clip
appears on
the audio #1
track.

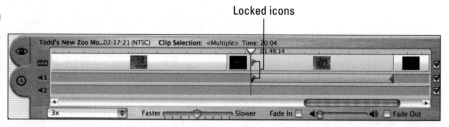

You may notice that small pushpin icons appear at the beginning of the audio clip and its host video clip. This suggests that the audio clip is locked (pinned) to that point in the video. This convenient little feature basically means that if you edit or move the video, the audio will continue to begin at the point in the video clip where the two have been locked. I explore this more as I go along. For now, know that as long as your audio is locked to a particular part of a video clip, it will stick with that video clip through thick and thin.

Removing audio

After you've extracted audio from your video clip, the easiest thing to do is to remove it from the project. How? Select the audio clip in question. It'll turn from a pale orange to a slightly brighter orange. (If you have more than one extracted audio clip, make sure the one you want to remove is the only clip that's highlighted, or bright orange.) Now, choose Edit⇨Clear or press the Delete key on the keyboard. The audio is gone. You can get it back using Edit⇨Undo, but that's your only choice. Otherwise, you have to re-import the clip, edit it again, add it to your movie, and extract the audio again. So before deleting audio, be sure that's what you want to do.

Copying, cutting, and pasting

Along with using the Clear command, you can bring in some of the usual suspects — the Copy, Cut, and Paste commands — to do your bidding. To place a copy of the audio on the Mac's clipboard and also leave the audio clip in the Timeline, select the audio clip and then choose Edit⇨Copy or press ⌘+C. If you'd like to remove the audio clip while placing it on the Mac's clipboard, highlight the clip and choose Edit⇨Cut or press ⌘+X.

Now, you can move the playhead to another location on the Timeline, and choose Edit⇨Paste or press ⌘+V. The selected audio appears at the playhead's position.

The only thing to watch out for in this scenario may have already occurred to you. If you paste an audio clip on the audio track of a clip that hasn't yet had its audio extracted, you'll hear both audio clips when you play that section of your movie. The solution is to extract the audio from the video clip, remove it (discussed in the preceding section), and then paste the new audio clip in its place.

Cropping audio

Do you have an audio clip that you want to make a little smaller? A few reasons to want to crop an audio clip come to mind, but I'm not telling you. Think of your own reasons. (Okay, maybe you want to copy and paste a bigger audio clip into a smaller spot. Or maybe you'd like part of the audio of a clip to fade to silence before the video clip ends. Or maybe you want to do some J- and L-cutting, which I discuss later in this chapter.)

Cropping audio is easy:

1. **Select the audio clip you want to crop.**

   It gets pretty orange all over. You also see two crop markers, which look like triangles.

2. **Grab one of the crop markers and move it toward the other one.**

   After you select a crop marker, you can press the right or left arrow key to move the crop marker frame by frame, or hold down the Shift key to move in ten-frame steps. Note that the lighter orange parts of the clip are now deselected.

3. **Grab the other crop marker and move it toward the first one, if desired (see Figure 8-4).**

4. **Choose Edit⇨Crop from the menu.**

   Any part of the audio clip that was lighter orange (deselected) is deleted.

Figure 8-4: In this case, I'm cropping from one side of the clip only.

Note that you don't have to invoke the Edit⇨Crop command if you don't want to. The mere act of moving the crop markers in causes the non-marked parts of the clip to no longer play in your movie. If you'd like to keep parts of an audio clip from playing, but you're not ready to delete the audio, just stop at Step #3 in the preceding list.

Splitting audio clips

Need to split an audio clip? If you need to magically transform one audio clip into two — count 'em, two — clips:

1. **Select the audio clip in the Timeline.**

2. **Place the playhead where you want to split the audio clip.**

   You can either click in the playhead area above the video clip or drag the playhead to where you want the split.

3. **Choose Edit⇨Split Selected Audio Clip at Playhead.**

   (If you don't see that option, you haven't selected the audio clip. Select it — remember, bright orange — and then position the playhead.) The clip is split, as shown in Figure 8-5.

Figure 8-5:
The audio
clip has
been sawed
in two.

Need to put the clip back together? Choose Edit⇨Undo. Say "Abracadabra" loudly if anyone else is in the room. Trust me: They'll eat it up.

Locking and unlocking audio clips

The Timeline offers another feature you may find useful after you extract some audio. You can lock an audio clip to a particular portion of a video clip so that, regardless of whatever editing happens in the Timeline, the audio can't move relative to the video. The audio begins right where it's locked to the video clip, no matter what happens in the rest of the movie.

Make sense? It might require an example. Suppose I extract audio from a video clip and then unlock the audio. Figure 8-6 shows a clip extracted from the video clip above it and then unlocked from the clip.

Figure 8-6:
The audio
has been
unlocked
from the
video clip
above it.

Now, I go to the video clip right before this one and crop out a nice big chunk in a fit of creative-control rage. It's a director's cut. (Get it?) With that bit of video cut out, check out Figure 8-7 to see what happens to the audio. Whoops.

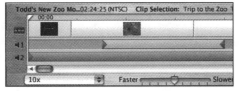

Figure 8-7:
Without
locking
down the
audio,
it won't
keep its
association
with its
video clip.

After cutting a video clip earlier in the Timeline, the video clip associated with the unlocked audio moves back to fill the empty space. But because the audio wasn't locked to the video, the audio stays in the same place. Now when I play this movie, the video begins before the audio does, and the two are out of sync. That's not what I want, so I begin to pout. I throw things at the actors. I yell that "I can't take this anymore" and storm off to my trailer.

The same sort of thing (sync problems, not cranky directors) can happen if you unlock an audio clip from a video clip, and then you switch to the Clip Viewer and move the video clip somewhere else. If the audio isn't locked to it, the audio will stay at that same spot on the Timeline.

Unlocking an audio clip

Technically, a clip is already locked when you first extract it. You unlock a clip when you *don't* want it to stay synchronized to a particular video clip. You probably won't unlock clips often, but sometimes you will want to unlock a clip quickly, edit the video track, and then relock the audio track to a new position relative to the video. (See the section "Making a J-cut" later in this chapter.)

Anyway, here's how you unlock a clip:

1. **Select the clip.**
2. **Choose Advanced⇨Unlock Audio Clip or press ⌘+L.**

That's it. Barely worth fitting into the numbered list, eh? Unfortunately, the numbered lists are mandated by Dummies Unilateral Headquarters (DUH) by direct order of the Vice Admiral in Charge of Making All Dummies Books Look Alike.

Interestingly, you don't actually have to unlock a clip before you move it around on the Timeline with the mouse. The lock doesn't keep *you* from moving the clip. The lock just keeps the audio clip synchronized with the video clip to which it's locked until you decide otherwise.

Locking an audio clip

So, an unlocked audio clip stays where it is even if the video clip above it moves. If you lock audio to a video clip, however, the audio clip and the video clip are as one. (Isn't it beautiful?)

Here's how to lock an audio clip:

1. **Select the audio clip with the mouse.**

It sounds simple, but there's actually a trick to this. First, click the area just above the video clip so that the playhead appears close to the side of the audio clip you're going to lock down. (If you're going to lock the beginning of the audio clip to the beginning of the video clip, click in the playhead area closer to the beginning of the audio clip.) Now, select the audio clip by clicking it. The playhead snaps right to the start of the audio clip. Cool, eh?

2. **Line up the playhead with the beginning of the video clip and the audio clip.**

You don't *have* to lock the audio clip to the beginning of a video clip. You can lock it to any portion of the video clip that you choose. (If you're trying to keep the video and audio of someone talking synchronized, though, you'll probably choose to lock audio to the beginning of the video clip.) To select a point in the video clip where you want to lock the audio clip, you can use the mouse, but I suggest pressing the right or left arrow keys on the keyboard.

3. **Choose Advanced⇨Lock Audio Clip and Playhead.**

This locks the audio and video clips. It also places the small pushpin icons on each (see Figure 8-8).

After the audio is locked, it will move along with the associated video clip, even if you switch back to the Clip Viewer and move the clip around again within the movie.

Moving an audio clip

Want about simply moving the clip around? I've talked about everything else, after all. After you extract an audio clip, you can move it by dragging the clip along the Timeline. Even if the audio clip is locked to a particular video clip, you can still move it. iMovie recognizes the lock only when an edit to the video would affect your audio, not when you move the audio clip on your own. In fact, when you have finished moving a locked clip, it locks once again to the spot where you drop it.

You can also highlight an audio clip (turn it bright orange) and then use the left and right arrow keys to move the clip frame-by-frame. (Hold down the Shift key and press the left or right arrow key to move ten frames at a time.) Note that, as far as iMovie is concerned, it's okay for two audio clips to overlap. They'll simply play simultaneously. (If you don't want that, crop one of the clips so that they're flush.)

If you'd like to move an audio clip to an exact moment on the Timeline, iMovie offers you a special way to do that. First, click in the playhead portion of the Timeline (just above the video track) to place the playhead *exactly* where you want the audio clip to begin or end. Now, drag the audio clip toward that playhead. As you drag, the playhead becomes a *ghost playhead* (see Figure 8-9). As you get close to the ghost playhead with the audio clip, the clip snaps to the ghost playhead. Release the mouse and the audio clip is in that exact position.

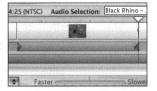

Changing a clip's volume

The Timeline interface makes it simple to change the volume of a particular audio clip after it has been extracted. This is great if you have audio in one clip that's a lot louder than audio in another clip. It's also useful when you intend to have narration or a soundtrack behind a particular clip and need to bring the audio level of the clip itself down a bit.

All you have to do is select the audio clip in the Timeline so that it becomes highlighted. (You can highlight more than one audio clip, if desired, by holding down the Shift key as you click each clip.) Now, using the small Volume slider at the bottom of the Timeline (see Figure 8-10), change the audio level for that clip.

Figure 8-10:
The Volume slider is there to change the volume level of a selected clip.

After you change the volume, you can test it out by placing the playhead at the top of the Timeline and pressing the spacebar or clicking the Play button in the Monitor panel.

You can change a clip's volume without extracting audio first, if you like. Simply select one (or more than one, if you hold down the Shift key while clicking) video clip in the Timeline that has unextracted audio and then change the volume using the Volume slider. You can even slide the volume all the way down if you simply don't want to hear the audio at this point, but you don't feel like extracting and removing it.

Fading a clip in and out

You can also select an individual audio clip and decide whether or not the audio will fade in (progress gradually from silent to full volume), fade out (progress gradually from full volume to silent), or both. Select the audio clip in the Timeline so that it becomes highlighted and then click the Fade In or Fade Out check box on either side of the Volume slider at the bottom of the Timeline.

If you select more than one clip at a time, note that *each* clip takes on the behavior you select. For instance, if you select three clips in a row and click the Fade In check box, the audio of each of the three clips fades in individually. If you'd like a fade in effect on the first clip and a fade out effect on the last clip, select only the first clip and turn on the Fade In option, then select only the last clip and turn on the Fade Out option.

As with the volume control discussed in the preceding section, you can select a video clip that has unextracted audio and use the Fade In and Fade Out controls in the same way. The audio that's still a part of that video clip then fades in and out as desired.

Want a more exacting way to fade in and out? Sometimes it's important that a fade effect take an exact amount of time in seconds or even fractions of a second. In iMovie, the power is yours:

1. **Select an audio clip (or a video clip that has unextracted audio).**

2. **Choose File⇨Get Clip Info.**

   The Clip Info dialog box appears (see Figure 8-11).

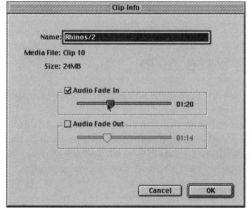

Figure 8-11:
The Clip Info
dialog box.

3. **Choose the Fade In effect, the Fade Out effect, or both by placing a checkmark next to the desired option.**

4. **Using the slider, select the exact amount of time, in seconds and frames, that you'd like the fade to take to go from silent to full volume (Fade In) or from full volume to silent (Fade Out).**

5. **When you've made your selection, click the OK button.**

Now you can play back the clip in the Timeline or Monitor to see how it sounds.

Cutting Up with Audio Transitions

Now that you've seen how to extract, alter, and tweak your audio, it's time to start editing with audio. Just as you can trim, crop, and place your video clips in the Clip Viewer to tell a story, you can use audio to create some effective moments within that story, as well as create a more professional, sophisticated video presentation. To start, you'll take a look at *intercutting* by pasting video from one clip over the video of another while continuing the audio track beneath. Then, you move on to some sophisticated audio edits called L-cuts and J-cuts. The meanings may seem a bit obscure at this point, but here's a hint: Look at the shape of the letters.

One thing to note as you discover more about editing with audio is that you need to be prepared in your shooting and early editing to take advantage of these special cuts. The bottom line with these cuts is that you end up with a continuous audio clip playing while different video is shown on the screen. You need to think about how this could work well in your movie, and then you need to make sure you have the necessary video.

To begin, get to know the cuts that are possible. Then, as you review your tape or the next time you go out to shoot, consider how you can get extra footage to take advantage of these powerful cuts.

Intercutting: Paste over

Consider how often you see video on the screen that isn't exactly the same as the audio you're hearing behind it. A reporter is talking about a burning building, and you see the building, not the reporter. An historian is talking about an important battlefield and you see the battlefield, not the historian. A comedian is talking about his personal life on stage and you see his bewildered and shocked parents in the audience, not the comedian.

Live broadcasts, newscasts, and sporting events use a number of different cameras and *intercut* between them to provide many different visuals that are often held together by a continuous clip of audio. You can do that same thing in iMovie as long as you have the video clips at your disposal.

See the QuickTime video clip intercut.mov in the Chapter 8 folder of the *iMovie 2 For Dummies* CD-ROM for an example of intercutting.

Before you can intercut your clips successfully, you need two things. First, you need a clip of audio and video that's long enough to provide the basis for your intercutting. In many cases, this is video you've shot of a person talking, whether it's a reporter, a documentary interview subject in her office (with the ubiquitous "smart person" shelves of books behind her), or your Safari tour guide. Second, you need smaller clips for the intercutting, and you need them on the Shelf, not currently in your movie.

Thus armed, here's how to accomplish the intercut:

1. **Place your long clip in the Timeline, if it isn't already there, and extract the audio from it using the Advanced⇨Extract Audio command.**

2. **Select the first (edited), short clip in the Shelf and choose Edit⇨Cut or Edit⇨Copy.**

   You want to have edited it down to the barest minimum before you place it as an intercut. You also have the choice of choosing Cut, which removes the clip from the Shelf, or Copy, which doesn't.

3. **Place the playhead at the point on the Timeline where you want the intercut to begin.**

   You may need to experiment with the long clip (playing it a few times) to find the exact point on the clip where you want the intercut to appear.

4. **Choose Advanced⇨Paste Over at Playhead or press ⌘+Shift+V.**

   This pastes only the video portion of the small clip *over* the corresponding amount of video in the long clip (see Figure 8-12).

5. **Repeat Steps 2 through 4 for the rest of your short clips (or for as many as fit the duration of the long clip).**

Cool, eh? Experiment to see how many quick cuts look right for your long clip. (For instance, how often do you want to go back to the video of the longer clip? Returning to a talking head too often can be distracting.)

Also consider adding transitions between the intercuts, if you like. You'll notice that as far as iMovie is concerned, each pasted clip is still its own, individual clip. You could easily drag a transition down to the beginning of each. (Not that I'd recommend this. Remember, quick cuts without transitions can look fine.)

Want another great reason to intercut? How about adding some non-DV graphics, such as a slide, a photo, or even an animation created in some program other than iMovie? You can do it, as discussed in Chapter 11.

Want to Paste Over at Playhead using an Over Black title? You can, but you need to create the title first and move it to the Shelf. Next, choose Edit⇨Copy to grab the video and then choose Advanced⇨Paste Over at Playhead to paste the title footage back into the Timeline.

Figure 8-12:
The Paste
Over at
Playhead
command
places the
small video
clip over the
same
amount of
the larger
video clip,
but doesn't
affect the
audio.

Here's the new video from the short clip ...

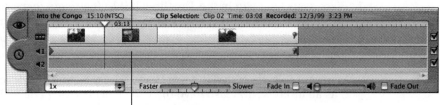

... but the audio is the same

Making an L-cut

An L-cut is one in which you cut to a new video clip without cutting to a new audio clip, which is suggested by the shape of the letter *L*. (The bottom part of the letter *L* represents audio that's under the next video clip. Get it?) In other words, you move on to new images while the same sounds continue under them. For instance, picture John F. Kennedy giving his famous speech to Rice University in which he states "We choose to go to the moon. We choose to go to the moon in this decade and do the other things, not because they are easy, but because they are hard." Suppose that somewhere in the middle of this speech, you want to cut (or transition) from the video of Kennedy himself to a video clip of an Apollo mission blasting off from the launch pad. That's an L-cut: the audio from the previous clip continues as the video from a new clip begins.

The main difference between an intercut and an L-cut is that you are, actually, transitioning to a whole new clip — you're not just pasting over the existing clip with a small bit of video. This, ultimately, is an *audio transition* into a new clip, but it's effective because it doesn't feel like an abrupt cut. In our example, the Kennedy speech could taper off while you're watching the video of the Apollo rocket on the launch pad, and then the audio of the countdown could begin (and then the movie could continue from there instead of returning to the Kennedy footage). It's basically a cut between two clips, but the audio overlaps to make the transition a bit more fluid.

See the QuickTime video clip lcut.mov in the Chapter 8 folder of the *iMovie 2 For Dummies* CD-ROM for an example of an L-cut.

And, as you may have guessed, iMovie makes an L-cut pretty easy to accomplish, although a little advanced iMovie technique is required. Here are the steps:

1. **Select the two clips you want to L-cut and center them in the Timeline so you can work with them.**

   Don't forget to choose an appropriate zoom factor in the Zoom menu and scroll so that you can see both clips.

2. **If the second clip has audio, extract it.**

   If the clip doesn't have audio, skip to Step 3.

3. **Ensure that each audio clip is locked to the beginning of its respective video clip.**

4. **Select the first video clip and delete a portion of its video from the end of the clip.**

   You can do this in the Monitor using Crop Markers and the Edit⇨Cut or Edit⇨Clear command. The amount of video you cut from the first clip is the amount by which the second clip will overlap the first clip's audio (see Figure 8-13).

Now, if it happens to be okay to have the second clip's audio overlapping the end of the first clip's audio (the portion that is the L-cut), you're finished. In most cases, though, you need to clear out that extra bit of overlapping video from the beginning of the second clip. Here's how:

1. **Select the second audio clip so that it's the only clip highlighted.**

   The second audio clip is bright orange, as is the area where the two audio clips overlap. The first audio clip is pale orange.

2. **Place the playhead at the *end* of the overlapping audio clips.**

   Figure 8-14 shows how this looks.

3. **Choose Edit⇨Split Selected Audio Clip at Playhead from the menu or press ⌘+T.**

   This splits the second audio clip into two clips: the portion that overlaps the first audio clip and the portion, after the playhead, that doesn't overlap.

4. **Select *only* the portion of the second clip that overlaps the first one.**

   This can be a little tough to do, but there are tricks. First, click the grey title area of the Timeline (the portion where the title of your movie appears) to deselect all clips. Now click a crop marker that's part of that overlapping clip. *Only* the overlapping portion becomes highlighted — make sure that the first audio clip is still pale orange.

Figure 8-13:
When you cut a portion of the first video clip, the second video clip moves over to fill in, effectively overlapping the first clip's audio.

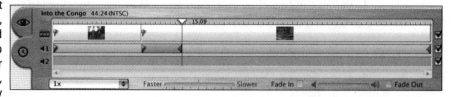

Figure 8-14:
The second clip is selected and the playhead is properly placed.

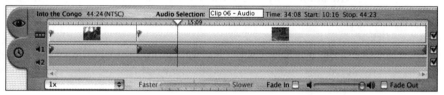

5. **Delete the overlapping audio clip by using Edit⇨Cut, Edit⇨Clear, or the Delete key.**

   The result should be two remaining clips: the original first audio clip and the second portion of the second audio clip, as shown in Figure 8-15.

6. **Click the second audio clip to select it and then choose Advanced⇨ Lock Audio Clip at Playhead.**

   This locks the audio clip so that it remains synchronized with the video in the clip.

That wasn't too difficult, eh? You'll find that a little practice helps you perform this cut quickly, and that it's a useful, good-sounding way to transition between two clips while maintaining some continuity.

Is the second audio clip sound too abrupt of a change? Select the audio clip and add a Fade In effect at the beginning of it by clicking Fade In at the bottom of the Timeline interface.

Figure 8-15:
The audio
from the
first clip
plays as the
video from
the second
clip begins.

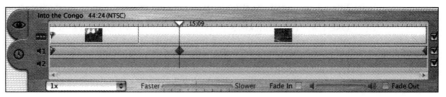

Making a J-cut

A J-cut is one in which the audio for a clip starts *before* the video for a clip.
(The curly bottom of the letter *J* represents audio that starts under the previous video clip.) You've seen this one a lot on TV and in the movies, probably
most often when you're watching a title sequence that flows aurally into the
first action sequence in a movie.

Here's how it might work in the movies. Picture the director's credit
("Directed by Steven Lucas") on the screen as you begin to hear an alarm
clock ring. Then, the credit sequence fades out and the next scene fades in on
video of the alarm clock, still ringing. That's a J-cut: You heard the audio of
the next scene before you saw the video of it. This is another professional
way to transition viewers fluidly to the next scene.

Performing such a feat is fairly easy to accomplish, especially if the first clip
of the two has no audio of its own. (If it does, things become more complicated. See Chapter 13 for a look at this more advanced edit.)

See the QuickTime video clip jcut.mov in the Chapter 8 folder of the *iMovie 2
For Dummies* CD-ROM for an example of a J-cut.

Here is a basic J-cut, in a few easy steps:

1. **Select the two clips you want to J-cut and place them front and center
   in the Timeline by choosing an appropriate zoom factor in the Zoom
   menu and scrolling so that you can see both clips.**

2. **If the first clip has audio, extract it using the Advanced⇨Extract Audio
   command.**

   If the clip doesn't have audio, skip to Step 4.

3. **Select the extracted audio and choose Edit⇨Cut or Edit⇨Clear from
   the menu.**

   If you don't want to cut all this audio, you need to crop it instead so that
   the audio from the second clip doesn't overlap it. This is difficult to do,
   but I cover the procedure in Chapter 13.

4. **Extract the audio in the second clip.**

5. **Select the second clip and crop the beginning of the clip in the Monitor.**

   Use the crop markers under the Scrubber bar to select video from the beginning of the clip and then choose Edit➪Crop. (This is discussed more in Chapter 5.) What you're doing is cropping the second video clip by the amount of time that you want the second *audio* clip to overlap the first video clip, thus creating your *J.*

6. **Drag the second audio clip so that its end once again lines up with the *end* of the second video clip.**

   You may need to zoom in using the Zoom menu in the Timeline interface. Drag the audio clip to the left until the end of the audio clip is perfectly aligned with the end of the video clip. Note that this causes the second audio clip to overlap the first video clip, as shown in Figure 8-16. (In the example, you hear the guy in the second video clip talking while the first credit clip is ending.) You've finished the J-cut!

Figure 8-16:
Crop the second video clip a bit so that its associated audio now overlaps the previous video clip or title sequence.

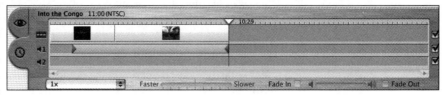

The only loose end with this technique is the dragging of the audio clip. If you don't properly align the audio clip with the end of its video clip, you may be in for some trouble with the *sync* of the audio and video. If someone is talking, for instance, their lips might move at the wrong time so that it looks like they're not speaking (or it looks like a poorly dubbed Godzilla movie). This shouldn't happen if you're careful in Step 6 to make sure that the end of the audio and video clips align perfectly.

Oddly, locking the back ends of the audio clip and video clip, in this instance, won't cause the audio to overlap the previous clip when you cut from the beginning of the second clip. Logic suggests that it would, making a J-cut easier to accomplish. Perhaps Apple will change iMovie so that this does work in future versions. If you're working with a version beyond iMovie 2.0.1, you might consider trying this.

Chapter 9

Releasing Your Inner DJ: Narration, Music, and Sound Effects

*C*hapter 8 covered editing the music that comes along for the ride with the DV clips you import from your camcorder. But that's only half the audio battle. With iMovie, you can add quite a few more sounds, including some built-in sound effects, sounds, or narration that you record yourself, or a soundtrack of music.

Adding all those things is easy, thanks to a few simple commands in the iMovie application. In this chapter, you take an up-close-and-personal look at the Audio panel in iMovie and build on the knowledge coverage of the Timeline in Chapter.

Sound good?

Adding Narration to Your Movie

iMovie enables you to record your own (or someone else's) voice or sounds and add them to the audio track in the Timeline. All you need is a micro-phone, the click of a button, and something to say.

iMovie makes the button clicking easy: Click the Audio button under the Shelf interface to open the Audio panel. Here you see your interface into the world of extra audio for iMovie, including sound effects at the top of the panel and music recording controls at the bottom. Don't worry about those right now.

What you want to worry about (if you want to call it *worry*) is the Record Voice control, smack dab in the middle of the Audio panel (see Figure 9-1). It's a simple interface that doesn't even hint of the set-up nightmare to come. But just you wait.

Figure 9-1:
The Audio panel includes a simple control for recording your voice.

Setting up the microphone

With iMovie active and the Audio panel selected, look at your Mac and say something to it. Did little green indicators light up just above the Record Voice button? If so, you have a microphone installed and properly selected for recording. You are what we in the Writing-Books-About-iMovie business call "one of the lucky ones." You can skip this section and go straight to "Speaking into the microphone."

Otherwise, you have a little more to think about. To record your narration into iMovie, you need to — brace yourself — find a microphone and set up your Mac to use it.

The first issue is determining what kind of Mac you have and what kind of microphone you'll be using. I start with that first part first. Here's a quick look at your microphone options, based on the type of Mac you have:

- ✔ **iMac DV.** If you have any model of iMac DV, you have a built-in microphone that you can use for recording your narration. It's not the best solution in the world because the microphone sits up above the screen, giving you less than ideal directional control over its placement. You can also opt for an external microphone. You'll need a PlainTalk microphone or a PlainTalk adapter to get the microphone to work properly (see the sidebar titled "Plain talk about PlainTalk").

- ✔ **Power Macintosh G3.** You don't have a built-in microphone, but your Power Macintosh G3 model should have come with a PlainTalk microphone. Connect it to the microphone port on the back of your Mac's tower case.

✔ **Power Macintosh G4.** Most Power Mac G4 models didn't ship with a PlainTalk microphone, although they require one (or an adapter). You can buy a PlainTalk microphone through the Apple Store or Mac retailers; see the "Plain talk about PlainTalk" sidebar.

✔ **PowerBook.** If you're using a PowerBook G3 (FireWire) model or a PowerBook G3 (Bronze keyboard) model, you have a built-in microphone that can record your voice. You can also plug in a PlainTalk-compatible microphone or microphone adapter, as discussed in the "Plain talk about PlainTalk" sidebar.

✔ **iBook.** The iBook (FireWire) models don't offer an internal or external microphone option — at least, not through a dedicated port. Instead, you need a special USB microphone that installs through the USB port on the side of the iBook. Or you can opt for a USB-to-audio adapter, such as the iMic made by Griffin Technology (www.griffintechnology.com).

Plain talk about PlainTalk

For various reasons, most iMacs, recent PowerBooks, and Power Macintosh models over the years have included a microphone port, but not the sort that supports, say, a microphone. In spite of the cute little microphone icon, the port is really an audio-in port, in that it's primarily designed to accept a connection from a stereo receiver or similar audio component. The microphone port in most cases is what's called a line level port.

Line level means that the port offers no amplification for devices attached to it. Unfortunately, most microphones — the karaoke-style microphones in electronics stores and parts stores such as Radio Shack — require an amplified port, so they don't work when connected to a Mac.

You need either a PlainTalk microphone or a microphone adapter. A PlainTalk microphone is built by Apple and has a slightly longer plug than the typical line-level device. When you plug this microphone into the Mac, the Mac goes, "Hey,

whoa, a microphone is attached there" and responds accordingly.

Likewise, you can plug a regular microphone into an adapter that simulates a PlainTalk connection. Such adapters include the NE Mic made by Griffin Technology (www.griffintechnology.com) or a Mac-compatible microphone made by Altec Lansing (www.alteclansing.com). Any modern Mac can also use a USB-based microphone or adapter as a solution for the iBook.

Finally: Why call it PlainTalk? PlainTalk is Apple's name for its speech recognition technology. Most Power Macintosh and related models have the capability to recognize basic spoken commands, using a PlainTalk microphone. This technology, in part, encouraged Apple to include a line-level input port on the Mac, so that the port and the microphones that fit it ended up with the PlainTalk name, too.

Telling the Mac to listen to the microphone

After you've plugged a microphone of some sort into your Mac, the next step is to tell your Mac where it is. Before you can record narration, you have to set up the Mac's Sound control panel so that it's listening for the microphone. Otherwise, you may as well be talking to your in-laws. Here's how to set up the microphone:

1. **Open the Apple menu and choose Control Panels⇨Sound to open the Sound control panel.**

2. **On the left side of the control panel, select Input.**

3. **Select Built-in in the "Choose a device for sound input" box. (If you're using a USB microphone, choose USB Audio instead.)**

4. **Open the Input Source menu and select the microphone you want to use from the options (Built-in Mic or External Mic), as shown in Figure 9-2.**

   Under certain circumstances, you may want to select Sound In from the Input Source menu. This is especially true if you're using a microphone connected to a stereo receiver or a mixing board that is connected to the Mac as a line-level device.

5. **Close the control panel and return to iMovie.**

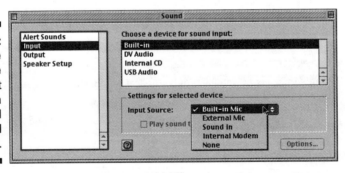

Figure 9-2: Select the microphone you want to use via the Sound control panel.

When you're back in iMovie, test your microphone by speaking somewhere in the vicinity of it. If the indicator above the Record Voice button lights up green, you know that iMovie is ready to record your narration.

Speaking into the microphone

After you've set up the microphone, you're ready to begin your narration. But before you do, you need to know a little secret.

When you record narration using iMovie, the audio is stored on the audio #1 track — the same track that you may or may not have used in Chapter 8 for dealing with extracted audio. Although it's possible for both extracted audio and narration to coexist amicably on that track (the two type of clips can overlap and both will play), the fact that the new narration audio clip will be there can make dealing with narration that much more difficult.

In some cases, you'll probably want to clear the existing audio out of the way and replace it with your narration. In others, you might want the ambient noise from the original, but you'll turn down its volume considerably so that it doesn't compete with your narration. In either case, simply being aware of the fact that the two types of audio will compete for that coveted space on the Timeline is important.

With that out of the way, you're ready to narrate. Here's how:

1. **Clear your throat, say "me, me, me!" or sing the first few lines of "Doe a Deer" to get ready to speak.**

   Also, position yourself close to the microphone you've chosen for recording.

2. **Place the playhead on the Timeline where you'd like to begin recording your narration.**

   You may also want to make a note of about how long to talk by examining the gap you want to fill in the Timeline.

3. **Click the Record Voice button and begin speaking.**

4. **When you're finished, click the Stop button (it's the same as the Record Voice button, but it has changed names since you began recording).**

   Try to click it quietly so that your mouse-button antics don't show up in the audio.

That's it. You have a length of recorded audio that appears on the Timeline on the audio #1 track. Now you can edit that audio clip as desired. See Chapter 8 for details on cropping, changing volume, and fading in and out.

iMovie stops recording narration at the ten-minute mark. If your narration last more than ten minutes, plan a natural stopping point (the end of a sentence) at about 9:00 and then start a new narration clip.

Tips for better narration

Within iMovie, narration is pretty simple to record and edit, especially if you mastered the audio editing techniques laid out in Chapter 8. But being a grand narrator takes time, talent, skill, hard work, dedication, and years of practice. Fortunately, it's pretty easy to fake. Here are a few hints:

- ✔ **Know what you're going to say.** It may seem easy to "wing it" by turning on the microphone and just talking, but most people can't take that kind of pressure. Instead, write a little script for yourself so you know what you want to say for your narration.

- ✔ **Don't read.** After you have your script, get to know it fairly well. You don't have to memorize it word for word, but most people read unfamiliar text in a way that sounds as if they're, well, reading. If you've read it a few times, you should be able to speak more naturally.

- ✔ **Breathe before clicking Record Voice.** You should breathe afterward as well — it's part of a daily regimen of optimal death-avoidance. In this instance, though, I mean take that big breath right before clicking the Record Voice button. If you don't, I promise that you'll take a deep breath right *after* you click the button and before you start talking.

- ✔ **Take it slow.** To sound right while narrating, you'll probably find that you need to talk more slowly than you think you do. In fact, it can almost seem exaggerated. But the truth is that, unless you're calling a horse race, a narrator's voice is expected to be very relaxed and comfortable sounding. That means talking slowly and evenly.

- ✔ **Test your microphone.** Make sure you're getting good sound from your microphone and that it's not popping, hissing, or making other untoward noises.

- ✔ **Consider a different type of recording.** Recording directly to your Mac may work if you have a good external microphone, but most built-in options (and even many add-ons such as USB microphones) offer only mediocre quality. You have an easy solution, however. Even if you don't have high-quality audio equipment as part of your camera setup, you have at least one good-quality microphone — the one built into your DV camcorder! One way to get good quality narration is to set up your camera and narrate directly to it. Then, in iMovie, you can extract the audio and use it in other parts of your video. (I discuss this technique in more detail in Chapter 13.)

Adding Music

Here's an interesting factoid about the original *Rocky:* It had a different ending, or, at least, more of one. If you remember the movie, it ends pretty much with Rocky "going the distance" (remember, Apollo Creed actually wins the match on a split decision), yelling for Adrian, and, when she makes it into the ring, proclaiming his love for her. Fade out.

In the original cut, though, there's a little more payoff at the end of the movie, with Rocky and Adrian basically walking off into the sunset. That ending was cut by the director, John Alvidsen, after he'd heard the score put together by composer Bill Conti. It built to such a dramatic crescendo at the end of that fight that the director decided to leave the audience where the music had led them — to an amazing high. (The song "Gonna Fly Now" was even nominated for an Oscar.)

Great movies and videos almost invariably have a great soundtrack. The music behind your video should, ideally, say a lot about the action that's taking place in your movie, setting the tone and determining some of the emotional responses that your audience is likely to have to the presentation. It's really that important.

One of the issues for us, however, is where to get that music. For most home-movie presentations, you'll probably grab your favorite song or songs from a few CDs you have floating around. Or you might work with MP3s, the Internet standard for downloadable music tracks. If you happen to have an audio-editing program (whether for creating your own music or editing and working with someone else's), you can use that, too, with a little file-translation magic.

Know your (and other people's) rights

Although iMovie encourages you to use CD tracks for your movies, consider the implications. In general, it's a copyright violation for you to extract audio from a commercial CD and use it for your own personal gain.

If you're using the audio for home movies with no commercial value, you shouldn't have too much to worry about. For the most part, the huge record companies aren't too likely to come after you for putting a little John Denver behind the video clips of your daughter's first steps.

Where you do need to consider the law is if you're using the video in a corporate or organizational setting or in any situation where you might stand to see commercial benefit from the work. In that case, you'll generally have to get written permission to use the song or other professional audio, usually for a fee. If you can negotiate directly with the artist (and the artist owns his or her own rights), do so. Otherwise, you're in for a sticky corporate mess requiring — you guessed it — paperwork and lawyers. Eech.

The other solution is to use royalty-free music, which doesn't require a per-use license. CD collections are available from many sources if you'd like to buy them to use as soundtrack cuts for your movie. (They can be a bit pricey, so this is probably best for institutional and corporate videos. Some places to start looking include www.crankcity.com, www.sounddogs.com, or any store or catalog that caters to audio and radio professionals.) Some software-based ways to get royalty-free music are discussed in the "Importing audio files" section.

So, if you're planning something beyond a home video — even if it's non-profit — make sure you at least stop to think about copyright issues. And if you do get in trouble with the law, remember the golden rule: Keep my name out of it.

(By the way, I'm not a lawyer, so everything in this sidebar is for entertainment purposes only, no warranty expressed or implied. Consult an attorney if you need actual, useful advice. No purchase necessary. Rebates to dealers.)

Adding CD music

If you have music on a CD that you'd like to use for your movie's soundtrack, adding it is easy. You can control and record from a CD using the Audio panel in iMovie. To open the Audio panel, click the Audio button at the bottom of the Shelf panel. Now, insert an audio CD into your Mac if one isn't already mounted. After iMovie recognizes the CD, the Audio CD interface lights up at the bottom of the Audio panel (see Figure 9-3).

Playback controls

Eject the CD

Figure 9-3:
The Audio
CD portion
of the Audio
panel is
where you
listen to and
record from
CDs.

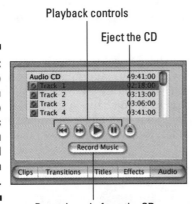

Record music from the CD

The Audio CD interface offers some familiar controls. In the scrolling list, you can select individual tracks that you want to work with. The VCR-like controls below the scrolling list enable you to move to the beginning of the track, move to the next track, play the track, pause the track, and eject the CD. The Record Music button enables you to record music from the selected track into your movie.

If you can't seem to get iMovie to recognize a CD that has been inserted, there may be a setup conflict; I've noticed that iMovie can be a bit finicky. For me, the most common problem is having an external CD drive (such as a CD-RW burner) connected through USB or FireWire. If that's your problem, turn off the external CD drive or disconnect it from the Mac and then restart iMovie. Now it should recognize audio CDs that you insert into the Mac's main CD or DVD drive.

Here's a quick look at the process of recording music:

1. **In the Timeline, place the playhead at the point in the iMovie where you want the music to begin recording.**

2. **In the Audio panel, select the track you want to record.**

If you'd like to listen to it first, click the Play button. Click the Play button again to stop the playback.

3. **If you want to record only a certain portion of the track (that is, if you won't be recording from the beginning of the song), play the track until you get to that point and then click Pause.**

In fact, you should probably pause the playback just a touch *before* the point you want to record, so you don't miss that first beat. You can edit any small problems later.

4. **Click the Record Music button.**

You hear the song played through your speakers (or headphones, if they're connected).

You also see your movie playing back in the Monitor as the audio is recorded (see Figure 9-4). The purple bar on the audio #2 track grows to indicate that music is being recorded for your movie.

Want to adjust the playback audio? Use the volume slider on the Monitor pane. This affects the volume you're hearing, not the volume at which the music is recorded.

5. **When you've finished recording, click the Stop button.**

This is the same button as the Record Music button; it simply gets a new name after you click it to record.

Figure 9-4:
Your movie plays back as the purple music bar grows at the bottom to indicate recorded music.

You don't have to be exacting in your recording. In fact, you may want a little overlap at the end of your recording, just so you can play with the music track a bit and, if desired, add some fade in and fade out effects.

Want to amaze your family and friends by skipping all those steps? If you happen to want an *entire* audio track from a CD in your movie, all you have to do is drag the small icon next to that track's name and place it on audio track #2 in the Timeline. As you're dragging along the Timeline, a small yellow line shows you where the song will begin if you release the mouse button. Drag that indicator until you get to the portion of the iMovie where you want the song to be and then release the mouse button. iMovie imports the entire audio track and places it in the Timeline.

Importing audio files

As noted, audio from a CD track isn't the only way to get music into your movie. You can also import audio files from pretty much any source — MP3s, music you create, royalty-free music software — as long as you can translate the file into an AIFF sound file. (*AIFF,* which stands for Audio Interchange File Format, is one of the standard ways to store audio files on a Macintosh.)

So how can you get these files? I include a few methods on the *iMovie 2 For Dummies* CD-ROM, as outlined here:

- ✔ **Translate an existing file.** If you have an MP3 file, AU file, QuickTime audio track, or a sound file created in a professional audio application, a utility can translate that audio file into AIFF. If QuickTime can import the original file, you can use QuickTime Pro Player (yes, you have to pay for the upgrade) to export the audio file as an AIFF file. If you don't want to use QuickTime, you can use SoundApp, which is on the included CD-ROM, to translate most sound files to AIFF.

- ✔ **Create an AIFF file with beat-box software.** Included on the CD-ROM are some demo applications, such as AudioFusion TWS and Groovemaker, you can use to create hip-hop and techno-heavy soundtracks. A good beat and a little sampling might work well for your soundtrack.

- ✔ **Save royalty-free music from CD collections as an AIFF file.** Some royalty-free collections work just like a regular CD, so you can use the instructions in the "Adding CD music" section. Another option is a soundtrack-creating application, such as Smart Sound, a demo of which is on the CD. With Smart Sound, in addition to getting royalty-free music, you can actually build your own songs (or select from a number of suggested songs), effectively arranging the music to fit your movie. Although you're still not getting any Oscar-caliber Randy Newman arrangements, this program is a great twist on the standard royalty-free fare. And it's easy to export to AIFF format.

Be careful with Smart Sound: It's addicting and not overwhelming cheap, at $200 for a basic version and $70 to $130 for each CD of royalty-free music licks. It's a pricey habit (trust me), but one you'll swear by as an institutional or corporate iMovie editor. I talk more about Smart Sound in Chapter 18.

✔ **Actually be talented.** If you have honest-to-goodness music talent, you could conceivably create and play your own music for your movie soundtrack. You just need to record the file in some way (using SoundEdit 16 from Macromedia, at www.macromedia.com, or Deck II from Bias Software, at www.bias-inc.com, for instance), and then edit it, mix it down, and save it as an AIFF file.

After you have an AIFF computer file on your Mac's desktop, you're ready to import it into iMovie. This part is simple:

1. **In the Timeline, place the playhead at the point where you want the imported audio to begin.**

2. **Choose File⇨Import File from the iMovie menu.**

   The Import File dialog box appears.

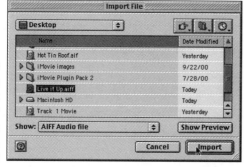

Figure 9-5: Importing an AIFF file for use as a soundtrack.

3. **Select the AIFF file that you'd like to import.**

   If you're seeing a lot of different files, it may help to limit what's shown in the dialog box by selecting AIFF Audio File from the Show menu.

4. **Click Import.**

   That's all it takes. The audio file is added to your movie on audio track #2, where it's now available for playing back or editing.

AIFF: Scheming to compress

AIFF is a slightly different animal from DV Stream files, if only because AIFF offers a number of *compression schemes* for determining the trade-off between the size and the quality of the file. When you export a file from a sound application to an AIFF file, you may be asked to select some settings. Here's the scoop.

A computer file isn't really a straight, linear recording like an LP or cassette recording. Instead, a computer file is simply a series of *samples* of a sound wave, stored as computer data. These samples are taken thousands of times per second, so the computer audio file sounds like a continuous recording when played back.

Most audio files are sampled about 22,000 time a second (22 Hz) or 44,100 times per second (44.1 Hz). That second number is considered CD-quality, and 22 Hz is closer to the quality of an FM broadcast (minus the static, usually). A 22-Hz file takes up a lot less storage space, however, so it's ideal for when a small file trumps the better quality of 44.1 Hz.

A sound file can also be limited in the breadth of numbers used to create each sample. In most cases, that's measured as either 8 bit (256 numbers) or 16 bit (65,536 numbers). The more numbers available to represent a sample, the better the sample sounds. Therefore, 16-bit samples take up more storage space but sound much better than 8-bit samples. You should almost always choose 16-bit.

Either a 22-Hz or 44.1-Hz file can be compressed according to different schemes. For AIFF files, that includes Mace, uLaw, and IMA. Each scheme has its strengths, but in most situations I recommend the following:

- If the recording is 16 bit and you don't require a smaller file, use no compression.

- If the recording is 16 bit and you need a smaller file, choose IMA 4:1 compression.

- If the recording is 8 bit, Mace 1:3 is an okay choice.

Editing the music

After you have your music track laid in on the Timeline, you can edit it pretty much as if it were any other type of sound file. A soundtrack file can be cropped, faded in and out, copied, and pasted. You can change its volume. You can even lock it to a particular video clip if you'd like to make sure the music stays with a particular scene. All of the commands and controls are the same as those discussed in Chapter 8.

Adding iMovie Sound Effects

Along with the music and narration capabilities, iMovie includes the capability to add some small, built-in sound effects to your movie. These little guys require almost no thought whatsoever, which helps them fit into my typical day quite nicely. Simply choose a sound and drag it to one of the audio tracks in the Timeline.

The sound effects are stored at the top of the Audio panel in a small scrolling list (see Figure 9-6). To hear one of these sound effects, click it once in the list. It plays back through your Mac's speakers or headphones. (Use the volume control on the Monitor to change the playback volume.)

Figure 9-6:
Sound effects are kept in the top corner of the Audio panel.

Adding an audio effect to your movie is just as easy. Locate the sound effect you want to use and then drag that sound effect's small speaker icon down to the Timeline. You can drop the icon on either of the two audio tracks, although I recommend choosing one of them for all your sound effects, just to be consistent. Two small blue boxes (only one box for shorter sound effects) appear on the Timeline, indicating that sound effect (see Figure 9-7).

Figure 9-7:
Two sound effects (a long one and a short one) have been dropped onto the Timeline.

Oddly enough, you can't edit a sound effect for length. All you can really do to customize it is select the sound effect (click the box or, in the case of longer sound effects, the first box) and use the Volume slider at the bottom of the Timeline to change the volume of the effect. You can also choose to Fade In or Fade Out the sound effect using those check boxes at the bottom of the Timeline interface.

Like other sound files, a sound effect's information dialog box appears when you double-click the sound effect. In that dialog box, you can choose the exact time when a fade in or fade out will occur. This may be the best solution if you need an audio clip to be shorter than its natural running time. Just have it begin to fade out a bit before you'd ideally like the effect to end.

Apple offers some basic sound effects in iMovie: crowd noise, animal sounds, people sounds, and a few circus-like effects. And the iMovie Plug-in Pack 2 features quite a few more (see Chapter 12). However, iMovie's built-in support for sound effects is limited. The solution? Well, you can always import smaller effects as AIFF files, just as easily as you can import long tracks of music. (The AIFF file will show up on audio track #2, but you can move it up to track #1 if desired.) Then you can move those sound effects around, edit them, and even crop them, if desired, which gives them a leg-up on iMovie's sound effects.

Part III
Post Production: Making Your Movie Look Fabulous

The 5th Wave   By Rich Tennant

THE NEW HOLLYWOOD   @RICHTENNANT

CUT! PASTE!

In this part . . .

This is perhaps the most fun part of the book. You look at some of the crazier things you can do to jazz up your movie. You start in a relatively sedate fashion by exploring the special effects built into iMovie, but I'd be surprised if you aren't impressed by iMovie's special effects by the end of Chapter 10. Just in case you're not, Chapter 11 comes rolling along with ways to add your own images and even animations to your movie. Then you see how to add even more capabilities to iMovie through the plug-in packs and other downloads offered by Apple. Finally, in the daddy of all editing chapters, Chapter 13, you see some exciting techniques for using both iMovie and QuickTime Pro Player to add finishing touches to your movie.

Chapter 10

Adding Razzle-Dazzle
with Special Effects

*O*bi-wan lifts his hand, presses a button, and a beam of light shoots out of
the handle of his light-saber and he's ready to do battle. Captain Kirk
tells Scotty to "Energize" and his body turns to sparkles and slowly fades
away as he's transported across space. Marty McFly climbs into the Delorean
and sits next to the Doc, as the car lifts up from its wheels and zooms off into
the future.

The wonderful world of special effects makes the movies that much more
magical.

With iMovie, alas, you can do none of these things. No light-sabers, no trans-
porters, no all-aluminum sports-car time machines. (Am I the only one who
wishes they still made the Delorean?) iMovie's special effects are a bit more
basic, but you can do some interesting things to the images, including changing the speed, running clips backward, adjusting the color, switching to black
and white, and introducing effects to make entire scenes look a bit more artsy
or more film-like.

In this chapter, you look at all the special effects built into iMovie. You can
use some of these effects to change the colors, brightness, and contrast of
scenes. Others can be used to create interesting looks and effects, such as
black and white or sepia tone. Then you see how you can use the effects to
create transitions and even a few science-fiction-type effects for your film.
Finally, you take a quick look at iMovie's simple controls for slow- and fast-
motion video.

Maybe if your movie's effects are good enough, you'll get a prize in a film festival. Your film will be released in all the "right" theaters, and ticket sales will

pour in. It'll hit big, and the studios will notice you. For your next picture, you'll get the budget to create those *other* types of effects. Hey — at least you can dream.

Understanding iMovie's Effects

Most of the effects built into iMovie are there to give you some control over how each frame of your clips looks in terms of its color, brightness, contrast, and other settings. For instance, the Adjust Colors effect is powerful stuff, making it possible to turn a color video into black and white or to change the colors and brightness of a clip to emphasize something within the context of your story.

Other effects are just simplifications of the Adjust Colors and Brightness/Contrast effects. The Black and White effect, for example, makes it possible to turn a clip into black and white for, perhaps, a Hitchcockian result. The Sepia Tone effect is another one-button effect that changes colors so that your images look more like an old photograph or early film.

So, you can change the look of a particular clip. Sounds cool. But (in my best infomercial voice) wait . . . there's more! One trick of these effects is that you don't have to apply the effect to the entire clip in the same way. So, for instance, a clip can start at one color level and then progress to another color level. This color shift is an effect all to itself — the audience watches the shift take place.

The Effects panel

You accomplish all of this in the Effects panel, so I take a look at what makes it different. To open the panel, click the Effects button at the bottom of the Shelf pane. Now you see the Effects panel interface, most likely with the Adjust Colors effect selected (see Figure 10-1).

The Effects panel is certainly familiar if you've worked with the transitions or title panel, but it also offers some subtle differences. Select an effect in the list of effects, and the controls at the bottom of the panel change. Some effects, such as Adjust Colors, offer a number of different sliders for changing the effect. Others, such as Black and White, don't have sliders. Every time you select a different effect or change one of the settings, a preview appears in the Effects preview area in the top-right corner — as long as a clip is selected in the Clip Viewer or Timeline.

Above the list of effects are two more sliders; these are used to determine the timing of the effect. (Note that these sliders represent the amount of time from the *beginning* of the clip for Effect In and the amount of time from the *end* of the clip for Effect Out.) If you want to affect the entire clip with the selected effect, the Effect In time should be set to 00:00 (all the way left) and the Effect Out time should also be set to 00:00 (all the way out). When you apply the effect to the clip, the entire clip is affected. (For instance, the entire clip is sepia tone if that's the effect you selected.)

If you select different Effect In and Effect Out times, however, something else happens — the effects happen more gradually. That is, if you set the Effect In time for a few seconds after the clip has started and set the Effect Out time for later in the clip, the effect takes place over time, as the audience watches. In this case, if you had chosen Sepia Tone, the clip would become increasingly more *sepia tone-ish* (that can't be a word) as it plays. (We get back to this a bit more in the section "Creating special looks.")

Choose when the effect will apply

Control buttons   Preview the effect

Figure 10-1:
The Effects
panel
includes
controls for
setting
effects
options,
previewing
the effect,
and
applying it
to the
selected
clip.

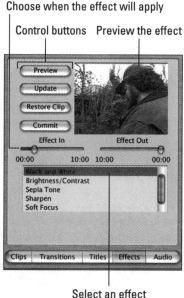

Select an effect

After you set the sliders, you're left with the four buttons in the top-left corner. This, frankly, is more thinking than we've been forced to do with iMovie's other panels so far. (And when I have to think more, I feel let down.) The buttons are Preview, Update, Restore Clip, and Commit. Here's what the buttons do:

 ✔ **Preview.** As with transitions and titles, the Preview button on the Effects panel displays a frame-by-frame preview of the effect in the Monitor.

 ✔ **Apply/Update.** If you haven't applied a special effect to the selected frame, this button reads Apply. It's the button you click to begin the rendering process. If you have applied an effect to the clip, the button reads

Update. That's meant to suggest that clicking the button updates the clip to the currently selected special effect settings.

✔ **Restore Clip.** When iMovie applies an effect to a clip, it doesn't actually apply it to the clip. (Follow me so far?) It makes a copy of that clip and applies the effect to the copy. It does this so you can update the effect with new settings if desired and restore the clip to the original, even after you've applied an effect. To restore the clip to its original, non-effect state, click the Restore Clip button.

✔ **Commit.** Commit is the archenemy of Restore Clip. If you click the Commit button, you're telling iMovie that you're completely, utterly, and for all time pleased with the effect. So, when you click Commit, the original clip is deleted, leaving you with only the FX version. To get the original clip back, your only choice now is to re-import it from your camcorder. (Not even Undo will save you after you Commit.)

So you see how to set effects: Just select a clip in the Clip Viewer or Timeline, make some selections in the Effects panel, and then click the button that's appropriate for your circumstances: Preview, Update, Restore Clip, or Commit.

Interestingly, emptying the Trash in iMovie (File⇨Empty Trash) does not affect your ability to restore an FX clip to its original state, even though it does affect any other sort of Undo command within iMovie. So, don't worry about being able to reverse your special effects even after emptying the Trash.

Effects in the Clip Viewer

Setting effects is just as easy in the Clip Viewer or the Timeline, so use the interface you're more comfortable with. If there's any advantage to the Clip Viewer, it's simply that each clip icon can show you, at a glance, whether or not an effect is already associated with the clip. iMovie indicates a clip that includes special effects by placing a small *fx* in the top-right corner. Figure 10-2 shows this.

Figure 10-2:
Clips with
special
effects have
fx in the top-
right corner.

You may also notice that when effects are applied to clips, the clips aren't split into more than one clip, even if the effect doesn't span the entire length of the clip.

Like transitions and titles, effects have to render in iMovie after you've selected a clip and an effect and clicked the Apply or Update button. This rendering looks the same as a title's rendering: In the Clip Viewer, a small line appears, filling with red as the rendering progresses. At the same time, the number of frames completed and the total number of frames (for example, *34 of 102*) are indicated in small red letters on the clip. Also as with other rendering, you have to wait for the rendering to finish before you can view the clip in the monitor, full screen, or through your camcorder.

Filtering and Fixing the Picture

Although light-sabers are no doubt cool, the fact remains that most of iMovie's effects simply help you change the hue, brightness, and contrast of the image. That's not to say that you can't get a lot out of such changes. You can, in fact, use color shifts and hue changes to create some interesting transitions, as you see in the "Using active effects" section. But that still doesn't make for *Star Wars,* eh? (Although you can still pull off the cheapest *Star Wars* effect out there: Breathe loudly into the microphone like Darth Vader. Put that behind your Halloween videos.)

The effects used to alter the look of the picture include Adjust Colors and Brightness/Contrast. I take a look at each individually.

Adjusting colors

Select a clip in the Clip Viewer or Timeline, pop up the Effects panel, and select Adjust Colors. Three sliders appear below the Effects scrolling list. These are the most complicated series of effects options we have. Not too tough, eh? The sliders are Hue Shift, Color, and Lightness, as shown in Figure 10-3.

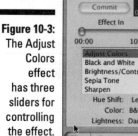

Figure 10-3: The Adjust Colors effect has three sliders for controlling the effect.

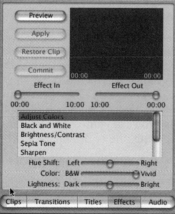

The sliders are self-explanatory to a certain extent, but I'm not earning my keep if I don't go behind the labels and tell you what's going on here. (Sounds like a VH-1 series, doesn't it? "Behind the Labels.") Cut to a bulleted list:

✔ **Hue Shift.** Hue shift, at its simplest, changes the colors within your image. The word *hue* itself, however, suggests a gradation of color, so that moving the slider shifts all the colors in the image toward one side or the other of a certain spectrum. In iMovie, this shift is from Red/Yellow on the left side to Blue/Green on the right side.

Although you don't want to make shifts too dramatic (unless you're going for a particularly wacky, surreal color scheme), a little shifting can make up for bad light, an incorrect white balance, or refraction that affected the colors you were shooting. You may find that if a clip is a little too green or blue in its natural state, sliding the hue a bit to the left helps stabilize the colors. If something is too yellow, red, or orange, shifting the hue to the right can help. On the CD, the clip hueshift.mov (in the Chapter 10 folder) shows the same scene twice — first in its original and second with a hue shift to make up for color problems with the shot (it was shot through tinted glass).

✔ **Color.** The Color slider simply enables you to scale each pixel in your images from their full color value toward an associated gray value. Sliding the bar all the way to Vivid lightens things up slightly, almost giving them a Ted Turner colorized effect. It's okay, given a certain music video quality. Sliding toward B&W (black and white), even slightly, can create a more interesting effect. You can get the suggestion of black-and-white images, but there really is color value there, which can be useful for an audience. Again, Woody Allen comes to mind: Any video that you'd like to make look a little more like older film, a 1930s period piece, or something similar could take a slight color shift toward black and white. (You could go all the way to black and white, but a digital black-and-white effect tends to look flat.)

The colorshift.mov file on the *iMovie 2 For Dummies* CD-ROM (in the Chapter 10 folder) shows a sequence of the same clip three times: the first is unaltered, the second is more vivid, and the third is slightly more black-and-white but still has some color. Note a certain *Schindler's List* quality.

✔ **Lightness.** Again, lightness creates a pixel shift, but note that it's not a brightness control, which is different from lightness (even though they rhyme). In this case, if you slide the slider toward Dark, all pixels shift toward black, which means the darker pixels (the blues, browns, and grays) get there first, with the lighter pixels right behind. Slide toward Bright and all pixels start shifting toward white, with lighter colors getting there first. At a full Bright setting, the entire image is white.

The lightness.mov file on the CD-ROM (in the Chapter 10 folder) shows the same clip with both dark and light effects applied.

To apply any of these effects to the entire clip in a uniform way (no shifting while the clip plays back), select 00:00 as the Effect In time and 00:00 as the Effect Out time. Then click Apply or (if appropriate) Update. The clip is altered according to your desires.

Adjusting brightness and contrast

To specifically adjust the brightness and contrast of your images, select a clip and then select Brightness/Contrast from the Effects list. Two sliders appear in the preference area of the Effects panel: Brightness and Contrast. Here's what they do:

✔ **Brightness.** Slide from Dark to Bright and the image lightens up quite a bit, with the lightest pixels becoming lighter very quickly as the darker pixels become lighter much more slowly. If you slide all the way to Bright, you get a fully white image. Slide all the way to dark and you get a fully black image.

✔ **Contrast.** Contrast moves individual pixels, as much as it can, more toward their closer dark or light value: Dark colors get darker and light colors get lighter. This is useful for a clip that seems somewhat washed out, with too many color values too close. In fact, contrast is often a more useful tool than brightness, especially if you were filming in sunlight or good artificial light but need a slightly more vivid clip.

Again, it's not a great idea to compensate for bad lighting or bad footage with these effects. Only very small value changes will work; larger changes simply make it clear that you've been messing with the brightness or contrast. If there's any trick to setting brightness and contrast, it's to use the values together to create a slightly more robust image. For instance, if you need to brighten the overall image somewhat, nudge the Brightness slider to the right a bit. Now, nudge up the contrast along with it, close to the same amount. You should see that the image brightens but also maintains a certain amount of depth, thanks to the contrast. Figures 10-4 and 10-5 show the difference a little contrast can make.

Creating special looks

The Adjust Colors and Brightness/Contrast effects are the intellectuals of the bunch, with all their sliders, options, controls and . . . well . . . big ideas. The others among the Effects crowd are the specialists. They do one thing and do it well and then they go home to their families and watch a little TV. On the weekends, maybe they attend a meeting or play some pool down at the union hall.

Figure 10-4:
Here I've bumped up the brightness without changing the contrast.

Figure 10-5:
Now, both brightness and contrast have been pushed up a bit, giving the image more depth.

Black and White, Sepia Tone, and Water Ripple don't even have options; you just point and shoot, so to speak. With Sharpen and Soft Focus, you have one slider for selecting more or less. Which you choose is more or less up to you.

Here's a look at the special-look effects:

✔ **Black and White.** You can achieve the same look by using Adjust Colors and going in yourself to switch to black and white, but this simple effect is a bit easier. Note that you need images with a lot of contrast (bright lights casting dark shadows) if you're going to use black-and-white with digital video. My suggestion is that unless the clip looks *great* in the preview using the straight Black and White filter, consider cheating a little using the Adjust Colors sliders, especially the Color slider, to give your clip a black-and-white feel. (See the "Adjusting colors" section.)

✔ **Sepia Tone.** This is intended to make the clip look like an old silent film, a daguerreotype from the Old West, or the like. It looks good in certain situations, especially when the video shows young children wearing big cowboy hats and stomping around like Bad Bart.

✔ **Water Ripple.** This effect seems to be there because it's possible to do. (It was a big deal when it was added to QuickTime a few years back, but I'm still not sure of the appeal.) Want to make your college dorm room look like it's underwater? How about making your office cubicle look like it's underwater? Or make your garden and dog look like they're underwater? See: infinite, exciting variations.

✔ **Sharpen.** If you've ever used Photoshop or a similar program, this effect will be familiar. Each pixel is *quantized* a bit (a fancy word for "perform a little math on it to make it more uniform") to make the overall appearance seem like you've sharpened the focus of the image. It doesn't work very well because it's a digital effect. The bottom line is that it looks like you applied a sharpen filter to the image, not that you've corrected the focus problem. But it's an interesting effect to use for a night-vision sequence or when you *want* the clip to look more digitized. ("Captain, I've got them on the scope right now!")

One place Sharpen might help a bit is if you'll be exporting to QuickTime video, especially video that's less than full screen. A slight sharpen effect — coupled with compressing the video and changing the size from 640x480 (full TV display) down to 320x240 or smaller — could result in a slightly better image than you started with. (See Chapter 14 for a full discussion of QuickTime's export options.) You're still better off if the image starts in focus. You're also much more likely to get that call from Ron Howard you've been waiting for.

✔ **Soft Focus.** This is the opposite of Sharpen, putting a slight blur on all pixels to make them seem a little softer and less focused. Again, it's a digital effect, and something that's better achieved with a special lens for your camera. That said, this effect is a bit more useful in my opinion. You can use soft focus to give your clips a film-like quality — a *very* little softening can make some of the harshness of video and make the scenes a little more pleasing to the eye. This is especially useful for close-up shots of people in which you'd like to smooth their skin tones and give them a warmer, friendly feel. If you want to show your subject sweating, stay away from soft focus.

Want to see soft focus in action? Watch pretty much any old movie with a female star. It was very common with Hepburn movies (both Hepburns, but a little more so with Audrey). It's often pronounced in shots that intercut between the male lead and the female one — the woman is usually shot with a very soft lens, almost to the point (in some cases) where it looks blurry. If you have someone on tape that you want the camera to love and cuddle, consider a little soft focus if you aren't already using a soft lens filter on your camera.

Using active effects

So there they were, minding their own business, and I came along and called all those special-looks filters in the preceding section bad names. Frankly, I may have called one or two of them nearly useless. Well, that was harsh, but in some cases it's true, especially if you're going to apply the filter or effect to the entire clip in one fell swoop. But watch me put on my tap shoes and start flailing my arms to a different tune now.

That's because some of these effects can look great when they're *active* or *transitional,* meaning the audience sees them applied gradually. Sharpen is only *so* useful when applied to an entire clip (although it certainly can be useful at times), but it can be an interesting transitional effect when it happens over time. Using the right combinations of settings, you can use Sharpen to take a clip from being in full focus to gradually being sort of digitally enhanced by the end of the clip — an effective and interesting transition to the next scene or perhaps to a Sci-Fi effect. The same thing can be true of gradually changing from color to the Black and White effect or gradually changing from color to the Sepia Tone effect. All these changes can be effective special effects and transitions.

Plus, the change can go in either direction. You can start from sepia tone and work back to regular colors or vice versa. Or you can have a clip go from regular to effect and back again. The key is changing the Effect In and Effect Out sliders.

Changing Effect In

How you select the Effect In time affects when the effect is first applied to the clip and how gradually. The rule is: If you want the effect to be active at a particular second, select that time as your Effect In time. If you want the effect to take place gradually over the entire clip, select an Effect In time somewhere close to the end of the clip. (You can even select a time that's beyond the end of the clip, if you don't want the full effect to occur during the length of the clip.)

Suppose you have a six-second clip and want it to go to sepia tone about halfway through the clip and then stay there. Select the Sepia Tone effect and move the Effect In slider to about 03:00, which is three seconds. Now the preview shows you that the Sepia Tone effect ramps up gradually from 00:00 to 03:00 and then continues through to the end of the clip.

Note that these effects never begin abruptly if they're planned for the middle of a clip — they always take effect gradually. It's simply a question of *how* gradually. With the same sepia tone example, if you set the Effect In time to the end of the clip, about 06:00, the entire clip is spent slowly changing from regular colors to sepia tone.

With this whole-clip transition possible, you have some intriguing potential. For instance, you can select an exaggerated effect — a major color shift, full-white brightness, full-black darkness, high soft focus, or high sharpen effects. Now, set the Effect In slider to the end of the clip's running time, and that effect ramps up slowly. By the time you get to the end of the clip, it's fully black, white, fuzzy, sharpened, or taken over by wacky colors. In effect, you've created a nice transition.

So what can you do with an Effect In transitional effect? Here are some of my favorites:

- **Blow out!** The blow out, or white out, effect makes a nice transition or a good, basic sci-fi effect. You achieve the effect by selecting Brightness/Contrast and sliding both sliders all the way to the right. Now, set an Effect In time that's pretty late in the clip and watch the magic unfold in the preview area. As the clip moves on, it is filled with brightness and contrast until the last frames, which are completely bright white. It's good for a Twilight Zone type plot twist: With scary music, a frightened-looking actor, and enough tension in the story, this effect looks like a nuclear flash, a time warp, or another type of major event. (It also looks good over a still clip image for that "all time has stopped at the end of the world" look.)

- **What was in that drink?** Another favorite is a gradual move from focused to blurry using the soft focus controls. Select a clip, select Soft Focus, and then slide the slider all the way to High. Now, set the Effect In time for late in the clip. As the clip plays on, it becomes increasingly blurry. What's this good for? How about the point of view of a character in your story who has just been poisoned by the bad guy and is going under? Now you can do your own version of the effect made famous by pretty much every James Bond movie.

- **Old West family portrait.** You know that effect in which a full-color, full-action image slowly dissolves into a still image that looks like an old photograph? You could do that with a gradual move to Sepia Tone (with the next clip a still clip that's also in sepia tone colors). Select Sepia Tone as the effect and slide Effect In almost all the way to the end of the clip. After the clip is rendered, tack on a still clip of that last frame (Edit⇨Create Still Clip) that's also in sepia tone. Now, you have a few seconds for a dramatic swell of music to end the voiceover ("And that's the story of the trip of '62") or to begin rolling credits.

- **Dream sequence.** Okay, maybe there is a use for the Water Ripple effect. Select it and choose an Effect In time. (In the selected clip, your actors should be making that *Wayne's World* dream sequence noise or scratching their chins while . . . wondering . . . what . . . if. . . .) By the end of the clip, the image is rippling and you can move on to the next clip, which shows the dream sequence playing out.

Changing Effect Out

Changing the Effect Out time does pretty much the opposite of what I've just been discussing. The clip starts will a full-blown effect and then gradually changes to its regular colors, brightness, and texture. Start the clip with a sepia tone and change back to regular colors or start at full bright white and return to a regular brightness. You do this by setting Effect In to 00:00 (the effect starts with the beginning of the clip) and Effect Out to some amount of time, in seconds, before the clip ends.

One major difference between the Effect In and Effect Out sliders is that the latter counts from the *end* of the clip. If, for example, you have a ten-second clip and want the effect to end after four seconds, you must set the Effect Out slider to 06:00, that four seconds is six seconds from the end of the ten-second clip.

You saw how Effect In can work for transitions, but how can Effect Out work? In a sense, Effect In settings let you transition *out* of a clip, where Effect Out can let you transition *into* a clip. Here are a few ideas:

- **What time is it?** Set Soft Focus to High and then set an Effect Out point just a second or two into your clip. The clip comes gradually into focus, giving you a sense that you've transitioned into the scene — sort of like you just woke up (or that you're watching from the point of view of a character just waking up).

- **Yes, it's World War I, but we're shooting in color.** You see this effect used often to transition the beginning of an historical movie into a modern color presentation, such as a black-and-white WWI dogfight followed by a transition from black-and-white to color for the characters. Select the Black and White effect and then set an Effect Out time. The image moves from black and white to full color in front of your eyes. (Clearly, this one could be used also with Sepia Tone for similar reasons, especially if you're transitioning from piano music and an Old-West-style opening credit sequence into a story you're telling in color.)

- **Admiral, we have them on the satellite feed.** Select the Sharpen effect and set an Effect Out time. The image begins as very sharp and then transitions to a regularly focused shot, suggesting that the satellite operator/hacker/spy has just successfully tweaked the digital image into full-focused video.

Changing the In and Out

You can change the In, you can change the Out, and if you like, you can do both. If you set an Effect In point and an Effect Out point, you can cause an effect to happen within the clip and then return it to normal before the clip ends.

When in doubt, split the clip

This far into your travels through the wonderful world of iMovie's special effects, you may have lit on an interesting question: What do I do if I can't do what I want to do? As long as I'm still talking about iMovie's video effects (and not some issue with your career ambitions), I probably have the solution.

The most likely solution is to split the clip. The one thing you can't really do with an iMovie special effect is make it *immediately* appear or disappear within a single clip. For instance, you can't cause a clip to play for a few seconds, immediately turn black and white, play for a few seconds, and immediately turn back to color. Instead, iMovie transitions those effects slowly.

If you split the clip, though, you can apply the effect immediately to the new second half of the clip. For this example, split the clip twice, into three parts. On clip one, put no effect. On clip two, put a black-and-white effect with no Effect In and no Effect Out times. For clip three, leave it color. When you play back the video, the clips go from color, immediately to black and white, and then to color again.

In any instance where you can't figure out how to make something happen — even outside the realm of iMovie effects (transitions, titles, sound, graphics) — think about whether it would work if you split the clip. Often enough, that's the answer. (Now if only splitting my bank accounts would somehow help.)

Slowing and Speeding Motion

I've been holding back on another special effect that you can perform on clips. In Chapter 5, I let you in on the secret of the backward-playing clip, which I warned was about as annoying as having too many blinking elements on a Web page. Well, here are two more effects with the potential to elicit groans: slow motion and fast motion.

Not that slow-motion and fast-motion have to be annoying. You might use different motion speeds on many occasions. For one, slow motion can work nicely with some of the Active Effects just mentioned. As you fade into a sepia-toned nostalgic Norman Rockwell-type ending, doesn't it make sense for the motion to slow down until it stops on a still clip?

Changing the speed of a clip is easy to do in iMovie:

1. **Switch to the Timeline.**

2. **Select the clip whose speed you want to alter.**

3. **Use the Faster/Slower slider at the bottom of the Timeline interface to change the speed of the clip.**

   Pretty easy, eh? See Figure 10-6.

Figure 10-6:
Move the
speed slider
to change
the speed of
a selected
clip.

After you change the speed of the clip, a small indicator appears on the clip's Timeline and Clip Viewer representations. Faster clips have a Fast Forward-type icon (sort of like >>), and slower clips have an icon like the one shown in the Rhinos/2 clip in Figure 10-6.

You should also note that, if sound was part of that clip, it has been sped up or slowed down as well. If you've extracted the sound from that clip, it wasn't affected by the speed change, but it will now be out of sync with the rest of the clip. In most instances, you're probably better off removing synchronized sound from a sped-up clip and relying on music or sound effects instead.

Look out for this one: Although a slow or fast motion isn't an effect (at least, you don't implement it from the Effects panel), if you apply an effect to a clip that has been slowed down or sped up, the clip snaps back to its original speed. So, apply other effects first and then slow down or speed up the clip in the Timeline. Otherwise, things can get shifted around in the Timeline.

And if you apply a transition or a title to a clip and then try to change the clip's speed, you must re-render the transitions and titles. The actual slow-motion or fast-motion frames also need to be rendered, but won't be until you go to export the video to your camcorder or to QuickTime (see Chapters 14 and 15).

Chapter 11

Adding Images, Animations, and Better Titles

In This Chapter

▶ Prepping images for iMovie

▶ Discovering how to create and import animations

▶ Searching for inspiration

*R*emember those boring presentation slides you made that one time in Microsoft PowerPoint for the sales meeting in Phoenix? Or what about all those boring slides you took on vacation — or the boring snapshots you scanned after the company picnic? If it's boring and it's a still image, now you can breathe life back into it using iMovie.

Okay, so the images don't have to be boring. But if you have a digital image or an animation that you want to get into iMovie, there's good reason to try. This is especially true if you're using iMovie for any sort of non-fiction endeavor, such as institutional videos, sales videos, training videos, organizational videos, or even presentations for the Web. You don't have to give up your presentation slides or other video just because you moved to iMovie.

iMovie itself can import still images in a number of different formats, including JPEG, GIF, PICT (Macintosh Picture file), and native Photoshop documents. And with the help of QuickTime, you can even import an animation file (after it's translated to DV Stream file format) and add it to your movie.

After you have the graphics in iMovie, you can work with them in a number of ways. You can transition between them, lay down an audio track of narration or sound effects, or use the images as backgrounds for title effects.

In this chapter, you look at the process of importing and working with still images and animations. Then I show you how easy it is to use that capability to add personalized graphics, titles, and credits to your movie.

Getting Images into iMovie

iMovie can import a number of image formats natively, while relying on QuickTime to do some other translations for it. Before you get started importing and using the files, however, you should get a little preliminary business out of the way. First, you should know a little bit about how images should be designed so that they fit nicely into iMovie. Second, you should know a little bit about the file formats that iMovie uses and which is best if you happen to have a choice.

iMovie needs the images to be a certain way before they can be effectively integrated into your video presentation. Not that iMovie makes any value judgments — the images can certainly be *bad,* as long as they're the correct height, width, and file format.

Most computer images — and, fortunately, television images — are measured in pixels, or picture elements. Each *pixel* is essentially a dot, making up a grander composition until, with enough dots smushed together on the screen, you end up with something resembling an image. And although iMovie doesn't care what those dots look like when they're strung together, it's rather a stickler for the *number* of dots you're allowed to use.

Images for iMovie should be 640 pixels by 480 pixels, at 72 ppi (pixels per inch, also sometimes called *dots per inch*). That's the basic, on-screen resolution, and images that fall outside those dimensions won't work properly in iMovie or, at the very least, will give you strange results.

In case you're curious, something interesting is going on with these resolutions. Digital Video (DV) is 720x480, not 640x480. The difference is the way DV uses dots: They're actually rectangles instead of the typical square-shaped dots that a computer uses. Because of this, they take up a little less space vertically. With images you create in a computer painting program, however, iMovie automatically compensates for this difference when you import the image, so stick to 640x480. The only caveat is if you're working with an image that's *smaller* than 640x480. In this case, you have one of three choices. You can simply import the image into iMovie and let it do what it wants to with it — which is to put a black border around it to make it a full 640x480 (see Figure 11-1). Second, you can scale the image *up* to 640x480, but realize that this may make the image appear a bit grainy. Third, you can place the image on a 640x480 background yourself, which is similar to iMovie's solution but gives you a bit more control over the placement and border color. (For this third option, see the "Creating a new image" section a little later in this chapter.)

Now, the next step is to decide if you're going to create the images yourself or if you're going to work with images you already have (either as computer files or images you plan to scan or take with a digital camera). In either case, you need to head out to a third-party application to get things accomplished.

Figure 11-1:
The result if you import an image that's smaller than 640x480.

Altering existing images

If you already have images that you want to place into your movie, you have the choice of quite a few applications. Adobe Photoshop, PhotoDeluxe, CorelDraw, and some of the software that came with your scanner or digital still camera, if you have one, may be capable of getting you to the basics.

For the sake of uniformity, however, I show you how to do this in GraphicConverter, which is included on the *iMovie 2 For Dummies* CD-ROM. GraphicConverter is a great shareware program for editing images on a Mac. The fact that it's shareware means two things. First, you can install it right off the CD-ROM and use it immediately, with no strings attached except for a short wait whenever you launch the application. Second, if you do use the application more than a few times and decide to keep it around, you must pay the shareware fee. (See the appendix for details.) Otherwise, bad things will happen. Movie people are superstitious — not paying shareware fees is bad karma.

GraphicConverter, as its name suggests, can deal with many different types of graphics files and formats. To get your existing image file into GraphicConverter, simply drag the file to the GraphicConverter icon (thus launching both) or use the File➪Open command in Graphic Converter to open the graphic image.

After you have the image open, you begin by changing the image's resolution (if necessary) so that it displays properly on the TV or in a QuickTime movie. Then, with the resolution set, you'll be ready to change its dimensions to fit iMovie by either cropping the image or scaling it.

Changing resolution with GraphicConverter

The first step in prepping the image is to change its resolution. Compared to printed images, images on television require relatively few dots — 72 pixels per inch (ppi) — to look acceptable. If you've scanned a still image using a computer scanner or if you've taken an image with a digital still camera, the image may have more resolution information than you need. As a bonus, converting down to 72 ppi causes the image to take up less disk space:

1. **With the image open in GraphicConverter, choose Picture⇨Resolution or press ⌘-Control-Y.**

   The Resolution dialog box appears (see Figure 11-2).

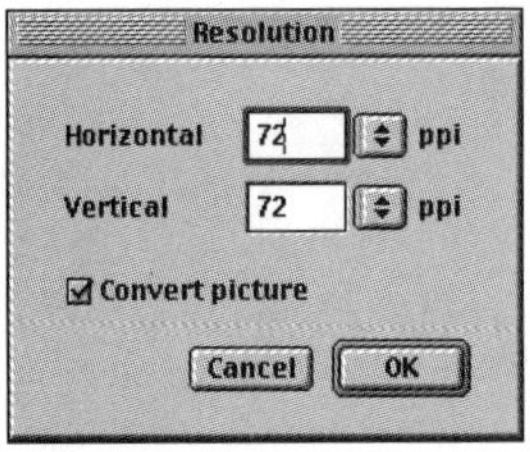

Figure 11-2:
The
Resolution
dialog box.

> **Resolution**
>
> Horizontal [72] [⇕] ppi
> Vertical [72] [⇕] ppi
> ☑ Convert picture
> [Cancel] [OK]

2. **Enter 72 in both the Horizontal and Vertical entry boxes.**

3. **Uncheck the Convert Picture option if it currently has a checkmark.**

4. **Now, click OK.**

You won't see any visual manifestation of this change on the screen, unless you happen to have taken a look at the small Information window before and after changing the resolution. The Resolution indicator changes to reflect that the image is now 72x72 ppi. (GraphicConverter reports dpi as *ppi,* or pixels per inch.)

Cropping with GraphicConverter

First, you may want to crop the image so that it fits into 640x480. The advantages to this are that you don't have to go through any conversion steps and it's often a good idea to crop images, anyway, if only to get closer to the action that you want to display. Here's how to crop the image:

1. **Make sure the Selection tool is selected.**

   The Selection tool is usually active by default if you just opened an image, but you can never be too careful.

2. **Move the mouse pointer to the top-left corner of the portion of the image that you want to** *keep.* **Press and hold down the mouse button and then drag to the bottom-right corner of the image you want to keep.**

   As you do this, note the two boxes labeled W (for width) and H (for height), which are usually at the top right of the image window in GraphicConverter. They tell you the dimensions of the dotted box that you're dragging. When W gets to 640 and H to 480, the selection is the right size for iMovie (see Figure 11-3). If this isn't acceptable, move down to the next section, "Scaling with GraphicConverter."

   Are the little W and H boxes showing inches instead of pixels? You can change that. Locate the Information window and then look at the top line, named Size. A small pop-up menu next to the size probably says Inches. Select Pixels from that menu and the little W and H boxes will now also show you measurements in pixels.

W and H values; this is actually a small
palette window that you can drag around

Figure 11-3:
Dragging to
select the
640x480 that
I want to
keep.

3. **When you get to exactly 640x480, release the mouse button.**

   This can take a deft hand. If you're having tons of trouble, try zooming in on the image using the Zoom pop-up menu at the bottom-left corner of the image window.

4. Choose Edit➪Trim Selection or press ⌘+Y.

The rest of the image goes bye-bye, and you're left with the 640x480 that you selected (see Figure 11-4).

Figure 11-4:
After you trim the image, the selected portion is all you have left.

Now you may still have a few more steps. If you haven't already, you need to change the resolution to 72 dpi (see the "Changing resolution with Graphic-Converter" section previously in this chapter) and then you need to save it correctly (see the "Saving your image" section later in this chapter). Because you've now officially cropped the image, you probably have no need to scale the image, so you have my blessing to skip the next section, if you so desire.

Scaling with GraphicConverter

If you *must* have the entire image (or most of it, anyway), cropping it won't work. Instead, your other option is to scale the image down to 640x480. This is generally a two-step process because images aren't always an exact multiple of 640x480. So, you might still do some trimming — but not too much.

Before you begin, take a good look at your image. Is the image (regardless of the number of pixels) arranged so that it has a width to height ratio of about 4:3? That is, is it about the proportions of a TV or computer screen? It not, you need to crop it so that it is, at the very least, *close* to 4:3.

If the image is close to 4:3, you can probably scale it to 640x480. Now the question is: Would you prefer to keep one dimension (the width or the height) exactly as it is? If you think you can crop a little from the bottom but not from either side, you should scale the width exactly and then trim a little off the height. If the image can stand to lose a little off the left or right side, scale to the height exactly and then trim a little off the width to make things fit.

Okay, now you're ready to scale the image. Here's how:

1. **Open the image in GraphicConverter, if you haven't already.**

2. **Choose Picture⇨Size⇨Scale or press ⌘+Control+Y.**

   The Scale dialog box appears.

3. **In the Dimension area at the top of the Scale dialog box, click the radio button next to the dimension that you want to scale exactly.**

   This is where that decision comes in. If you want to keep every last pixel of the width of the image, choose W. If you want to keep all of the image from top to bottom, click H.

4. **If you selected W, enter 640 in the box next to W. If you selected H, enter 480 in the box next to H.**

5. **Click the Keep Proportions check box at the bottom of the image (see Figure 11-5).**

   This scales the image in exact proportion, so that it doesn't become stretched in one direction or another.

   When you click Keep Proportions, you immediately see the *other* value change to reflect its final number. (If you entered 640 for W, you see the H number change; if you entered 480 for H, you see the W number change.) If the changed number is now *lower* than 640 for W or 480 for H, your image isn't proportioned correctly for scaling. If that's the case, you probably need to crop parts of your image to get it to about a 4:3 ratio before you can scale it to 640x480.

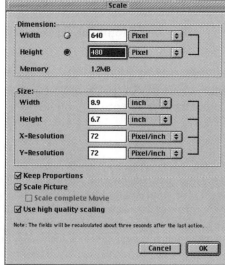

Figure 11-5:
Enter the appropriate number (640 for Width, 480 for Height).

6. **Make sure that the Scale Picture and Use high quality scaling options are turned on.**

7. **Click OK.**

   GraphicConverter goes through the process of scaling the image to the specified dimensions. When it's finished, you see the image window again, probably at a new size.

After you go through this process, you may not be finished. If it so happens that your image was a multiple of 640x480 (say, 800x600, 1024x768, 1152x864, or 1280x960, which are common resolutions for still images), the image will have scaled perfectly and will be ready to use. If the image wasn't an exact multiple, you need to return to the image window and crop it so that it's perfect in both dimensions. (If you scaled to the W dimension, it should be a perfect 640 pixels. Now you have to crop the H dimension to 480 pixels.) For more on cropping, see the "Cropping with GraphicConverter" section.)

Creating a new image

Want to create your own images for use in iMovie? Doing so isn't tough, as long as the image has the right dimensions: 640 pixels by 480 pixels at 72 ppi. You can use pretty much any graphics program you like, such as the AppleWorks Painting module, as long as it can export the image in a graphics format that iMovie can recognize: PICT, JPEG, GIF, or something similar.

Here's how to create an image in GraphicConverter:

1. **Choose File⇨New⇨Image from the GraphicConverter menu or press ⌘+N.**

   The New dialog box appears.

2. **Enter 640 for the Width, 480 for the Height, and 72 for the Resolution. Choose 16.7 Million Colors from the Depth pop-up menu.**

3. **Click the New button.**

   A new, blank window appears, ready for you to spruce up.

Now you can create an image using the text, line, and shape tools available in GraphicConverter (see Figure 11-6). You have to figure out the tools on your own, but doing so shouldn't be difficult if you're familiar with any sort of drawing or painting program. When you're finished, save the image in a compatible format for importing into iMovie. (See the next section, "Saving your image.")

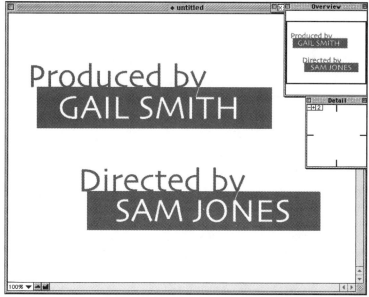

Figure 11-6:
Creating
a title
image in
Graphic-
Converter.

Saving your image

After you've cropped or created your image, you're ready to save it. (In fact, you should probably save it as you're working because, as the adage says, "savingliness is next to godliness.")

iMovie can deal with a number of different graphic file formats, including PICT, GIF, JPEG, and BMP (the Windows Bitmap format). So which do I suggest? If you're already working in a particular format, there's no reason to change. If the image was originally in JPEG, for instance, continue to work with JPEG. If you're creating the image from scratch, select either PICT or JPEG.

JPEG (Joint Photographic Experts Group) is both a file format and a technique used to compress image files. (For example, PICT files can be compressed with the JPEG scheme.) It's a *lossy* technique, meaning files compressed with JPEG will be smaller and may lose image detail. JPEG is great for photographs that will be transmitted over the Web, for instance, because JPEG image files are small in file size but maintain a lot of color and image detail. For images in iMovie, however, uncompressed images (such as uncompressed PICT files) are ideal.

Getting way too deep: NTSC colors

One of the major issues when creating your own graphics for iMovies is the choice of colors. Some colors simply don't work well on TV, as you've no doubt seen if your cable system has public access channels. If you choose the wrong color, you get buzzing, popping, bleeding, and all sorts of other awful things happening on TV.

So, if you're planning to output images to TV, you should be concerned about your colors. If you can, use a program that offers an NTSC Color Safe palette, such as Adobe Photoshop. If you don't have Photoshop, use a Red-Green-Blue selector (in GraphicConverter, for instance) to choose your colors. When you do, follow two rules: Avoid using pure colors (for instance, a red value of 255 and a blue and green value of 0) and keep your R, G, and B numbers at about 200 or lower.

Another trick is to use a video monitor connected to your camcorder. Check it for colors that are too bright and seem to flicker or bloom. And check for patterns (especially checks, plaids, and series of lines that are too close together) that cause trouble on the screen.

Here's how to save an image in GraphicConverter:

1. **With the image open in GraphicConverter, choose File➪Save As.**

   You can instead choose File➪Save if you just created the image. But if you opened an existing image, use Save As so you can select a new file format if desired.

2. **Choose the folder where you want to save the file.**

3. **In the Name entry box, type a name for the file.**

4. **From the Format menu, select the file format you want to use to save the image.**

   Again, I recommend PICT unless you're already dealing with a JPEG image.

5. **Click the Options button next to the Format menu.**

   For a JPEG file, you'll see a Quality slider bar (see Figure 11-7). Move it all the way to High, select the QuickTime radio button, then click OK. Skip down to Step 7 in this list.

6. **For a PICT file, you'll see the PICT dialog box. Select QuickTime in the Compress area and click Options again.**

   Now you'll see the Compression settings. Select None from the top pull-down menu (see Figure 11-8). Then, click OK. (Click OK again in the PICT dialog box.)

7. **Click Save.**

   The image will be saved, and now it's ready to import into iMovie.

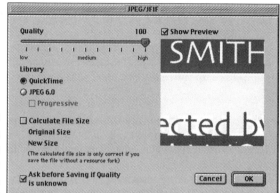

Figure 11-7:
The options
for a
JPEG file.

Figure 11-8:
The options
for a
PICT file.

Importing the image

After the image is sized and ready for action, head over to iMovie and import it. All it takes is a few steps:

1. **Choose File⇨Import File from iMovie's menu or press ⌘+I.**

   The Import File dialog box appears.

2. **Locate and select the file you want to import.**

   You can use the Show menu to decide, for instance, that you only want to see Macintosh PICT files in the Import File dialog box.

3. **Click the Import button.**

The image appears as a clip on the Shelf, where you can begin to work with it as if it were just any old regular still clip.

Changing the length of the image clip

When you import an image into iMovie, it's turned into a still clip and is assigned the default length of time that has been set for still clips. If you'd prefer that your still clip take up more or less time, you can change that in one of two ways.

Before the import, you change the amount of time it takes to import a clip by choosing Edit⇨Preferences. On the Import tab's "Still Clips are" entry box, enter the amount of time (in seconds) that you want each still clip to be.

The other way is to edit the clip's time after you've imported it. Select the clip in iMovie. (It can be on the Shelf, in the Timeline, or in Clip Viewer.) The Time indicator at the top of the Clip Viewer changes to an entry box. Click in the box and enter a new number (in the format 00:00:00, such as 00:15:00 for fifteen seconds) to change the amount of time that the clip is left on the screen. You have the option of making the clip up to one hour (actually, one frame short of an hour at 59:59:29), which is nice in terms of the flexibility that iMovie gives you. In terms of moviemaking, however, a single still clip on the screen for nearly an hour is vigorously discouraged.

Creating and Importing Animations

Aside from still images, iMovie can import animations, as well, especially with the help of QuickTime Pro. For iMovie's part of this process, it simply imports a DV Stream file, as discussed back in Chapter 4. But if you happen to have QuickTime Pro, you can go a step further by translating your animations into DV Stream files.

If you have an animation program that you're using to create your animations, you're probably the sort of person who doesn't need me to tell you how to use such a program. (Especially because I'm not an expert in any of them.) Most such programs have the capability of exporting the animation as a QuickTime movie. Do that and then launch QuickTime and export the animation movie as a DV Stream, as discussed in Chapter 4.

If you don't have an animation program, you can still use QuickTime to put together an animation the old-fashioned way: from a sequence of image files. Create an image file, as described and discussed earlier in this chapter. Then create about 30,000 more images, changing things in the image slightly each time. At 30 frames per second, that's 1000 seconds of video — almost 17 minutes.

Actually, you have two things going for you here. First, you don't *have* to create a 17-minute animation — I was just funning with you. Second, depending on what you're trying to accomplish with your animation, you probably don't need 30 different images to make up each frame of your animation. You'll probably be able to get away with two, five, or ten images per second, depending on what you're trying to animate. In Figure 11-9, for instance, I created a sequence of images (about 18 total — the picture only shows half of them) that, at six frames per second, take about three seconds to animate.

If creating all those images still doesn't sound like much fun, at least stop to consider that you don't have to be an artist. (Or just don't do it. I don't think it sounds like much fun, at least, not with a program to do some of the animating for you.) In fact, the animation doesn't even have to look like a cartoon. You might simply want to use an animated sequence to show images or text blinking on the screen or to create a title sequence where letters or words appear or disappear magically on the screen.

Here's how to create an animation from a sequence of images in QuickTime:

1. **Create a sequence of 640x480 images at 72 ppi and name them *any-thing1.pict, anything2.pict,* and so on. Make sure their names are spelled the same except for the sequential numbering.**

2. **With QuickTime Player active, choose File➪Open Image Sequence.**

   The Open dialog box appears.

3. **Select the first image in the sequence and click Open.**

   The Image Sequence Settings dialog box appears.

4. **Select the frame rate for the animation (how many images should be shown per second?), as shown in Figure 11-10.**

5. **Click OK and a QuickTime movie is created.**

Now, with the QuickTime animation in QuickTime format, you can export it as a DV Stream file that can then be imported into iMovie. See Chapter 4 for details.

Clearly, for most of us, animations will be easier to create in another program. Fortunately, a number of programs are designed to create image sequences or QuickTime movies while enabling you to more easily animate text and graphics. See Totally Hip's (www.totallyhip.com) line of products, for example.

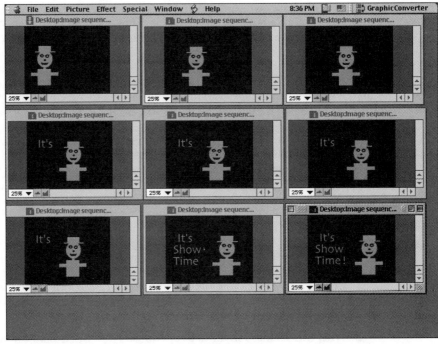

Figure 11-9:
Here's a sequence of images to load into QuickTime. Okay, so I'm no artist. Are you giggling?

Macromedia Flash is another powerful animation tool. QuickTime can read Flash files directly, and those Flash files can then be translated into DV Stream format. Finally, a program I use all the time, called Snapz Pro (www.ambrosiasw.com), includes a feature that will create a QuickTime movie as it watches actions on your Mac's screen. (It's taking a series of screen shots, creating an animation.) If you happen to be making a computer training movie, you can create a QuickTime movie of the on-screen moves, export it as DV Stream. Then, integrate that animation into your video using iMovie. You can even record voiceover or commentary, just as if you were the space reporter on CNN while they play those NASA animations of the Mars Probes missing Mars and spiraling off into deep space.

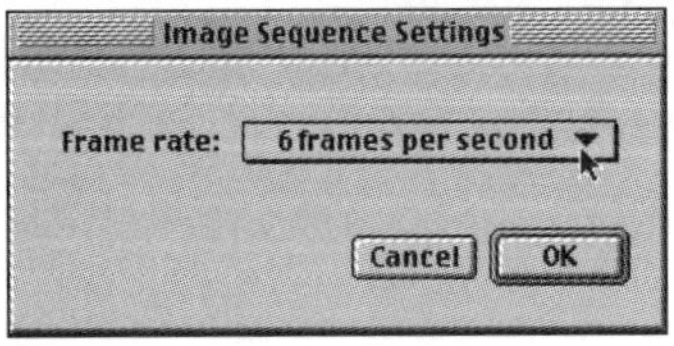

Figure 11-10:
Select the number of frames per second.

> **Image Sequence Settings**
>
> Frame rate: [6 frames per second ▼]
>
> [Cancel] [OK]

Ideas for Images

So why would you decide to import still images into iMovie? I can think of a few different reasons, not the least of which is to simply get more control over your titles and credits. Although it's tough to get your credits to roll up the screen using a still image, you can fade in and fade out on unique personalized images that you've created if you have a particular look that you'd like for your opening sequence. Or, you might have a particular background that you'd like your credits to appear on (even if it's just a white, blue, or green background, which isn't easily accomplished in iMovie).

Slides and information screens

One trick that can be effective for corporate or organizational video is to take the same slides that are being used in a filmed presentation and translate them to images that can be edited into iMovie itself. For instance, if you're filming your company's CEO giving a talk and using PowerPoint slides for emphasis, arrange ahead of time to get a copy of the presentation file. That way, you can focus your camera work on the CEO himself and not worry about trying to film the slides with your camcorder. Then, when you go to edit in iMovie, use the *actual* PowerPoint presentation slides in your movie.

In fact, the easiest way to get them is this:

1. **Launch PowerPoint and load the presentation.**

2. **Change to the slide you want to include in the iMovie.**

3. **Use the Monitors control panel to change your Mac's screen resolution to 640x480.**

4. **Take a screen shot of the slide.**

   The screen capture keystroke (⌘+Shift+3 in Mac OS 9.*x* and earlier) creates a PICT file of the screen that's stored on the main level of your hard disk. You can also use a third-party screen capture application.

Now you're free to import the image file to iMovie and change the amount of time it takes up. If desired, you can use the Timeline and the Advanced⇨Paste over at Playhead command to add this still image to the point in the movie where the CEO is referring to it. With a nice cross dissolve transition between the slide and the CEO, your movie audience probably won't even stop to think about how these transitions are taking place — they're simply able to see the slide at the right time. (In fact, it probably looks better than it did for some of the people who were in the room with your CEO!)

Note, by the way, that the screen-capture method described here is a great way to get anything to be exactly 640x480 at 72 ppi without messing around with editing or scaling the image. When you set your monitor to display 640x480 in the Monitors control panel, it so happens that the screen is also at 72 ppi. So, if it looks good on your computer screen, it should look good in iMovie.

Slide shows

iMovie isn't a bad place to put together slide shows or "film" strips that are nothing but still images, back-to-back-to-back if necessary. It's easy to create interesting transitions between the slides, add narration, and put music behind the slide show. This can give an active feel to a self-running demo or an educational QuickTime movie. I've seen entire local TV shows on Saturday mornings that were basically nothing but still images of houses (usually six or seven) while a voice describes the house and some music plays in the background.

If you have a real estate office or a car dealership or are creating a trade show kiosk, you could use iMovie as the foundation for a narrated, music-ified self-running presentation.

Personalized titles and credits

Importing images into iMovie can give you some flexibility and freedom to create interesting titles that use different colors and fonts as well as backgrounds, which can be sorely lacking in iMovie.

Import an interesting still image and use it as the background for a title sequence, credit sequence, or both, created in iMovie. Just give the still image a running time that's long enough to take on the titles or credits you'd like to use and then select and apply a Title sequence (from the Title panel in iMovie), as discussed in Chapter 7. Figure 11-11 shows an example.

Another approach is to paint the title graphics yourself and then import them to iMovie and arrange them in a sequence. A cross dissolve between the two is a great way to create a sense of animation for the titles (although many transitions will work). If you'd like to create your own titles, feel free. You can create a series of credit screens and transition between them, as shown in Figure 11-12. The figure shows two images: one with the producer's name on a white background and one with the director's name on a white background. Between the two still clips, I placed a cross dissolve transition.

Be careful, though: The credits created for Figure 11-12 look good in a QuickTime movie but are a little close to the edge (and a touch too big) for the TV screen. As always, it's a good idea to have a TV monitor connected for previews, especially if you're creating your own credits and titles. (See Chapter 2 for more on hooking up a TV monitor.)

Figure 11-11:
Import a still image as a background for credits or titles.

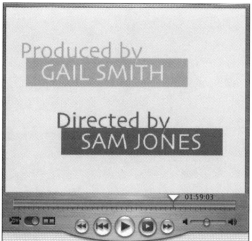

Figure 11-12:
Here we are in mid-dissolve, as the producer credit disappears and the director credit appears.

How about combining these two thoughts? You can export a still frame image from your movie (File⇨Save Frame As) and edit it in GraphicConverter or Photoshop to add a title or otherwise alter the image. Then, import it *back* into iMovie using File⇨Import. Now you have a still clip with your own fonts that you can add to the end of the action clip that led up to it, creating a freeze-frame titling effect.

Chapter 12

Working with iMovie Plug-ins

In This Chapter

▶ Installing plug-ins

▶ Finding out what the plug-ins do

▶ Discovering other free Apple downloads

*N*o doubt, iMovie has quite a few built-in features, and Apple should be applauded for that. But the fact remains, as one of my ethics mentors (the Michael Douglas character, Gordon Gecko in *Wall Street*) told me in the mid-1980s: *Greed is good.* I think that applies to effects, transitions, and sounds in iMovie, as well.

Apple has heard that call and built into iMovie the capability to take on more effects, transitions, and sound effects through a plug-in architecture. In fact, Apple has made available the first round of such plug-ins, the iMovie Plugin Pack 2, which includes new transitions, effects, and titles you can add to iMovie 2. And beyond that, Apple offers separate downloads for more sound effects, looping background music, and background images that you can use for more interesting credits and still clips. All you gotta do is find 'em and use 'em!

In this chapter, you see how to install plug-ins and take a close look at the additional tools that the iMovie Plugin Pack 2 puts at your disposal. Then you see how to download all the extras that Apple makes available for sounds, songs, and stills.

Installing iMovie Plug-ins

Although Apple hasn't made it abundantly clear whether or not third-party developers are allowed to develop plug-ins, it's a very real possibility. A *plug-in* is a piece of computer code that isn't an application but rather augments an existing application. Very often, a plug-in adds functionality such as special effects or filters. For instance, Adobe Photoshop, Adobe After Effects, and QuarkXPress are all examples of applications that can accept plug-ins that augment their capabilities. Similarly, Web browsers such as Internet Explorer and Netscape Navigator can accept plug-ins that enable them to display QuickTime movies or Flash animations right there in the browser window. Now we can add iMovie to that list, even though, at the time of writing, only Apple-written plug-ins are available.

Apple's Plugin Pack 2 adds new transitions, titles, and effects to iMovie. It's easy to install, but first you have to get your hands on it. If you have the CD-ROM that was included with this book, you'll find the Plugin Pack there on the CD. If you don't have the CD-ROM (or if you want to check for a later version), you can find the Plugin Pack at Apple's iMovie Web site (`www.apple. com/imovie`). Right there on the main page, look for a link that enables you to download iMovie Plugin Pack 2.

If you download the Plugin Pack, it should automatically decompress and be available in its own folder on your hard disk. If all you see is a file with a .sit filename extension, it may not have decompressed correctly; drag-and-drop the file to the StuffIt Expander application icon so that the file can be decompressed.

After the Plugin Pack folder is on your hard disk, installing it is as easy as drag and drop. (Presumably this will work for any iMovie-compatible, third-party plug-ins, too, if any are written in the future.) Here's how to install it:

1. **Quit iMovie, if it's running.**

   Use the File⇨Quit command (iMovie⇨Quit in Mac OS X), and don't forget to save any changes. iMovie looks for new plug-ins only as it starts up, so you need to launch iMovie after you install new plug-ins.

2. **Locate the iMovie folder on your hard disk and open it.**

   You see the alias for iMovie, along with another subfolder called iMovie.

3. **Open the iMovie subfolder.**

   Now you see the actual iMovie application and a folder called Resources.

4. **Open the Resources folder.**

   You see a number of folders, including one called Plugins.

5. **Drag-and-drop the iMovie Plugin Pack 2 folder to the Plugins folder.**

   You can also open the Plugins folder and place the iMovie Plugin Pack 2 folder in it. Note that you *don't* have to drag any items out of the iMovie Plugin Pack 2 folder: all individual plug-ins can stay in the folder (see Figure 12-1).

6. **Close all the folders and launch iMovie.**

7. **You can click the Transitions, Titles, and Effects buttons to see the new additions.**

Presumably, any third-party plug-ins will work the same way. Simply drag them to the Plugins folder that's hidden away in the iMovie folder that's inside the iMovie folder . . . and so on.

Figure 12-1:
You can drag the entire iMovie Plugin Pack 2 folder to the Plugins folder to activate the plug-ins.

What the Plug-ins Do

The iMovie Plugin Pack 2 adds a number of different transitions, titles, and effects to the built-in capabilities discussed elsewhere in this book. Some of these new additions are welcome friends, including some basic effects we may have expected the first time around and some gimmicky effects that are just fun to play with.

Let's look at the different add-ons in each of three categories: transitions, titles, and effects. I'll render my opinion as to which are useful in certain situations and which, on the rare occasion, I just don't like much.

Checking out the transitions

The iMovie Plugin Pack 2's most prolific contribution category is transitions, which has a full seven transitions. For the most part, the new transitions are variations on a theme — different ways to wipe between the first clip and the second clip using different shapes, mostly. My favorite, however, is the addition of the Wash In and Wash Out effects, which are important to have in your iMovie arsenal.

Here's a looksie at each type of new transition:

- ✔ **Circle Closing and Circle Opening.** These two transitions work with circles, clearly. With Circle closing, the first clip appears to become a circle that gets smaller and smaller until it disappears, while in the background we see the second clip running behind the first. This transition tends to suggest that a story line is coming to an end and might be used between action and the closing credits.

  The opposite happens with the Circle Opening transition. The second clip appears as a small circle, which opens until it completely hides the end of the first clip. This transition tends to suggest that a new scene (or theme, thought, or chapter) is beginning.

  I suggest using the circle transitions only between static and dynamic scenes. For instance, you could use a circle transition between an unmoving document — such as a map or the chapter page in a book — and a person in action. These do not look as good if you transition between two action scenes. See the QuickTime circlesbad.mov and circlesgood.mov clips (on the *iMovie 2 For Dummies* CD-ROM) for examples of what I mean.

- ✔ **Radial.** Radial is just a special effects swipe, clearing away the first clip with a sweep that resembles a second hand on a clock, with the next clip revealed in its wake. There's no particular rule for using this transition, although it may subtly suggest the passage of time. I recommend using it sparingly and not using other gimmicky effects such as the Warp, Circle, Scale Down, or Push transitions. (The exception would be if you're going for a playful look, such as with a Saturday morning kids news or magazine show. It would also work with other videos of kids, such as a school play, talent show, or birthday.)

- ✔ **Warp In and Warp Out.** Both of these effects are gimmicks too, basically mimicking Circle In and Circle Out, but with different shapes. They're a bit cartoony, and perhaps appropriate for lighthearted fare. (Probably not for corporate or institutional videos unless you're looking for a light moment.)

- ✔ **Wash In and Wash Out.** Washes are basically the same as fades, but with all white instead of all back. A Wash In begins the clip with all white and then transitions into the full color of the clip. A Wash Out goes from full color to an all-white image. These are good transitions, again, for beginnings and endings of thoughts, chapters, or ideas, and are especially effective for transitioning into a title screen, a graphic, or credits.

Aside from radial, these transitions are all end-of-idea transitions, as opposed to an overlap or a cross dissolve used to transition between clips while keeping your audience in the moment. They are designed to take the audience *out* of the moment of the first clip and plop them back down in the moment of the second clip.

Adding new titles

The iMovie Plugin Pack adds only two new types of titles, Subtitle and Zoom, although each also has a Multiple option to make it easier to string together multiple instances in one title sequence. Here's a look:

- ✔ **Subtitle.** This title is definitely useful, if only because it gives you a simple and effective way to put text at the bottom edge of the screen for whatever reason — translations, a person's honorific or job description, or a text track. If you're doing translations using subtitles, you'll probably need to split clips many times to keep the subtitles on the screen for the correct amount of time. Just split the clip at every point where you want new subtitles.

- ✔ **Subtitle Multiple.** With this title, you can enter multiple lines of text and have them appear on the screen at any regular interval. This is good for low-key opening credits but probably isn't useful for translations unless the people are speaking in well-timed iambic pentameter. (It could conceivably be used for "follow the bouncing ball" sing-along text, as long as you're willing to overlook the lack of a bouncing ball. But just think — you can make your very own karaoke videos!)

- ✔ **Zoom.** This one-trick pony enables you to create a title or credit that zooms from very small to big, filling the screen. If you happen to want to do that, now you can. But . . .

- ✔ **Zoom Multiple.** This one is almost the same as Zoom but *tons of fun.* Why the difference? With a nice, heavy sans-serif font (I use Impact, although Techno or Textile work pretty well, if you have them) and Over Black turned on, you can make Zoom Multiple look like a cheesy old trailer for a black-and-white horror movie or even some old Hitchcock films. The key is having three text boxes. Try one with "Chills!" one with "Spills!" and one with "Hair-Raising Terror!" as shown in Figure 12-2. (Put Terror on the second line in the text box, all on its own, and don't forget the exclamation marks.) The result is outstandingly cheesy.

  I played with Zoom Multiple for days — see the chills..mov clip on the CD-ROM in the Chapter 12 folder.

Seeing the new effects

The iMovie Plugin Pack adds five new special effects to the list on the Effects panel. Almost all fit a general MTVish category. None are amazing technological feats, but they're interesting for isolated instances — especially, as I've intimated, if you happen to be putting together your own music videos.

Figure 12-2:
I just had to show you this one. (You have to picture it zooming in from the background with scary music playing. Duh, duh, duh!)

Here's a look at each:

✔ **Flash.** Flash is an interesting, limited effect that's simply designed to make it look like you're taking flash photos of the subject of the clip. Sliders at the bottom enable you to choose how many times the flash effect happens, how bright it is, and how quickly the effects happen. What's this good for? Making a loved one look like a movie star seems to be the primary purpose.

Don't make the flashes occur too quickly, and note that if you set less than maximum brightness, you can still see the subject in the flash of light. This effect isn't great (it doesn't look that much like a camera flash) although it can look good if (1) your subject is getting out of a limo in evening wear and (2) you slow the footage down a bit, giving it a slow-motion feel. Movie stars (and sports stars) are always getting their picture taken in slow motion.

✔ **Ghost Trails.** This one pretty much just blurs the image as your subject moves around. It's good for that "We're at warp speed!" effect or for bone-crushing punches in a boxing movie. The controls enable you to determine the length and opacity of the trail as well as how many steps each trail is (that is, how often the trail is updated). The most dramatic trails are long, with large steps and high opacity. It's an interesting effect to use when your kids are playing sports or air-guitaring around the house.

✔ **Mirror.** This one is a simple effect, but it has some interesting applications if you play around with it. Select a clip and then select the Mirror effect and use the slider to determine where within the clip (toward the left or toward the right) you want the "mirror" to be placed. The result: A clip that seems to have a reflection of itself playing on each side.

This effect can give a great look to a vacation video. Shoot a family member or companion in profile as he or she is walking down the street in New York or Venice or Paris (or select some place that seems equally exotic out in Iowa if you happen to be from New York or Venice or Paris). Then, use the Mirror effect on that walking clip. The result has a familiar "boy/girl meets world" look, as shown in Figure 12-3. (See the mirror.mov clip on the CD–ROM in the Chapter 12 folder.)

Want another idea? If you place the "mirror" well off to one side (almost to the left or right edge), you can make it look exactly like a disruption in the space-time continuum. I don't know if that's useful for you, but I liked it.

Want a third idea? Try this effect as a moving effect. That is, give it an Effect In time. Now the mirror effect slowly travels across the screen.

✔ **Mirror Advanced.** The Advanced version of Mirror simply adds a top-to-bottom option to the Mirror effect, so you can choose to have the image mirrored both right-to-left and top-to-bottom. If you place both sliders dead center, you end up with a kaleidoscope effect that's pretty disturbing if your subjects are people or animals.

✔ **N-Square.** What's the *N* for? This one takes the video image and replicates it *N* number of times, so that the screen image becomes one of many on the screen (see Figure 12-4). This is perfect for the times when you want multiple images of your video running on the screen: (1) a music video, (2) a statement on the mundane redundancy of humanity in our commercialized corporate world, or (3) a music video that makes a statement on the mundane redundancy of humanity in our commercialized corporate world.

Figure 12-3:
Get your subject to look around and try to have something cool, like the Parthenon, in the background.

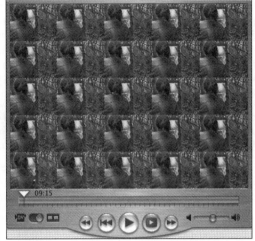

Figure 12-4:
"And she
told two
friends . . .
and she
told two
friends. . . ."

Apple's Other Downloads

Aside from the iMovie Plugin Pack, Apple has made available a number of other items you can download and add to your movies. They include sound effects, sound tracks specifically designed to be looped (repeated) for as long as necessary, and some still images you can use for various effects, including more interesting credit and title sequences.

All of the downloads are currently available from a special page called Free Stuff, located at www.apple.com/imovie/freestuff/ on Apple's Web site. If you don't find them there, they've either been moved, taken down, or Apple has gone out of business. (Does the site still seem to be about computers?) It's also technically feasible that, if you can't find a particular Web site, the entire Internet is just closed for the evening.

All of these collections are stored as StuffIt archives. After you download them, these extras should automatically decompress and appear on the Desktop (or in another folder that you've specified as your Web browser's Download folder). In most cases, each download has its own folder, which you can open to reveal the items.

Background sets

Apple has a number of background sets that are available for downloading in categories such as Abstract, Artwork, Gradients, Theater, and Video. After they're downloaded, you can import each individual graphics file using the

File⇨Import command in iMovie. As with any still image, these images are imported as five-second clips (by default) that you can then use just as you would any other clip. You can place titles over them, put sound and music behind them, and so forth. Figure 12-5, for instance, is a credit sequence over one of the free backgrounds. (I'm also still a bit too enamored with the Zoom title effect, as you can see.)

Figure 12-5:
Using one
of the down-
loadable
back-
grounds,
you can
have fun
with the
credits.

Looping music

Apple has also made available a few clips (fewer than the backgrounds, unfortunately) of what it calls *looping music*. Basically, they're tracks of music that sound okay if you copy them multiple times and then lay them down clip after clip in the Timeline. It gets a little redundant but not jarringly so.

After you download these reasonably small music clips, you can store them anywhere you like. (I recommend, but not for any particularly good reason, putting them close to your iMovie data files.) Now you can simply import the audio clip into your movie:

1. **Choose File⇨Import from within iMovie.**

2. **Select the audio file (or one of the audio files) you downloaded from Apple.**

3. **Click Import.**

   After a short import session, the audio appears on the Timeline. Now you can move it around as desired.

Now, if the audio isn't long enough for you:

1. **Select the audio you want to copy.**

2. **Choose Edit⇨Copy.**

3. **Place the playhead.**

   It's important to use the Zoom menu to get in close and make sure the two audio clips touch exactly without overlapping — that keeps the clip from skipping a beat or getting out of sync (see Figure 12-6).

4. **Choose Edit⇨Paste, as many times as necessary.**

Figure 12-6:
You can copy the music as many times as necessary to complete your story.

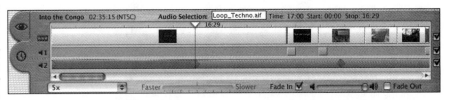

If the music gets tedious, don't forget that you can always fade out the last clip and then drop in one of the other clips to change the mood. Or you can even run silent for a few seconds or minutes before dropping in more music. Music doesn't have to be under every moment of your movie. Use it, like images and sound effects, to set the tone and highlight the images you want to present in the video.

Adding sound effects

Apple has made a number of sound effects available for use in iMovie, along with two different ways to install them. The groups of sounds range from animal sounds to bells, people sounds to cars, trains, and planes. You download the sounds as a StuffIt archive. After you decompress the archive, you have a folder full of (or overflowing with) interesting effects to add to your movie.

The sounds are simple AIFF files, so if you want to preview them, you can drag them to the QuickTime Player icon or open them using the QuickTime Player's File⇨Open command.

After you download the sounds, you can get them into your movie in two ways. First, you can import them using the File⇨Import command. This places the image at the playhead in the Timeline.

The other method is to drag the files to iMovie's sound effects folder:

1. **Shut down iMovie.**

2. **Inside the iMovie folder (and the iMovie folder that's inside the iMovie folder), find and open the Resources folder.**

   You see the Sound Effects folder.

3. **Drag any AIFF sound file to the Sound Effects folder (see Figure 12-7).**

4. **Restart iMovie.**

   The new sound is available in the Sound Effects area at the top of the Audio panel in iMovie.

Figure 12-7:
Drag sound files to the Sound Effects folder if you want to access them from iMovie.

So, if it's so easy to add sound files to iMovie, why doesn't Apple just make an installer that puts them there automatically? It turns out that adding sound files to iMovie, at least in the current (2.0.1) iteration, can slow down iMovie as it launches. If you notice that iMovie is taking a long time to start, consider moving unnecessary sound files out of the Resources folder. You can always import them later if required.

In fact, leaving sound effects in their folders is a convenient way to organize them not only for quick removal to avoid long startup times, but also to deal with quite a few sound effects in the Audio panel within iMovie (see Figure 12-8).

Figure 12-8:
Sound
effects
stored in
folders
show up as
subtopics in
the sound
effects list,
making
them easier
to find by
subject.

When you place a folder full of sound effects in the Sound Effects folder,
iMovie adds those effects as subtopics in the Audio panel, with the name of
the subtopic the same as the name of the folder. That makes the individual
sounds a bit easier to organize, find, and use.

Chapter 13

Take Two: Advanced Editing Techniques

• •

In This Chapter

▶ Experiencing intercutting

▶ Doing J-cuts the right way

▶ Getting audio from the unlikeliest of sources

▶ Understanding advanced effects with QuickTime

• •

*P*revious chapters present the bulk of the tools that iMovie makes available to you for editing. The tools are deceptively easy to use — so deceptive, so easy, so sinister, so coy — that you may not have realized their full power. With a quick lesson in video editing tricks, you can add interesting moves to your movie and finally convince that mobster producer to underwrite your next picture — without having to cast his girlfriend in the leading role.

The Fine Art of Intercutting

Chapter 8 shows you the basics of pasting the video portion of one clip over the video portion of a base clip so that you can include the audio of the base clip with the video of a different clip. For our purposes, that's called *intercutting*. Although I talk about how to intercut in that chapter, I save the "why" of intercutting — and some additional tricks — for this chapter.

In general, I offer one admonition: If you decide to intercut, you should have a good reason for doing so. Most of the time, that reason is to convey additional visual information or interest. An intercut enables you to tell *more* of your story by adding to the power of the audio presentation with different video images. People expect to see video that changes and remains interesting — if you don't do this, you run the risk of boring your audience with a stationary camera and a single subject, just droning on and on and on.

Another reason to intercut is less noble. You can use that handy-dandy Paste Over command to help make up for mistakes or problems with your camera-work. (Or, rather, with your brother-in-law's camera work. We all know you wouldn't let the camera shake that much.) If you have portions of a video clip that are good and others that aren't as good, a little intercutting may help you work around the problem by putting different video on the screen while the audio plays on. Although this technique can help you get out of a jam, don't rely on it too much.

So those are the reasons to consider intercutting — but what about the cuts themselves? In this section, I quickly discuss the two major types of inter-cuts: cutaways and cut-ins. For the most part, Chapter 8 shows you how to perform these cuts. In this chapter, I discuss some special circumstances.

They went cutaway!

A *cutaway* is a shot that shows some action other than the base or main action but usually on-topic. If your base action is video of a professor talking in his office, you might cut away to whatever it is that the professor is talking about — lions on the outback, computers lined up in a computer lab, or students walking across the stage at graduation. These cutaways make the video presentation more interesting or engaging while holding it all together with a steady stream of audio (see Figure 13-1).

Figure 13-1: While I hear this woman discussing the animals, I cut away to the animal she's pointing at and then cut back.

Another major type of cutaway is the *reaction shot*. You've seen these on *60 Minutes* or during TV coverage of pretty much any public speech. On a news show or in a documentary, the reaction shot is often of the reporter — nodding her head in agreement or looking sternly objective when the interviewee is saying something misleading that's about to be proven wrong. For a public speech, the reaction shot might be audience members clapping or protesting. Reaction shots are used in fiction, as well, to show someone who is in the same scene but not talking.

Note that *actual* reaction shots require either two cameras or a time machine — otherwise, by definition, you're not able to film the reaction to something you're filming. If you're shooting non-fiction, you may want to consider the ethical implications of getting so-called reactions out of sequence using only one camera. Professionals would get in trouble for doing that. Instead, the best approach is to use two cameras — one to shoot your main footage and one to capture reactions or other cutaway footage. If you have the luxury of two cameras, you can still piece the video together in iMovie by simply importing clips from each camera into the same project. Because you're extracting audio from your base clip and then pasting your cutaway video over portions of the original clip, you don't have to worry about synchronizing audio from each clip.

May I cut in?

So what's a cut-in? It sounds like what you used to be accused of in high school if someone held your place in the hot lunch line. A *cut-in* is actually an intercut that goes deeper into the current action (see Figure 13-2. Most cut-ins are close-ups on the action or product shots. Watch one of those cable shows about improving your home and you see a shot of the actor (in most cases they are *actors,* you know) setting up to hit a nail into the side of the house. Then, suddenly, you see a cut-in of the hammer hitting the nail).

Figure 13-2:
In this one, we show the full shot of the subject, cut-in to something a bit smaller, and then back out.

Cutaways and cut-ins don't necessarily have to involve other video clips — you can just as easily intercut between your base action and still images. An example of a still image cutaway is a still image of the Mona Lisa while your interviewee is discussing the Louvre or Leonardo DaVinci. A still-image intercut is one that shows a close-up of a product or product box as it's being discussed, or a graphic overlay that shows text of the information that's being presented on-screen. For instance, in an instructional show, you might be showing video of the instructor teaching and then intercut to a still image of a computer screen shot that demonstrates the issue being discussed. (Actually, this is a great place to import an animation of a computer screen, as discussed in Chapter 11.)

Still image transitions

You'll sometimes find it useful to *transition* between those intercuts, although I emphasize that you should do this only for a good reason. I give you two right here. First, you could transition between still images and moving images in your intercutting, especially for a title sequence. Second, you could transition between two similar clips that need to go back-to-back but don't look good as a straight cut because they aren't different enough. For example, you might desperately want to use some footage that's hampered by shaky camera work.

Although it's certainly possible to perform straight cuts between still images and moving clips, it can often look better to use a fade in on each graphic portion. For opening titles and credits, for instance, you can transition between some graphical titles that you've imported and your opening scene in the iMovie. As an example, suppose you were putting together a vacation video of your visit to New York City. You could put an opening sequence of titles and credits at the beginning of the video, transitioning between each still image title and each action shot of New York. What's more, using the Extract Audio and Paste Over at Playhead commands, you can keep the audio from the original clip running even when your still clips are on the screen.

Figure 13-3 shows a video sequence of my New York opening and the credits that appear between them.

Figure 13-3: Here's part of the sequence I'm working with.

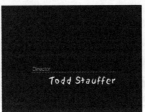

To begin, you need a long clip of the New York skyline (or something similar) on the Shelf, along with a few still-image title graphics imported as still images (see Chapter 11). Then, follow the procedure laid out in Chapter 8. Drag the skyline clip to the Timeline and extract its audio. Now, it's a simple matter of selecting one of the still clips on the Shelf and invoking the Edit⇨Cut command (or Edit⇨Copy, if you want to leave the clip on the

Shelf). Back on the Timeline, place the playhead at the point where you want the title graphic to appear and use the Advanced⇨Paste Over at Playhead command. Do the same thing, at interesting intervals, for the rest of your title clips. See the results in Figure 13-4.

Figure 13-4:
This view of
the Timeline
shows the
title images
pasted over
the video.

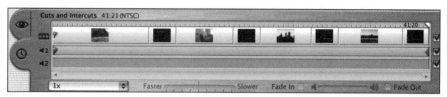

Notice that the last title clip in the sequence actually ends when the extracted audio ends. The only trick I used for that is a little arithmetic — the editor's friend. I know the street-scene clip is 20:15 long and I know that last title was 2:00 seconds. (I imported all the images as two-second still clips by choosing Edit⇨Preferences and selecting the option on the Import tab.) So, I put the playhead right at 18:15 before pasting over.

Now, as this sequence stands, the graphics are a bit too abrupt. Play back the clip and it seems jarring the way you're happily watching the video and then suddenly cut to a still clip. So, we need a quick transition. Next step: Place a fade in transition between each step from clip to credit graphic. As shown in Chapter 6, all you need to do is activate the Transitions panel, select Fade In, set a Speed, and drag the Fade In icon down in front of each still image clip. The transitions take a little time to render, but then you're ready to preview your handiwork.

Figure 13-5 shows how this looks in the Timeline. The transtitle.mov file in the Chapter 13 folder on the *iMovie 2 For Dummies* CD-ROM shows how the movie looks in QuickTime.

Figure 13-5:
Here's the
Timeline,
complete
with fade in
transitions
for each
graphic.

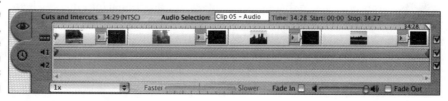

First, note that the fade in transitions don't need to be very long. I set them for a mere 0:10 — that's one third of a second. Second, you may think you need fade in transitions on each video clip (or fade out transitions on the back side of the still clip), but I don't think so. Experiment, but I say it looks fine with a quick cut back to action — it isn't as jarring for your audience to cut from still to action as it is to cut from action to still. And, third, don't you think a cross dissolve would look good between still and video clips? Well, it does, but iMovie messes with the timing of clips when you use cross dissolve, so cross dissolves mess up the synchronization of your audio if you've extracted audio from the clip.

So, this transitioning to still images works for titles, but what about other graphics? As a general rule, a quick transition into any still clip is helpful, regardless of the type of still graphic. That includes graphic overlays that convey information, such as statistics, Web addresses, or weather maps, and any still image you want to put on the screen while the audio from the underlying clip is playing.

Jump cuts

Another special case of editing technique is the jump cut, which simply describes a type of cut you'll almost immediately identify with music videos. A *jump cut* is a cutaway that, in a nutshell, doesn't actually cut away — you stay with the same action but at a slightly different angle. Although the rule is at least a 30-degree angle change for a straight cut, a jump cut doesn't do that. In most cases, you're jumping to another portion of the same video clip, often while the image is zooming in or out.

In iMovie, this is exactly what you do to achieve the effect — you cut one clip into three or more parts and then remove some of the middle clips to remove the smoothness of the clips and make them appear to jump from one point to the next. For instance, if you split a clip into five smaller clips, remove clips 2 and 4, and then play clips 1, 3, and 5 in sequence, you see a successful jump cut. Figure 13-6 sort of shows what this looks like. (It's tough to show *exactly* what this looks like because, no matter what I do, I can't seem to get this printed page to show movie clips.)

A jump cut is generally not recommended for regular video because it's an abrupt change that doesn't convey any additional information. It can be visually appealing, as you can see in the clip called rhinojump.mov in the Chapter 13 folder on the CD-ROM. And jump cuts can look really good when put to music. In fact, the original of the clip I put on the CD-ROM is part of a larger project that's set to a swingin' big band song.

(Note to Self: To avoid future procrastination, don't sign on to write books about cool programs like iMovie. Write all future books about obscure scripting techniques in Microsoft Office for Mainframes.)

Figure 13-6:
Here's an example of a jump cut — imagine each image is an abrupt "jump" as the clip plays.

The other problem with a jump cut is the fact that it'll wreak havoc with the audio portion of the clip if you start slicing and dicing. That's why, if you're using a jump cut technique, you should use it as an intercut, pasting it over existing audio. (This still might not make sense if the audio needs to by synchronized exactly to the video. But it will work in some cases where the audio is simply ambient noise.) Here's how to do this:

1. **Place the entire clip on the Timeline and extract its audio.**

2. **Select the entire clip and use the Copy⇨Paste command to place a copy of it on the Shelf.**

3. **Select the new video clip on the Shelf.**

   It appears in the Monitor window.

4. **In the Monitor window, place the playhead on the Scrubber bar and choose Edit⇨Split Video Clip at Playhead.**

   The video clip is split in two.

5. **Continue with Steps 3 and 4 until you've cut the clip into all the smaller cuts you'd like to use.**

6. **Rename the clips that you're going to keep, if only so you can keep them in order (for example, Jump 1, Jump 2, and so on).**

   You may also want to rename the clips that you're going to keep, if only so you can keep them in order (for example, Jump 1, Jump 2, and so on). Now you have the clips that you want to keep for your jump cut sequence.

7. **Select the first clip on the Shelf and choose Edit⇨Copy or Edit⇨Cut.**

   Choose Copy if you want to leave the clip on the Shelf or Cut if you want to remove it from the Shelf.

8. **Place the playhead on the Timeline and choose Advanced⇨ Paste Over at Playhead.**

9. **Repeat Steps 7 and 8 for each of the clips, putting them back-to-back by carefully placing the playhead at the end of the previously pasted clip.**

   You may find it helpful to view the Timeline at a higher zoom level to line things up nicely.

That's it. After you have your clips pasted into the Timeline, you should have a nice little jump cut, complete with the continuous audio beneath it. Of course, if you used less of the video clip than the original length of the clip, you'll probably also want to crop the underlying audio.

This jump-cutting process can be time consuming, so I recommend a short-cut. Suppose that you're making a music-videoesque presentation that you want to set to music. In that case, you probably don't need to worry about extracting audio and all that jazz because you don't intend for your audience to hear anything that's spoken or going on in the clip's audio. If that's the case, you don't have to worry about this quite as much:

1. **Select the Timeline icon at the bottom-left of the screen so that you're seeing the Timeline.**

2. **Select the clip (on the Shelf) that you're going to use for your jump cut.**

3. **With the clip highlighted, move the Timeline's volume control slider all the way to the left.**

   Now the clip's volume has been turned all the way down, which is great, because you didn't want to use any of that audio, right?

4. **Use the Clip Viewer (see Figure 13-7), if you want, to split and rearrange clips.**

   I think the Clip Viewer is easiest for this because you can move clips around more easily, including dragging some of your split clips to the Trash.

5. **Record your music to audio track #2 and put together the rest of your music video.**

Figure 13-7:
The final clip portions (clippettes?) arranged on the Clip Viewer.

Jump transitions

Here's a real fun one, but you have to watch out for it. This music-video effect is not only jarring in a non-music-video presentation but also presents trouble because, as noted earlier, the cross dissolve effect can mess up your audio synchronization. (When you take two clips and cross dissolve them, the overall amount of time is shortened by the length of the cross dissolve transition. If the two clips total six seconds and you put a one-second cross dissolve between them, you end up with a total of five seconds between the clips after the transition happens.)

So, what do you do? Take a single clip and split it using the Split Clip at Playhead command. (You can remove the middle part of a clip to create a more abrupt jump transition, but you don't have to — even if the clips run smoothly together, the transition has an effect.) Now, place a cross dissolve effect between the two clips. The result is similar to a jump cut but with a sort of magical, transitional effect. It's an interesting way to get from one part of a clip to another and is a bit smoother than a jump cut.

For an example of a jump cut with a cross dissolve, see the QuickTime movie jumptrans.mov in the Chapter 13 folder of the *iMovie 2 For Dummies* CD-ROM.

Sneaky Tricks for a J-Cut

In Chapter 8, I promise a little more coverage of what may be the most complicated edit you can do in iMovie: a J-cut. With this type of edit, the point is to get the audio from a clip starting *before* you see the video of that clip. That means the audio starts while another video clip is on the screen. This is easy if the first clip doesn't have any audio of its own (for instance, an Over Black title clip). But if it does have it's own audio, you have to get a little tricky.

Here's how to succeed with the J-cut:

1. **View the clips in the Timeline and extract the audio in each, if necessary.**

   Figure 13-8 shows how this looks when you're ready to begin the J-cut procedure. Note that, for this to work, you need to have a third video clip that's after the second one, as pictured.

Figure 13-8:
Setting up to
perform the
J-cut.

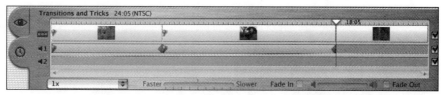

2. **Select the second audio clip (the one that will be part of the J-cut) and unlock it from its video clip.**

3. **Click in the playhead area above the video track to place the playhead on the Timeline at the very end of the second video clip.**

   It should snap right to the point between the second and third clips.

4. **With the second audio clip still highlighted, press the right arrow key on your keyboard once.**

   Press it *only* once. You are lining up the end of the clip with the beginning of the next clip. (You need a next clip, incidentally, although it doesn't have to be permanent.)

5. **Choose Advanced⇨Lock Audio Clip at Playhead.**

   The end of the audio clip is locked to the beginning of the next video clip. If it doesn't look exactly like Figure 13-9, you need to try again; cheat the playhead just slightly toward the third clip.

Figure 13-9:
Locking an audio clip to its neighbor.

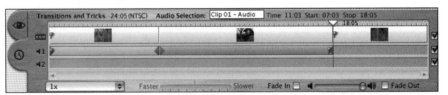

6. **Select the second video clip and remove a portion of video from the beginning of the clip. Use the crop markers (in the Monitor) to select a few seconds from the beginning of the clip and then choose Edit⇨ Clear to remove the video.**

   Note that after you clear the video, the second audio clip now overlaps the first one.

7. **Select the second audio clip and press the left arrow key once.**

   The audio clip moves back into sync with the video clip. Note that you don't have to unlock the clip first — it automatically unlocks and locks at the beginning of the audio clip.

8. **Select the first audio clip and drag its right-side crop marker to the beginning of the second clip. (See Figure 13-10.)**

   This doesn't delete the audio of the first clip, but it keeps the overlapping portion of the audio from playing.

Figure 13-10:
Drag the
crop marker
of the first
audio clip so
that it's no
longer
overlapping
the second
clip.

Alternative Audio

Chapter 8 covers some of the basics of importing audio into your movie, and
Chapter 9 discusses narrating the film. If you want to go a little further down
the quality spectrum, however, you might consider two additional options
when it comes to better sounding audio: exporting audio for editing in a
sound-edit application and using your camcorder to get good narration without a high-priced audio setup!

Editing audio tracks

Tucked away in the nether regions of iMovie's seamy underbelly of file storage are the media files for your project. There, you find an interesting array of
the raw files used to put together your movie. After you gain access to these
files, you can force them to do your bidding. Open a project folder on your
hard disk and then open the Media files folder inside that project folder.
Figure 13-11 shows a sample of the Media folder for one of my projects.

Note that video, audio, and music clips can be kept in separate files, although
audio files (such as Voice 01 in the list in Figure 13-11) are stored in separate
files only if they're broken out by the Extract Audio command. After you do
that, though, you can access the audio directly. And guess what? It's stored in
AIFF format, so you can edit that audio in an audio-editing application such
as Felt Tip Sound Studio, a great little shareware editor on the CD-ROM, or a
more professional application such as SoundEdit 16 from Macromedia.
Simply locate the file that holds the audio clip you want to edit and then load
it into your audio-editing application.

Figure 13-11:
Media files
for a project
in progress.

If you're having trouble locating the correct audio file, select the clip in the Timeline. Choose File➪Get Info (or press ⌘+Shift+I) to display the Info dialog box. The Media File entry in that dialog box tells you the name of the file.

After you locate the file, open it in your sound-editing program (see Figure 13-12). You can open it directly with the Media folder (you don't need to duplicate or move the file first), and you can even leave iMovie open, if you want.

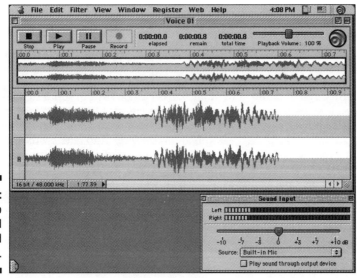

Figure 13-12:
The audio
clip loaded
in Sound
Studio.

Now, edit the file to taste — cut out hisses and pops, normalize, change the volume, add an echo — whatever you need to do. (I leave it up to your own skills, talents, and the boundaries of good taste.) Avoid doing anything that may alter the synchronization of the audio and video — such as cutting out part of what someone says, if you aren't going to cut the corresponding video — unless you're going for that poorly-dubbed monster movie look. (Which, frankly, might be fun.)

When you're finished editing, just save the file. As long as you don't mess with the name of the file or change its file format, it should not only load into iMovie but also play the next time you play the associated clip in the iMovie timeline, even if you have iMovie open the whole time. It's just that cool.

This works for narration, actor audio, and music you added to the project. Whatever you need to edit can be altered quickly and easily and then added right back into the project as long as it's all in AIFF. So, if you happen to know your way around audio-editing software (or you're willing to find out), go for it!

You can move audio and video clips between projects by locating the original media file for a particular clip (using the Get Info command) and moving (or copying) that file to the Media folder of another project. Video clips are usually named Video *XX* or something similar. When you next open that project, iMovie recognizes the new clip and moves it onto the Shelf.

Secret narration trick

Okay, so this isn't very secret and I can't take much credit for it; I learned it from the folks at DVCreators.net (see the acknowledgments at the beginning of this book). But here it is: If you want to record some good sounding stereo narration and you don't have a good microphone or recording setup, something I know you *do* have will work great. You have a digital camcorder, and it has a stereo microphone.

Set up your camcorder on a tripod or mount it otherwise, six to twelve inches in front of your mouth, find a blank portion of tape, and press record on the camera. (If you have a remote controller, so much the better.) Now you can record your narration almost as if you were in the recording studio sitting across a soundproof glass window from a guy named Mick who is always saying, "Yeah, I dig."

Actually, there's more to this trick: Record with the lens cap off. Why? Because you can see your lips or face moving on the video clips that you import into iMovie. This can be helpful because it gives you a quick visual cue to let you know when and where a good take was recorded. (You should also keep notes as you're recording if you record multiple takes in a row.) And, as an alternative or in addition to simply recording your face, you can also *slate* each take, which means you begin the recording (or perform the whole narration) while holding up a sign on which you've written the take number and some information about the scene (see Figure 13-13). The microphone picks up rattling paper, so you probably shouldn't try to hold the slate yourself while you narrate. Prop up the slate so it's visible, arrange your notes, and begin.

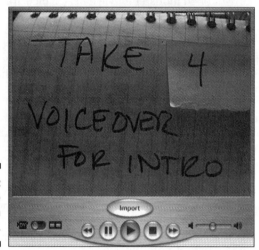

Figure 13-13:
An example
of slating an
audio take.

After you have the take you want, hook up your camcorder to your Mac, locate the take, and import it into iMovie. Find a spot on the Timeline (probably past the end of your current project, if you've started one), and drop the narration clip onto the Timeline. Extract the audio, edit it to taste, and then clear the video. Now you have a stereo narration clip you can drag back into your edited iMovie and place where it needs to be on audio track #1 or #2 — your choice.

More Effects in QuickTime

iMovie has (let me put this nicely) reasonably few special effects. The program is capable, but it runs up against some limits if you want to have things blow up or fly around or generally do something you can't manage to catch on videotape without putting your brother-in-law or your CEO in harm's way (not that it didn't entice you for a second).

The solution is to use another program. That's what the professionals do, generally relying on a program such as Abobe After Effects to perform amazin' wonders of FX when even the more sophisticated editing applications, such as Final Cut Pro and Adobe Premiere, can't quite hack it. That's part of the reason that I spent hour after hour on the *For Dummies* Yellow Situation Phone talking to the people at Adobe to get them to allow me to put a demo version of After Effects on the CD-ROM. I was, as you can see, triumphant.

Okay, I didn't really do it. The *For Dummies* people did, from Dummies Worldwide Conglomerate United Headquarters on the Dark Side of the Moon. But I suggested the idea.

With a full version of After Effects, you can do quite a bit with your DV footage. And without it? Well, without After Effects, you can still do some tweaking and hair pulling using QuickTime Pro, which can sing a few ditties that iMovie doesn't know the words to yet. QuickTime Pro must be registered, and you need a lot of time on your hands. First, though, you have to get the clips you want to mess with out of iMovie.

In this section, I show you how to export your clips for use in QuickTime Pro and After Effects (which I cover in a *little* more detail in Chapter 18). Then I show you a few tricks in QuickTime Pro.

Exporting your movie

The first step to using a third-party application for effects is to export your movie or at least part of it. You may want to put on the Timeline (or Clip Viewer) only the footage you want to use for your effect. If you already have a huge project going and you don't want to mess with it, the best plan may be to create a new project, import the clips you want to work with from your camcorder, and then put only those clips on the Timeline. Now you can export those clips much more quickly.

What you do is export to a QuickTime movie while maintaining the quality of the images. That means no compression. (For more on all of this, see Chapters 15 and 16.) Here's how:

1. **Choose File⇨Export from the iMovie menu.**

   The Export dialog box appears.

2. **From the Export To menu, choose QuickTime and then choose Expert.**

   The Expert QuickTime Settings dialog box appears.

3. **Click the 4:3 button and then click the Settings button that appears in the Image Settings section.**

4. **Under Compressor, select None from the first pop-up menu.**

   The little Quality slider automatically moves to Best.

5. **Click OK twice (one in the Compression Settings dialog box and again in the Expert QuickTime Settings dialog box).**

6. **Click Export.**

   A Save dialog box appears asking you to enter a name for the QuickTime movie and select a place to store it.

7. **Enter a file name and click OK.**

   Another dialog box appears. This one keeps you up-to-date on the progress of the export process.

When the dialog box disappears, the export is finished. You have a new QuickTime movie on your hard disk, ready to work with in QuickTime Pro or to import into another special effects application.

QuickTime Pro effects

Now I look quickly at some of the things you can accomplish in QuickTime Pro. This won't be an exhaustive discussion, but I hope to put you on the path of self-QuickTime-enlightenment.

Open your exported QuickTime movie in QuickTime Pro Player. It appears in the window. Now, you're ready to do some editing. You may notice that QuickTime has some controls that are similar to iMovie's Monitor — a Scrubber bar, triangle-shaped crop markers, and a little diamond-shaped playhead. If you like, you can use some basic cut, copy, and paste commands to edit your video or even paste video from other QuickTime movies.

But why would you want to do that when you already have iMovie? To add QuickTime's special effects! The key to effects in QuickTime is an obscure dialog box called the Info box. Choose Movie⇨Get Info (or Movie⇨Get Movie Properties in QuickTime 5 or higher) and the dialog box appears (see Figure 13-14).

Figure 13-14:
The Info dialog box in QuickTime Pro Player.

The Info dialog box has two pop-up menus at the top of it, one for selecting the item you'll be working with and one for selecting different qualities, choices, or other data. In this case, leave the selection at Movie in the first menu and use the second menu to see different information about that movie:

✓ **Auto Play** makes the movie play automatically on Macs that support that feature.

✓ **Controller** determines which QuickTime Player controller (the interface that enables you to play, pause, and change the volume) appears when the movie is opened.

✓ **Files** shows you what individual files make up the movie (it's likely just one right now).

✓ **General, Size,** and **Time** tell you different details about the movie.

✓ **Preview** enables you to select the portion of the movie that plays in any Preview windows that support QuickTime playback (such as Mac OS 9 and X Open dialog boxes).

Changing the size

You still haven't used any special effects, eh? That's because QuickTime Player lets you apply special effects only to individual *tracks* in your movie. By default, you likely have two tracks — an audio track and a video track. You can select those in that first pop-up menu at the top of the Info dialog box.

After you've selected a video track, you can perform effects in two places: the Size and Graphics Mode options in the second (right-hand) pop-up menu. Select Size, for starters, and the Adjust and Normal options and some directional buttons appear (see Figure 13-15).

Figure 13-15: Select the Size option and more controls appear.

Now you have some interesting effects. Click the left-and-right facing arrows and the image flips left to right — you're now seeing the image backwards, as if in a mirror. (Try to read text in signs in this mode.) Click the up-and-down arrow and the image flips upside down. You can use the clockwise and counter-clockwise buttons to rotate the movie 90 degrees in the selected direction.

Click the Adjust button and controls appear in the QuickTime Pro Player window itself. The handles all around the window (in red) are little places where you can point and drag the mouse to change the dimensions, angle, or size of the movie image. Experiment with them to see what sort of effects they offer. After you're finished, you can click the Done button to make the changes take effect. At any time (after rotating, resizing, or what-have-you), you can click the Normal button to return the video to its original size, orientation, and resolution.

Transparency effects

Here's the real magic in QuickTime. It's called *transparency,* and in basic terms, it enables you to overlay your video with either another video image or a graphic of some kind. In some ways, this is basically the *chroma key* effect that you may have heard of. You tell the program to knock out a particular background color and fill it in with video, such as the moving maps behind a TV meteorologist or the moving sky behind Superman. With QuickTime, you can get a similar effect.

Probably the number one issue with chroma key effects is the uniformity of the background. Suppose I want to shoot a superhero — Macman — against a blue background, feed the video to iMovie, export it to QuickTime, and get it into the program and ready for some transparency effects. Two problems present themselves. First, in QuickTime, the transparency effect isn't that sophisticated, so I need to know the *exact* color that I want to make transparent. Second, any variation in that background color — even changes in the lighting or shadows cast on the background — make the transparency process fail because that means there's more than one color in the background. (A blue screen with a shadow across it has parts that are now a different shade of blue, right?)

All this is simply leading up to a warning: Don't try to do Superman effects in QuickTime Pro. You need a more sophisticated application, such as Adobe After Effects, before any effect of that caliber will work. You need to know something about professional lighting and camera work, too. (All bets are off if you know something about flying with just tights and a cape, incidentally. Film that!)

What you can do in QuickTime Pro, though, is create a special graphic image that will overlay the video portion of the movie. Then you can make part of that image transparent, so that you can see the movie through the transparent section. It's not as sophisticated as the Superman stuff, but it's fun nevertheless.

How does this work? You create an image that will be used to define transparent and non-transparent portions of an image, called a *mask*. In this case, you're creating a *static mask* because it won't be moving. (A moving mask is a lot tougher, requiring an application more sophisticated than QuickTime Player.)

You can pull this off because you can control everything — you can make the background color a certain color that doesn't change shades or hues, and you can purposefully set it to a color for which you know the settings. Here's how:

1. **In a graphics program such as GraphicConverter or PhotoShop, create an image file that's 640x480 at 72 dpi.**

   These are the same settings discussed in Chapter 11.

2. **Draw a mask, or the image that will include parts that you want transparent and parts you don't (see Figure 13-16).**

   The key here is to choose a color for the transparent section for which you'll easily be able to input the Red, Green, and Blue values. White is 255, 255, 255 and Black is 0, 0, 0, but if you use the RGB color controls in your graphics application, you just need to note the color values you do use.

3. **Save the file as a PICT image.**

   You'll be importing it into the QuickTime Player application.

Now you're ready to get the image into QuickTime and prep it for merging with your QuickTime movie. There's one step you need to take, first. Load your movie (the one you exported from iMovie) and figure out its length in minutes and seconds. You need to know the time for the transparency to work correctly. With that number noted, head back to QuickTime and begin importing:

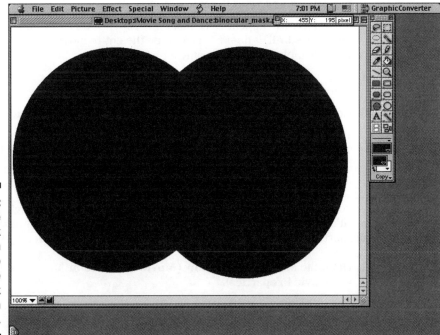

Figure 13-16: Creating the Mask image. I'm going to make the black portion transparent.

1. **In QuickTime Player, choose File⇨Import.**

   The Import dialog box appears.

2. **Locate the PICT file you want to import and then click Convert.**

   Another dialog box appears.

3. **Name the QuickTime movie that's being created and then click Save.**

4. **In the QuickTime Player window, select the entire movie on the Scrubber bar (use ⌘+A or the Edit⇨Select All command) and copy it using the Edit⇨Copy command.**

   When QuickTime imports the PICT and converts it to a movie, the movie is one second long. Now you've copied the mask movie.

5. **Choose File⇨Open and open the original QuickTime movie.**

   This is the one you exported from iMovie.

6. **With the movie open, place the playhead at the point on the Scrubber bar where you want the mask to begin overlaying the image.**

   This point is probably the very beginning of the movie.

7. **Hold down the Shift key and drag the playhead to the end of the selection where you want the mask to appear.**

   If the mask will appear over the entire movie, you can simply Choose Edit⇨Select All. It doesn't have to be the entire movie, though, if you want to apply the mask to only a portion.

8. **After you've made the selection, use the crop markers to fine-tune it, if desired.**

9. **Hold down the Option and Shift keys and choose Edit⇨Add Scaled.**

   The Add Scaled command appears in the Edit menu only when you're simultaneously holding down Option and Shift. (If you're only holding down Option, you see the command Add, which adds the mask for only one second.)

Now you've added the mask movie to the existing QuickTime movie as a new layer. It's overlaying the original movie image right now, but you're about to make part of it transparent so that you can see the movie under it. Here's how:

1. **Open the Movie Info window (Movie⇨Get Info or Movie⇨ Get Movie Properties).**

   The Info window appears.

2. **In the left menu, select Video Track 2.**

   That's the top layer — the mask movie you just added.

3. **In the right menu, choose Graphics Mode.**

   Here's where you change some graphics settings about the selected layer.

4. **Choose Transparency.**

   A box and a button called Color appear.

5. **Click the Color button.**

   Color selector controls appear.

6. **Choose RGB picker and then use the sliders to select the RGB values for the color that you want to make transparent.**

   I went with black, so the numbers are 0, 0, 0 — I moved the sliders all the way to the left.

7. **Click OK in the dialog box.**

   Did it happen? Your top layer should turn partially transparent (see Figure 13-17).

Figure 13-17: When I turned the black part transparent, suddenly you could see part of the movie behind the mask layer.

That's it. If things are transparent, you may need to make sure you've selected the correct color in the Color selector dialog box. Otherwise, I recommend you experiment with the different graphics mode settings and see what else you can come up with — the QuickTime Pro Player is your oyster.

Another quick way to get a mask (where portions of the screen are transparent and others aren't) into your movie is to make a black-and-white image similar to the one just created. Now, without using the Add command to add the new layer, simply open the Info dialog box and select the video track. From the right-side menu, select Mask. Click Set and select the mask image in the Open dialog box. When you click OK, you should see the mask immediately take place in the QuickTime window — the binocular example works great for this. This is easier to do but somewhat limited, because the mask must be applied to the entire track at once.

Want another idea of what to do with the transparency effect? Make a small box in one corner of the mask image a meaningful graphic, and make the rest of the image transparent. (See Figure 13-18.) What have you got? A local newscast look! You'll love this one for hamming it up with the kids.

Figure 13-18:
Using a
small
graphic
and a
transparent
background,
you can put
news
graphics
over your
on-screen
talent.

When you've finished messing around, see Chapter 4. In that chapter, I talk about importing this QuickTime movie back into iMovie.

Part IV
Opening Night: Presenting Your Movie

The 5th Wave   By Rich Tennant

DAD ADDS MULTIMEDIA SOUND AND GRAPHICS TO THE TRADITIONAL CAMPFIRE GHOST STORY.

In this part . . .

You've shot, you've edited, you've toiled. Now you're ready to take your work and present it to the world. Part IV shows you how. In these chapters, you see how to output your movie to a TV and to videotape for distribution in the traditional way. You see also how to use iMovie to create QuickTime movies, which you can then place on CDs, distribute through the Internet, or simply play back right there on your Mac's screen. Speaking of the Internet, you dig deep into the settings to see how best to optimize QuickTime movies for distribution through e-mail, the Web, or other Internet options. In addition, you see how to prepare and present your movies using iTools, Apple's online tools for building your own Web presence and distributing your work.

Chapter 14

Exporting to the Small Screen

● ●

In This Chapter

▶ Finding out the point of exporting

▶ Getting simple output to your camcorder

▶ Getting your movie on VHS tape

▶ Backing up to DV

● ●

*1*f you're anything like me (and I hope, for your sake, that the similarities are limited), you've spent countless hours painstakingly editing your movie. You've cut little slivers from each clip to get the movie to fit the sound track; you've imported audio and re-imported it after you've messed it up; you've selected and updated titles and effects over and over again. You've seen your little movie more times than you can count in the Monitor window, full-screen on your Mac, or if you have a sweet little video-out setup through your camcorder, previewed on a TV monitor.

Well, you've had that little puppy squirreled away for too long. (A puppy squirreled away? I can't wait to see how the translator handles that one if we sell the foreign language rights for this book.) It's time to get your movie exported to tape so the video can be seen by the real world on the small screen — a TV — in all its glory and splendor.

iMovie offers plenty of export options: exporting to QuickTime, exporting to create Internet-capable movies, and exporting to your camcorder. I cover that last instance in this chapter and take a look at what you can do after the transfer back to the camcorder, which is quite simple. After exporting your movie, you can use your camcorder to get it on a TV screen or on VHS tape or just, uh, squirrel that puppy away on a DV tape for posterity.

Why Export?

Exporting to your camcorder is simply the process of moving your edited DV content back to the DV cassette in your camcorder. You have a few excuses for doing this, including watching the footage on a TV, recording it to a VCR, and storing the footage on a cassette. Here's a look at each:

- ✔ **Watch on TV.** After you've exported your movie to a camcorder, you can connect that camcorder to your television set and play it back directly from the camera itself. It reminds me of that part of *Back to the Future* where Doc, in the 1950s, looks at Marty's camcorder and says "A portable TV studio! No wonder your president is an actor. He has to look good on television." That's what you have in your hands — a portable TV studio. Output your edited movie to the camcorder and connect it to a TV — instant screening.

- ✔ **Record to VHS.** If you can hook your camcorder up to a TV, you can hook it up to a VCR. What's even better, recording from the camcorder to the VCR is the first analog recording in this process, meaning there's only a slight loss in quality. (If you record from an analog camcorder to a VHS recorder, you've already lost two *generations* — or levels — of quality.)

- ✔ **Store the movie.** A DV cassette just so happens to be another storage mechanism for digital data, almost like a removable disk. That means you can move iMovies to a cassette if you're running out of disk space and then store them on the cassette until you need the footage again. I promise you — you'll be doing this a lot, especially if you're working on projects that are longer than ten minutes or so.

So that's what's possible. First, though, you have to get your movie out to the camcorder. I cover that now.

Outputting to the Camcorder

When you have an edited movie you're exceedingly proud of, you're ready to test things out, make some last-minute decisions, and send the movie out to your camcorder. You start with a little testing and prep work.

Previewing the video

With your movie arranged in the Timeline or Clip Viewer, preview it carefully in the Monitor window or full-screen on your Mac's display. I recommend doing this at least twice, once with each quality setting in the Preferences dialog box. Choose Edit➪Preferences and then click the Playback tab. You see two options: Smoother Motion and Better Image (see Figure 14-1).

Figure 14-1:
The
Playback
tab in the
Preferences
dialog box
enables you
to preview
your movie
in different
ways.

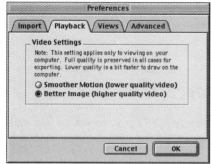

When previewing the Smoother Motion setting, listen closely to see whether you have any audio problems — soundtrack music that's skipping, unexpected audio volumes, clips or unwanted sound effects you've forgotten about, and so on. (I've noticed, on occasion, that a split soundtrack clip can mess up the playback of both video and the audio beyond it.) Then, switch to the Better Image setting and watch the video again — this time, look for obvious visual problems such as special effects you forgot to take out and misspellings in your titles.

If a TV monitor is connected via your camcorder, you can probably get away with using the Smoother Motion option and previewing on the TV screen to look for both audio and video problems. I recommend that you preview this way if your video is for corporate, organizational, or any other public purposes. Watching your edited movie using iMovie's preview options can give you a false sense of both the picture quality and picture dimensions. (Not always for the worse — the slower frame rates in iMovie's playback can make some effects look better and more film-like than they'll eventually appear on a TV screen.) If you preview on a TV through your camcorder, you can correct small errors before you export them to tape. Remember, you can preview through the camcorder in the Preferences dialog box. Choose Edit➪Preferences, click the Advanced tab, and turn on the Video Play Through to Camera option.

Previewing on a TV monitor can be helpful in another respect: It enables you to see your title effects and make sure they're showing up in the "title safe" portion of the screen. If your titles seem to be falling off the edge of the TV screen, you may have set some of them using the QT Margins option. Return to those titles, de-select the QT Margins check box, and click the Update button to update them with their proper TV borders.

Finally, previewing on TV can show you one other issue — color problems. If you can preview on a TV, watch carefully for colors that seem to bloom or bleed on the screen — as noted in Chapters 7 and 10, using pure colors can often cause trouble when the image is on a TV screen. (Depending on the size and font of your lettering, you may even find this is true with plain white lettering on Over Black title clips. You may get better results with slightly beige, blue, or gray letters if it seems your credits or titles are causing color trouble.)

Setting up to export

Happy with how things look? Then you're ready to set up iMovie to export to tape. Of course, first you need to set up the camcorder and tape itself.

Most likely your camcorder is already connected to the Mac through its FireWire cable and is in VTR, VCR, or Playback mode. Make sure that's the case, and make sure the camcorder is turned on and plugged into an AC outlet. (You don't want to run out of battery juice halfway through the transfer.)

Next, insert the tape you want to use for recording into your camcorder. It's always a good idea to use a new tape for your recording. That way, you know you're not recording over anything else that may be valuable. You also know that your raw footage is stored safely on another tape in case you ever want to re-import that footage to alter this project, or even use it for a different project. (I recommend keeping everything you've ever shot that's even halfway decent. If you ever need footage of the beach or Central Park or zoo animals for another project, you have it. Don't forget to label your tapes!)

With the tape inserted, use the controls on your camcorder or in the Monitor to move to the point on the tape where you'd like to begin recording. If you're recording from the beginning of the tape, there's no need to do any shuttling — unlike a VHS tape, a DV cassette has no leader that you need to fast-forward past. You can record from the very beginning of the tape. (You can set up iMovie for a few seconds worth of black at the beginning of the recording anyway.)

With that set, head back to iMovie. Before you begin the export process, you can make another major decision about your movie: Which tracks will you export?

Open the Timeline viewer and find the small check boxes down on the far right side of the interface (see Figure 14-2). Each track that's checked will be exported; tracks left unchecked won't be. This makes it easy to export just the video portion of your movie, if desired, or to drop out the audio #1 track while leaving the audio #2 track in (so that no voice sound is exported but the soundtrack is). Now you're ready to begin the process of exporting.

Choose the tracks that you want to include

Figure 14-2:
Make sure
you have
the
appropriate
tracks
checked for
export.

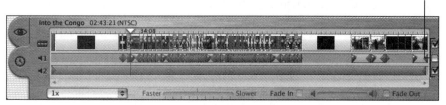

Exporting to your camcorder

To export your video back to a camcorder, iMovie has to turn all these clips, effects, and sound files back into a single DV Stream document and send it out through the FireWire port to the camcorder. This is a demanding task, but one that iMovie and compatible Macs can handle. Be aware, however, that the export process takes over the computer completely — you won't be able to do anything else with the computer until the process is finished.

It's important not to interrupt the export process and, fortunately, it's difficult to do so. Still, you should take precautions before exporting to your camcorder. Notably, quit any other applications in the background (especially those that may decide, suddenly, that they want your attention, such as a calendar program or an e-mail program that may try to automatically download new messages). Consider turning off file sharing (to keep others from trying to log into your Mac while the rendering is taking place) and remove media from removable drives such as CD-ROM or Iomega Zip drives.

Now, with those precautions out of the way, you're ready to begin exporting. Choose File⇨Export Movie from the iMovie menu. The Export Movie dialog box appears, as shown in Figure 14-3.

Figure 14-3:
The Export
Movie
dialog box.

Export Movie

Export to: Camera

You have slow motion or reverse clips in your movie which will flicker on TV unless they are rendered first. You don't have to render them, but it will look better if you do. It may take a while to render.

Render Now

Wait 5 seconds for camera to get ready.

Add 1 seconds of black before movie.

Add 1 seconds of black to end of movie.

Cancel   Export

At the top of the dialog box is the Export to: menu — most likely it already says Camera, which is the selection you want. Use the menu to choose QuickTime if you decide to export to create desktop movies or movies for the Internet. (I cover QuickTime exporting in Chapters 15 and 16.)

If you have slow motion segments in your movie, you may see a message in the small information area that's immediately under the Export to: menu, as shown in Figure 14-3. This gives you the option to render the slow-motion sequences before you output the iMovie. This is pretty much *always* a good idea, unless, for some reason, you'd like your slow- or fast-motion effects to be jagged and non-TV-like. Click the Render Now button to set iMovie into motion. A dialog box appears showing you the progress of the rendering, complete with a scrolling indicator and an estimate, in minutes, of how long the rendering will take. The rendering can take a while, depending on how many fast- and slow-motion sequences you have.

Back to the Export Movie dialog box, the information area now tells you that the movie is ready to export as well as how long the movie will be. At this point, you may want to double-check your camera settings and make sure the camera is plugged in and powered up and has a tape loaded.

In the bottom half of the dialog box are three text entry boxes. In each, you can enter the amount of time, in seconds, for which you want each option active. (You can put a zero in any of them if you don't want that option active.) Here's a look at them:

- **Wait *xx* seconds for camera to get ready.** This is probably the most important option because it tells iMovie to wait a few seconds after sending a Record command to the camcorder. You may want to check your camcorder owner's manual to see whether it offers any hints on how long that might take. If you happen to be using a camcorder that iMovie can't control automatically, set this pause for the length of time it takes you to press the Record button on the camera.

- **Add *xx* seconds of black before movie.** This one is important, too, although if I had to save one of these settings from a burning fire, it would be the preceding Wait setting. That said, you should have a few seconds of black at the beginning of your video, especially if you plan to use it in a commercial setting. The black video helps make sure you don't cut things too tight if you eventually output to VHS, for instance. No one will hold a few seconds of black video against you — we're used to it.

- **Add *xx* seconds of black to end of the movie.** Consider doing this, especially if you happen to be recording *over* some other video. That way, this recording won't end and drop immediately into another recording. In fact, recordings that overlap can confuse a tape's time code and cause other interesting problems. So, add a little black to the end of the movie just in case.

Now, with all the options set, click the Export button. If you failed to click the Render Now button previously and have slow-motion or reverse clips, an alert box asks whether you want to render them. Click Render Now if you've decided to render them, or click Proceed Anyway if you want to go ahead and export the movie without rendering.

If you don't see that alert box (or after you get past it), the movie begins to export. The movie plays in the Monitor window while the Exporting to Camera progress box displays a scrolling indicator (see Figure 14-4). If you see something you don't like (or otherwise decide to stop the progress of the export), click Stop.

If the export process is interrupted along the way, the results will range from a poor transfer (perhaps with dropped frames or other issues, such as slow-sounding music or pixelated images) to iMovie coming to a halt and stopping the transfer. This is especially true if a problem with FireWire occurs, in which case iMovie may stop transferring immediately and display an alert dialog box (see Figure 14-5). If this happens, do the following:

Figure 14-4: Exporting a movie to the camera.

✔ Make sure you didn't accidentally kick the camcorder's cable out of the Mac (or the other way around).

✔ Make sure no other FireWire devices are being plugged in or out.

✔ Remove media from FireWire removable storage devices.

✔ Make sure the camera is plugged into an AC outlet — it may have put itself into a sleep (low-power) mode or run out of battery power.

Figure 14-5:
Here's what happens if you get a FireWire-based interruption in your camera's connection or if other FireWire devices interfere with the transfer.

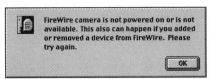

FireWire camera is not powered on or is not available. This also can happen if you added or removed a device from FireWire. Please try again.

OK

Being Analog: TVs and VCRs

After you've exported your movie to your camcorder, you're ready to use that camcorder as what I'll call, in the high language of politics, a bridge to the 20th century. In other words, you can hook your digital camera up to your lower-tech analog devices to display the movie for others or record the movie to another type of tape, such as VHS tape.

Chapter 3 discusses connecting a TV to your camcorder for external monitoring while editing, and it also touches on connecting a VCR to your camcorder. That was for viewing while editing, which you may or may not have decided to do. If you want to watch your movie, you may be more interested in these connections, so I dig a little deeper into them.

Oh — before I get started, Dummies Worldwide Conglomerate Headquarters has a style guide, and I have to follow it, even if my sense of integrity and good taste are compromised. That style guide requires that newly introduced terms be completely defined before I go on.

So, here goes: *TV* stands for *television,* a device used to suck the vitality and independent thinking out of modern culture. *VCR* stands for *Video Cassette Recorder,* a device that allows you to lose your vitality and independent thinking late at night, when most people are sleeping. A VCR has the added advantage of allowing you to watch television-based marketing messages (called *commercials*) very quickly, so that you can squeeze more of them in.

Connecting to TVs and VCRs

Most camcorders come with an AV-out or video-out cable, which usually has a mini-plug-style adapter on one end and RGB cables on the other end (see Figure 14-6).

SP versus LP: Fight to the death

SP and LP, although they're brothers, have had it in for one another for years. This, now, is their story.

SP and LP stand for Short Play and Long Play, respectively. (I can tell you that much, but I won't tell you *which* is *which*. You'll have to figure that out on your own.) And SP and LP are settings you can make in most digital camcorders to determine how much space the data that's written to the tape will take. In LP mode, it's possible to store close to 90 minutes of video on a tape rated for 60 minutes. In SP mode, you get something close to the tape's rated length.

There are two camps on LP and SP: One says LP is fine and the other says to stick with SP for the highest quality recordings. Both are right. If you know something about VHS recording, you'll be happy to know that the LP setting on a digital camcorder doesn't mean nearly the significant loss in quality that LP does on a VHS tape. All it really means it that there's more of a *chance* of a loss of quality, especially if you re-record to the tape repeatedly.

So, if your projects are valuable vessels of commercial power and zeal, record them at SP. If you're the type who bought your DV tapes unwrapped from a street vendor in the first place, go with LP. The only caveat is to choose one setting and stick with it for the entire tape. Although your camcorder is capable of switching back and forth between modes, you're just begging for trouble if you record in both LP and SP modes, especially if you later try to go back and record over part of the tape. (Also, switching modes on the same tape can break time coding, just in case that's important to you. See Chapter 4 for more details on time codes.)

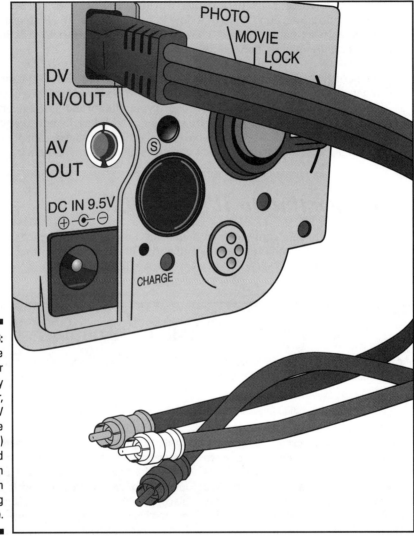

Figure 14-6:
The connector for my camcorder, from the AV port to the (RCA style) video-in and audio-in ports on an analog device.

Nearly every VCR I've ever seen offers RCA-style video-in and audio-in ports for connecting to other devices such as your camcorder. They're probably color-coordinated: The yellow plug fits into the yellow connector for video, the white plug fits into the white connector for left-channel audio, and the red plug fits into the red connector for right-channel audio. If there's anything tough about this, it's that the VCR may offer a few similar-looking ports on its backside. If that's the case, make sure you're connecting to the video-*in* ports in every case. If your VCR has connectors on its front, these are invariably the in ports.

Some VCRs support S-video inputs, and some camcorders offer S-video out-
puts (see Figure 14-7). S-video offers slightly higher quality for video transfers
and should be used if possible. Connect the S-video cable between the S-video
ports on the camera and the VCR. Then, using only the audio connectors (the
red and white ones) from the AV-out cable, connect the camcorder to the
audio-in ports on the VCR. Now, the higher-quality S-video cable handles
video, but the audio is connected using the RCA-style plugs, as usual.

Fewer televisions offer S-video support. If yours doesn't, RCA-style cables are
fine for getting output from your camcorder to your TV. Note that many
newer TVs sport their video ports on the front of the set, suggesting that
they're ready for this kind of thing — they know we're out here messing with
video, so they've made the ports a little easier to get to. If you don't find the
ports on the front of the TV, look on the back.

If you have a direct connection between your camcorder and your VCR or TV
through S-video or RCA-style plugs, you probably need to set the TV or VCR
to its Video mode, a special mode that can accept line-level inputs from a
camcorder. In other cases, you need to set the TV or VCR to Channel 3 or 4,
as I'm sure you're used to doing by now.

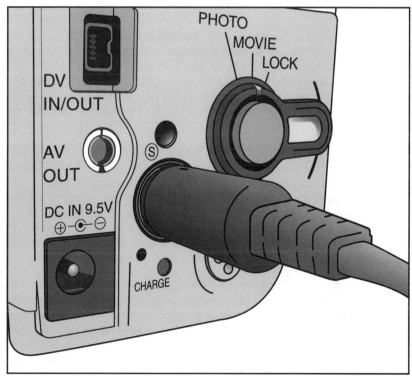

Figure 14-7:
An S-video
cable
connected
to the S-
video port
on my
camcorder.

TV hookup alternatives

Didn't find the RCA-style ports anywhere on your TV? Some TVs don't offer RCA-style or S-video ports. In that case, you need to connect your camcorder to the cable TV (coaxial cable) connector on the back of the TV. To do that, you need an adapter from an electronics store. (What? You have a non-cable-ready TV? Well, uh, don't you think it's time to get a new TV? You have a portable TV studio, after all! I'm sure you can do something — ask around at your local electronics store for an RF converter.)

Finally, there's one other answer if you're having trouble hooking up a camcorder to your TV. Do you have a VCR hooked up to that TV? Connect your camcorder to the VCR (using S-video or RCA-style plugs, whichever the VCR supports) and then watch the video on the TV through the VCR. This is how you'll want to connect everything if you're going to record the movie, after all.

Recording to a VCR

After your camcorder is connected to your VCR, you're ready to record. This is not tough. In general terms, all you need to do is turn on the VCR, set it to Record, and then, with the camcorder in VTR or Playback mode, press the Play button on the camcorder. You may want to put the VCR in some sort of Pause/Record mode, so the VCR is ready to start recording immediately after you start exporting from iMovie. If you can, though, it's best to let the VCR roll a second or two before beginning the playback on the camcorder — analog VCRs, especially VHS models, take a little longer to spin up to speed than digital camcorders.

Actually, that's what the movie-making term *speed* refers to — the camera operator calls out "Speed!" to let the director know that the camera is up and spinning at the right speed for recording. (In most cases, it's a film camera, not a video camera, but the theory is the same.) So, feel free to yell "Speed!" in your living room or office after you've pressed Record on the VCR and waited a second or two. Then press Play on the camcorder (or un-pause it, to coin a phrase).

One other major consideration for quality reproductions is to use a new tape in your VCR, fresh out of its plastic wrap. (Okay, I don't know if the plastic makes a difference, but it does give you that fresh electronics smell. Actually, that fresh electronics smell is probably slowly killing us.) Recording over old video always results in a lower quality level, and that quality level can take a dive significantly if the tape has been recorded to more than once or in different recording modes.

Second, speaking of recording modes, the video recording mode that you set the VCR to should be SP, which stands for *standard play* or *short play,* depending on who you ask. Don't use EP (extended play), LP (long play), or SLP (super long play), if those options are available. Although these last three settings enable a tape to record more video on the same tape, the SP setting ensures the best quality. Because your movie is unlikely to be more than two hours, the standard for SP, the short play setting should be sufficient.

Third, for best results, avoid stopping or starting your VCR while you're recording — you can never line things up correctly to start again because a VCRs mechanism is a little too loose to keep the tape in the cassette slack. (The tape in a digital camcorder is a bit loose, too — you'll never find yourself able to re-record at *exactly* the right spot.) Instead, just let the VCR record straight through from the start of your movie to the end of it.

That's it! When you're finished, play it back to check things out. Then, wrap it up and send it to whichever network is running home video contests these days!

Plan to make more than one copy? Tape duplication services exist for high-volume duplication, but if you're talking just a few copies here, I have some advice: Make each one from the camcorder. That way, each copy is still a first-generation analog copy, so there is only a minimum amount of deterioration of image quality. If you make your copies using the VHS version, those copies will be worse than the VHS original, which, in turn, is a little worse than the digital version. Of course, if you have a high-speed duplicating VCR deck and quality isn't your tip-top issue, you probably aren't listening to me anyway.

Backing Up to DV Tapes

Clearly, one of the reasons to get your movie exported to your camcorder is to be able to see it on TVs and VCRs. But there's another good reason, and one you'll probably take advantage of before too long: You can get that movie off your Mac and onto a DV tape to store it and then you can delete the project from your Mac and start on a new one. After all, your disk space is probably limited, especially on an iMac, a PowerBook, or an iBook. If that's true, you'll find it's a good idea to export your movies to DV for safekeeping.

I should note up front, however, that storing a project and exporting it to DV are not the same thing. If you export an iMovie to your camcorder and then re-import it, you won't see it as the same work-in-progress that it probably is in your project window. For instance, you won't be able to alter an effect that's already part of the clip. If you have audio that's both talking and background music, you can't extract that audio separately — you get one audio track that combines the two. So, if you think you may want to dig back into your project some day and change the transitions or alter the audio, storing your project as-is on some type of removable media is worthwhile.

Unfortunately, it's tough to find removable media that's large enough to store an entire project, even if that project has a minimum of extra clips and untossed trash. A recent three-minute iMovie project I worked on required more than a gigabyte of storage space on my hard disk, making it tough to back up the whole project to anything but an Iomega Jaz, Castlewood Orb, or perhaps a pricey DVD-RAM drive. (See Chapter 18 for hints on buying drives for backup.) If you have a project that totals five to ten minutes, you might be able to squeeze it on a high-capacity removable drive; for a thirty-minute or longer project, fuggitaboutit.

The two- (or three-) tape system

To store your projects, some compromise is probably in order. Although it may be impossible to keep your open project files around forever, you can structure things so that you can maintain both the finished product and the raw materials for working with later, if necessary. You can accomplish this with a two-tape approach. Keep all raw footage untouched on the first tape, which you lock, label, and store somewhere cool and dry, according to the tape manufacturer's instructions.

Then record your finished iMovie to a second tape, which you can use as a master for any dubbing or VHS transfers in the future.

You might also consider a third tape, which you can use to store edited but unaltered raw footage — basically, the footage you end up with after you get through Chapter 5. With your clips edited down to size and arranged in the order in which you plan to present them, you can record them to a new tape before you add background music, effects, transitions, and titles. The advantage here is that you can start over from about the halfway point and quickly piece together your movie again if you lose the final copy or need to revisit the presentation and do something different with your edits, transitions, and titles.

The trick to creating this rough-cut tape is to drag the clips to the Clip Viewer and arrange them in rough order (see Figure 14-8). Next, export those clips as a movie to your camcorder, saving it to a new tape. Now you should be able to re-import these clips using the "Automatically start new clips at scene break" option in iMovie, and each clip will be re-imported separately.

Figure 14-8: Arranging clips to create your rough-cut backup tape.

Locking the tape

After you record to a tape, you can lock it to avoid further recording — a nice step to ensure that you don't accidentally export a movie to a tape that you've designated for backup. The first tape you lock, even before you begin importing clips at the outset, is the tape you used for your original footage. Because you'll use that tape as a backup for the entire project, there's no point in leaving open the possibility that you'll tape over it accidentally. Similarly, you should lock your master tape (the one with the finished movie on it) after you're pleased with the output results. And if you make a rough-cut backup, lock it, too.

To lock a tape, locate the Rec/Save slider on the side of the tape itself (usually the same side as the label area). Flip the slider to the Save side (see Figure 14-9) and the tape is locked — it can't be recorded to.

Figure 14-9:
My master tape for a recent project, flipped to Save to keep me from accidentally recording over it.

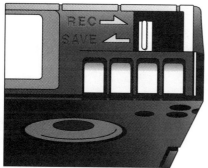

If you decide at a later date to record over the footage on that tape, flip the slider back to its Record (often labeled Rec) side.

Chapter 15

Turning iMovies into QuickTime Movies

In This Chapter

▶ Understanding QuickTime

▶ Creating QuickTime output simply

▶ Viewing and editing QuickTime movies

▶ Exporting your movie in a different format

Chapter 14 covers exporting your movie to the camcorder for displaying it on TV or recording it to a VHS videotape. But there's a lot more you can do with your movie, thanks mostly to the power and wonder of Apple's QuickTime technology. With iMovie's QuickTime integration, you can easily save your movie in QuickTime format, making it possible to play it back on nearly any Macintosh and most any Microsoft Windows computer out there. QuickTime is, in a word, cool.

iMovie makes it easy to export your movies into QuickTime format, even going as far as to build in some of the most common options and settings. After you export your QuickTime movie, you can switch to the QuickTime Player application, where you can play back, edit, alter, and augment your movie. Then, you can save that movie to different formats or, if desired, get ready to distribute it over the Internet, through CD, or in another application's documents, as I discuss in Chapter 16. To start, though, I discuss some of the basics of what QuickTime is and how it works. You should get to know QuickTime — it's destined to become a big part of your life.

Understanding QuickTime

As Yogi Berra might put it, the best place to start is at the beginning. We need to take a quick look at what, exactly, QuickTime is and why I've already typed the word fifteen times here in the first page of this chapter (and why I'll be typing it countless more times before I'm finished). Then I also discuss why it's important and how it will affect your every-day life from here going forward.

Apple calls QuickTime a "software architecture" that includes a file format (QuickTime Movie format) and special translators that can change files from one movie format (or still image format) to another. QuickTime also comprises an *application programming interface* (API), which is just a fancy way to say "hooks for application programmers to mess with so that their programs, too, can play and edit QuickTime movies."

The QuickTime software architecture means two things that you may find somewhat interesting. First, it means Mac programmers don't have to start from scratch when they want to help you edit or play back desktop movies. As you may know, a lot of applications — such as SimpleText and AppleWorks — can use QuickTime fairly easily, right there in a document window. That's part of what makes QuickTime so powerful (see Figure 15-1).

Second, QuickTime is its own multimedia document format. When you export a project from iMovie to QuickTime format, you can then play that movie back on Mac computers, on Microsoft Windows computers, from CD-ROMs, and in other applications. After you translate a file into QuickTime Movie format, it can be read, understood, and played back by any QuickTime-enabled application.

Figure 15-1:
Even basic
programs
such as
SimpleText
can display
QuickTime
files.

What does QuickTime do?

In a way, QuickTime is a sophisticated version of the old flip-card animations that have been drawn into grade-school textbooks since shortly after Guttenberg put down his screwdriver and pronounced that his printing press was in beta testing.

With QuickTime, a series of digital images are arranged and displayed quickly so that they give the impression of movement. This is the same concept used for any motion-picture technology, from the movies to filmstrips to TV.

QuickTime is the underlying technology for making those moving images appear on the screen, and QuickTime Movie format is the way in which such a file is stored on a computer. Using this technology, an application (such as QuickTime Player Pro) can be written to enable you to load a QuickTime file, edit its contents, and play it back on the screen. Similarly, a program such as iMovie can use QuickTime technology to export files to QuickTime Movie format as well as import files from QuickTime movie format.

Aside from being able to play back QuickTime movies in many different places, one of the main goals in working with QuickTime is making the movie file smaller — making it take up less disk space. The less disk space a movie requires, the easier it is to transmit to others. This is such an important part of what QuickTime does that it has its own terms: compression and codecs. I talk about those next.

Understanding compression and codecs

I mentioned that QuickTime is a sophisticated version of a flip-card animation system. Part of that sophistication comes from the fact that it does more than simply show image after image in sequence. The deeper sophistication of QuickTime is that it can create these moving pictures (and synchronize sound to them) without creating enormously huge files that take gigabytes of storage space.

Part of the solution to this gigabyte dilemma is that QuickTime movies can be *compressed,* using fancy math to use less data to represent the images in the movie. For instance, consider a single frame of a movie that includes a clear, blue sky. Instead of noting the color of every single pixel that makes up that sky, the frame can be compressed using an algorithm that says, in effect, "Remember that pixels 1 through 1000 are blue." This makes each frame take up less storage space, which translates into a much smaller QuickTime file.

Does size really matter?

The push and pull between the size of a file and the quality of its contents is a huge focus in the computing world. Part of the reason that DV and iMovie have become popular at this particular moment in time stems from the fact that inexpensive hard disks have become bigger (such as those now standard in iMacs and iBooks) while technology has come together to make digital movie files a bit smaller. So, although DV Stream files are huge in the scheme of things, it has become possible for a consumer computer to deal with video editing.

But the technology still doesn't really exist to make it easy to, say, take a DV Stream file (such as an iMovie project) and put it on a CD-ROM or send it over the Internet. The problem is, DV Stream files are way, way too large for these other existing technologies. Even with the fastest Internet connections available in homes and small offices, it would take days to transfer a raw iMovie from one person to the next. Using modems and typical home computers, it's impossible. Even a technology such as a writable CD has a limited amount of storage — about three minutes of a DV Stream file can fit on a CD.

So, to make it possible and practical to share your movies with friends, you need to translate your movie into a QuickTime file and then make that QuickTime file smaller. This means making the picture itself smaller (so that it fills only a fraction of the Mac's screen) and using other technologies — such as image compression, discussed in the "Understanding compression and codecs" section — to get that movie down to the smallest size possible.

Right now, the tradeoffs are noticeable. A movie small enough to attach to an e-mail is tiny on the screen and poor quality. A movie small enough to post on a Web site looks better, but it's still about as pleasant as watching one of those 4-inch handheld TVs. QuickTime movies that can fit on a CD-ROM, however, begin to approach at least 12-inch kitchen-TV type quality.

And it will get better over time. How do I know? Just look at the popularity of MP3 audio files — CD-quality audio documents that are small enough to be transmitted and traded over the Internet. That wasn't possible a few short years ago, but the combination of faster Internet connections and better compression technology made MP3 possible. Smart people are already at work on similar breakthroughs in video and QuickTime technology, so don't be surprised when it happens!

Compression is a trade-off, however, between image quality and the size of the movie file. DV footage is compressed within the camcorder as you're film-ing the images. Still, this is relatively *lossless* compression, resulting in an image that is still crisp and clear. As noted, though, DV files require about 210MB per minute of TV-quality footage.

With QuickTime, you can compress images even further, using different *codecs* (codec stands for *compressor/decompressor*) that range in the amount of compression they offer and how lossy the compression is. Figures 15-2 and 15-3 show an example of a movie that is full DV quality versus one that has been compressed significantly.

Figure 15-2:
This QuickTime movie is lightly compressed (it's a straight DV-quality export from iMovie) but requires 170MB for a five-second movie.

Figure 15-3:
The image quality has suffered, but the movie now requires only 980KB of storage space after compression.

QuickTime supports a number of different codecs that I look at a later in the chapter. The codecs vary in capability and quality, making it important to choose the right one for a particular situation.

Frame rates and key frames

Compression is one way to make QuickTime movie files smaller. But other approaches, when coupled with compression, make it possible to get an even smaller QuickTime movie file. One of those approaches is to use a lower *frame rate,* meaning you store a QuickTime movie with fewer *frames per second* (fps).

On NTSC-standard television, images are updated nearly 30 times per second (25 times per second for PAL television), which is part of why motion seems very smooth when you're watching TV. Motion pictures update at 24 frames per second (fps), which makes movies a touch less smooth, but gives a certain look to film that most people are comfortable watching. You've probably noticed how different movies and live NTSC TV shows look, even if both are on television. Some of that difference is thanks to different camera lens, different media (film versus tape), and different lighting, but part of the overall look of film is its different frame rate.

QuickTime movies, unlike TV and movie standards, aren't fixed at a particular frame rate. A QuickTime movie can be saved at 15 fps, 10 fps, even 4 fps, if you want. The result may look a little choppier, but the fewer frames, the smaller the QuickTime movie file size. Generally, movies exported for use on the Internet or for storing and sharing on CDs are saved using a lower frame rate.

Another way to save storage space is to set fewer key frames within a QuickTime movie. I said before that QuickTime is a little like flip-card animation — but only a *little*. In fact, QuickTime movies work by displaying a key frame every so often and then updating only the *changes* from that key frame in subsequent frames until the next key frame comes up. So, if you have a key frame each ten frames, you see a complete frame and then the next nine frames show only the changes from that key frame. The fewer key frames you have, the smaller the file size and, in most cases, the lower the quality of the movie. The bottom line: Part of saving your movie as a QuickTime movie is deciding how often a key frame will pop up.

Movie size

You have one last trick for making movies smaller and easier to transmit and deal with. You can make them smaller on the screen. This is the most common and, in some ways, most significant difference between movies created for TV output and those created for the computer desktop.

Unlike when you export to a camcorder, you have the option of choosing a smaller movie size when you export to QuickTime. Generally, that size should be proportional to 640x480, which is the standard resolution for TV — 320x240 (one-quarter the size of standard TV), 240x180 (close to one-eighth the size), or even 160x120 (one-sixteenth the size). These are common resolutions for movies destined for the Internet or for CD-ROM playback — the smaller the movie, the less storage space it requires (see Figure 15-4).

Figure 15-4:
The one on the left is 160x120; the one on the right, 320x240.

The problem is that the smaller the QuickTime movie, the harder it is to see. If you get much smaller than 320x240, you also need to worry about the size of the text you use for titles and subtitles — your audience won't be able to read small titles at those movie sizes. And, although QuickTime Player lets you view a given movie at, say, double its natural size, that just stretches the existing picture, making it even more difficult to view details (see Figure 15-5).

Figure 15-5:
Here's a 320x240 movie, doubled (to 640x480) in the QuickTime Player playback window.

Exporting the Simple Way

Now, with all that discussion under your belt (assuming you read the previous pages about QuickTime), you're ready to begin ignoring everything you've found out. As it turns out, iMovie offers some options that make it possible to circumvent all these exporting decisions and simply take iMovie's recommendations. This limits you in some ways, so we look at more advanced settings later in the chapter. For now, though, the simple settings may be all you need.

To export an iMovie project to QuickTime, you need to go through a few steps to make sure you're ready for action. Then you use the File⇨Export Movie command to perform the actual exportation. You begin with the preparatory issues.

Prepping for output

You need to consider a few minor issues before you begin exporting your movie to QuickTime. First, you should think about *why,* exactly, you plan to export your video. iMovie gives you some basic options for the type of QuickTime movie you're going to create, including movies that would be about the right size for e-mail, the Web, a CD-ROM, or a very high-quality movie. Decide which you want your QuickTime movie to be and then keep that decision foremost in your mind.

Next, open your movie project and play it in the Monitor window to make sure that all is smooth, the sound levels are right, and if you've been editing with sound, everything is synchronized correctly in the Timeline. You should also take careful note of any place where you've created titles or subtitles in your movie and make sure you're using a large font. Unless you opt for the highest quality setting for your exported QuickTime movie (which creates a movie that's 640x480 — the standard TV resolution), you probably won't be able to read smaller fonts and subtitles when viewing the QuickTime movie. So, you may want to head back into your iMovie project and update those titles with bigger fonts. (It also helps if you use the Over Black option with larger fonts — such titles are easier to read at smaller sizes.)

If the text looks good, head to the Timeline and make sure you've turned on or off the correct tracks in your iMovie project. You can turn tracks on and off in your movie by clicking the check boxes for each track on the far right side of the Timeline (see Figure 15-6). If a track is turned on, it will be exported to the new QuickTime movie; if it's off, it won't be exported.

Figure 15-6:
Turning
tracks on
and off in
your movie.

Finally, check the free space on your hard disk to make sure you have enough space for the exported QuickTime movie to be saved. Use the Free Space gauge in iMovie to see how much space is left on your hard disk (at least, the hard disk on which iMovie is installed). You can also head to the Finder, select your hard disk icon, and choose File⇨Get Info to see how much space you have on that disk. (Look for the Available entry.)

So how much space do you need? It ranges wildly. For the smallest QuickTime movies (the E-mail option), you need about 1MB per minute of running time. (Multiply the number of minutes in your iMovie project by 1MB to get the total space needed.) Web movies require 3 to 5MB per minute. For a medium-quality CD movie, you need about 10MB per minute. Want a full-quality movie? It takes 200 – 210MB per minute. Yee-ouch!

Exporting to QuickTime

Now you're almost ready to export. But first, you need to decide the type of movie you plan to create. Here's a quick look at the options:

- ✔ **Email Movie, Small.** Select this option for a highly compressed, 160x120 movie that plays at 10 fps. This will not be a high-quality movie, but at only 1MB per minute, it can be attached to an e-mail message and sent to the family. (Assuming the family has a reasonably high-speed DSL or cable connection.) The audio for an Email Movie is mono (instead of stereo), which also saves storage space.

- ✔ **Web Movie, Small.** QuickTime movies set to this setting are 240x180 in size, about one-eighth the resolution of a full DV movie. At 12 fps, motion is fairly smooth and the audio is stereo. Again, users with higher-speed DSL or cable modems can access this type of movie over the Web, assuming that they're willing to wait one minute for each minute in the movie. The audio is stereo but at a lower-quality setting (about the quality of an FM radio broadcast).

- ✔ **Streaming Web Movie, Small.** This movie is the same size as a Web movie, with all the same settings. The difference is that the movie file is *hinted,* a setting required for Web movies. All this streaming and hinting stuff is discussed in detail in Chapter 17.

✔ **CD-ROM Movie, Medium.** This option creates a QuickTime movie one-quarter the size of a TV-quality movie, meaning text should be reasonably easy to read. At 15 fps, motion is pretty smooth. Audio is stored in full stereo at CD quality.

✔ **Full Quality, Large.** This option doesn't compress, is full DV size (720x480), and offers better than CD-audio quality. Movies created with this setting are *huge* and only recommended if you're planning to import the footage into another DV-editing software application.

With some settings, you also have the option of checking the QuickTime 3.0 Compatible option, which simply causes iMovie to choose older compression technologies that are installed along with QuickTime 3.0. These compression technologies are less efficient than the default choices (which require QuickTime 4 or higher) but are compatible with more QuickTime-compatible computers.

Let the exporting begin:

1. **Choose File⇨Export Movie from the iMovie menu.**

   The Export Movie dialog box appears.

2. **From the Export To pop-up menu, select QuickTime.**

   The options change to the QuickTime export options shown in Figure 15-7. You can see that this will be quite easy.

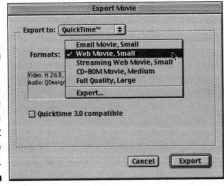

Figure 15-7:
The
QuickTime
options in
the Export
Movie
dialog box.

3. **From the Formats pop-up menu, select the type of movie you plan to create.**

4. **Click the Export button.**

   The Export QuickTime Movie dialog box appears; it resembles a typical Save dialog box.

5. **Select a folder where you'd like to store the exported movie and then enter a name for the file in the Name entry box.**

6. **Click the Save button and the export process begins.**

A Progress dialog box appears, showing a progress bar and the estimated time remaining for the export (see Figure 15-8).

Figure 15-8:
The
Progress
dialog box
during an
export
operation.

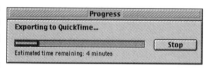

Now, you wait. Exporting can take quite a while — often twenty minutes of exporting time per minute of video that you're exporting. And the Mac is useless for any other tasks while the export is taking place. After the export is complete, find the QuickTime movie file in the folder where you chose to save it. Double-click that file and it opens in QuickTime Player.

Fun Things to Do with QuickTime Movies

After you have your movie in a QuickTime format, what next? First, you can distribute the movie on CDs or over the Internet — I talk about those options in Chapter 16, and I discuss Apple's special iTools and Internet options in Chapter 17.

For now, though, you can look at some of the things you can do with a QuickTime movie on your own desktop, including viewing, editing, and translating the movie. QuickTime is a powerful and useful technology, especially if you've upgraded to QuickTime Pro. With QuickTime Pro, you can perform a number of feats of editing and translation, including some of the QuickTime Pro effects I discuss in Chapter 13 and other tricks I discuss in this section. And, after you have your movie in QuickTime format, it's fairly simple to integrate that QuickTime movie into other applications, including AppleWorks and Microsoft PowerPoint, two options I discuss in this section as well.

Watching your movie in QuickTime Player

Whether or not you've upgraded to QuickTime Pro, you can use QuickTime Player to view your newly exported QuickTime movie. Double-click the movie file, drag-and-drop it to the QuickTime Player icon, or open the QuickTime Player application and use the File⇨Open command to locate the movie. With the movie open, you see the QuickTime Player interface, as shown in Figures 15-9 and 15-10.

(I show both the 4.0 and 5.0 versions of QuickTime. QuickTime 5.0 is brand new as I write this, and you may not have it installed on your Mac. It's recommended, however — QuickTime 5 is a free upgrade, and you can register QuickTime Pro features in QuickTime 5 even with a registration number from QuickTime 4 or 3. See Chapter 18 for more details on QuickTime Pro.)

Figure 15-9:
QuickTime
Player
version 4.0.

Figure 15-10:
QuickTime
Player
version 5.0.

The controls in QuickTime Player are similar to those offered in the iMovie
Monitor window. In QuickTime 4.0 Player, click the Play button to play the
movie, and then click the Play button again to stop the movie or click the Pause
button to pause playback. (There isn't much difference with a QuickTime
movie, so the controls are redundant.) To see more controls, click the small
controller button (which is on the far right side of the controller and sports four
dots) to see Fast Forward, Rewind, To Beginning, and To End controls.

In QuickTime 5.0 Player, everything is more straightforward. Click the Play
button to play the movie; click and hold the Review and Fast Forward buttons to move quickly through your movie; click the To Beginning and To End
buttons (at either side of the Fast Forward and Review buttons) to move to
the first or last frame of the movie, respectively.

Aside from these basic controls, QuickTime Player can be used to view your
movie at different sizes. The smaller the size, the clearer the images seem —
showing a movie at a larger size hurts the quality. Still, you may be willing to
trade the quality of the movie for a bigger image. In the standard QuickTime
Player, pull down the Movie window and select Half Size, Double Size, or Fill
Screen. When you do, QuickTime Player changes size accordingly.

You can also drag the small resize box at the bottom-right corner of the
QuickTime Player window to change the size of the movie image — notice
that the movie image stays proportional to the original as you drag. If you'd
like to change the proportions of the movie, hold down the Shift key as you
drag to change the Player's size (see Figure 15-11).

Figure 15-11:
Hold down
the Shift key
while
dragging
and the
proportions
of the movie
change.

In QuickTime Pro, you have a few additional sizing options. You can choose
Movie⇨Half size to see the movie play at a smaller size — the movie is a bit
smoother and crisper even though it's harder to see.

Choose Movie⇨Present Movie and QuickTime Player displays the Present Movie dialog box. In that dialog box, you can select the size at which you want the movie to play, and you can choose a Mode, either Normal or Slide Show. (In Slide Show mode, every click of the button or press of an arrow key advances the movie by one frame. In Normal, the movie simply plays.)

Click the Play button and QuickTime takes over the Mac's display, putting a black border around the movie and hiding any other windows or controls. This is a nice way to watch the movie as if it were on a TV set.

Editing in QuickTime Player

If you haven't upgraded to QuickTime Pro, you can't do much editing, but you can copy individual frames of video in QuickTime Player:

1. **Place the playhead on the Scrubber bar.**

2. **Choose Edit⇨Copy.**

3. **Open a document in any application that supports images — Word, AppleWorks, even the ScrapBook in Mac OS 9 and earlier.**

4. **Choose Edit⇨Paste or press ⌘+V to paste an image of that frame into that document.**

If you've upgraded to QuickTime Pro, you'll notice that QuickTime Player now has a Scrubber bar and crop markers, just like the Monitor window in iMovie. You can do some basic editing in QuickTime Player, although you're limited to trim, cut, copy, and paste functions.

To select part of your movie:

1. **Place the playhead (by clicking on the Scrubber bar) at the beginning of the section you want to select.**

2. **Hold down the Shift key and drag the playhead to the end of the selection.**

   You see the crop markers.

3. **Drag the crop markers individually to fine-tune your selection (see Figure 15-12).**

Figure 15-12:
Selecting a
portion of a
movie in
QuickTime
Pro Player.

Copy, cut, paste, trim, add, and replace

With the movie portion selected, you can use the Edit⇨Cut or Edit⇨Copy command to place the QuickTime data on the Mac's clipboard. This enables you to switch to another QuickTime movie or another document that supports QuickTime data and paste it into that new document using the Edit⇨Paste command. You can also use the Edit⇨Clear command to remove the selected portion from the movie, much as you would in the iMovie Monitor window.

The QuickTime Pro Player's equivalent of iMovie's Crop command is called Trim, and it's hidden from ordinary view. The trick is to hold down the Option key while opening the Edit menu, at which point the Clear command changes to Trim. Select the command and your movie is cropped so that only the selected portion remains.

QuickTime Pro Player offers an Undo command, so if you make an edit you regret, choose Edit⇨Undo. To clear the current selection on the Scrubber bar, choose Edit⇨Select None; to highlight the entire movie, choose Edit⇨ Select All.

Finally, two other hidden commands may come in handy. As noted in Chapter 13, QuickTime Player offers the capability to add more than one *track* of video to a QuickTime movie, including audio and video tracks. To add a track:

1. **From another QuickTime movie, copy the track you want to add.**

2. **Select the portion of this movie where you'd like the track added.**

3. **Hold down the Option key while selecting the Edit menu.**

   The Paste command has changed to the Add command.

4. **Choose Add.**

   The copied QuickTime data is added as a new track to this movie.

You can also replace part of a QuickTime movie with a section of another QuickTime movie:

1. **Select and copy the footage from the other QuickTime movie.**

2. **Switch back to the current movie and use the Scrubber bar and crop markers to select the portion of the movie you want to replace.**

3. **Hold down the Shift key and open the Edit menu.**

   The Paste command is now the Replace command.

4. **Choose Replace.**

   The QuickTime footage on the clipboard replaces the portion of the current movie you've selected.

Working with tracks

As mentioned, QuickTime considers each portion of a QuickTime movie an individual track. A QuickTime movie file can actually be just one track — a video track or an audio track — although most include one of each. You can add tracks, as discussed in the previous section, and you can layer tracks one over the other, as discussed in Chapter 13.

QuickTime enables you to deal with the different tracks of your movie easily using three commands in the Edit menu. For starters:

1. **Choose Edit⇨Enable Tracks to see the Enable Tracks dialog box.**

   You see the existing tracks in the QuickTime movie, along with a small On button next to each track entry.

2. **Click the On button once next to a track and you turn off that track.**

   If you turn off the video track, it disappears immediately from view. If you turn off the audio track, you won't hear any audio the next time you play the movie.

To extract tracks from the movie so that, for instance, you can paste the video track from this movie into another QuickTime movie:

1. **Choose Edit⇨Extract Tracks.**

   The Extract Tracks dialog box appears.

2. **Select the track you want to extract.**

3. **Click Extract.**

   A new QuickTime movie appears, now containing only the track you've extracted, as shown in Figure 15-13.

Figure 15-13:
The Untitled movie is actually the exported video track.

And, before you get too worried, I should point out that extracting a track doesn't remove it from the original, it simply creates a new QuickTime movie comprised only of that selected track.

If you *do* want to delete a track from your movie, that event has its own command:

1. **Choose Edit⇨Delete Tracks from the menu.**

   The Delete Tracks dialog box appears.

2. **Select the track you want to delete.**

   You can select more than one by ⌘+clicking each entry.

3. **Click the Delete button.**

   The tracks are deleted from your movie. Bye-bye.

Adding a text track

QuickTime Pro Player offers you the opportunity to add a text track to your movie, which can work something like a subtitle in iMovie, although it's a little easier to read and a little more flexible to work with. On the other hand, it looks more like the way closed captioning text appears on a TV set than the way subtitles appear in iMovie.

To add a text track to your movie, you first need some text. Here's the drill:

1. **Switch to SimpleText or another text editor and type up to two lines of text.**

   You can even format the text — bold, italic, font size, font face — and the formatting will appear in the QuickTime movie.

2. **With your text set, select the text and choose Edit⇨Copy.**

3. **Switch to your movie in QuickTime Pro Player and then place the playhead on the Scrubber bar where you'd like the text to appear.**

4. **Hold down the Shift key and drag to the end of the footage where you want this text.**

   You can use the crop markers to tidy it up and get exactly the right parts selected.

5. **Press the Option and Shift keys while you access the Edit menu and choose the Add Scaled command.**

   This command appears only when you're holding down Option and Shift; it adds the text on a new text track for the exact length of time you've selected on the Scrubber bar. If you hold down only the Option key, you get the Add command, which adds the text for exactly two seconds.

That's it. Play back your movie and the text appears at the bottom edge of the QuickTime Player movie when the movie reaches the footage you selected (see Figure 15-14).

Figure 15-14: The text track appears at the bottom of the screen when that portion of your movie is reached.

If you don't like the way the text looks (for some inexplicable reason it appears off-center by default), you can use the Info window to change it:

1. **Choose Movie⇨Get Info (in QuickTime 4) or Movie⇨Get Movie Properties (in QuickTime 5).**

   The Info window appears.

2. **Select the Text Track from the left-side pop-up menu and then select Size from the right-side pop-up menu.**

3. Click the Adjust button.

In the QuickTime movie window, small red controls appear around the edges of the text track to help you move, rotate, and resize the text. I'd try to explain them to you, but they have me a bit baffled (see Figure 15-15).

Figure 15-15: Small controls appear around the text track when you select Adjust in the Text Track Size screen.

Here's all I know about these controls: If the control is a circle, it enables you to rotate the text; if the control *isn't* a circle, you can use it to resize the text track. You can use the arrow keys on the keyboard to move the text track. Good luck. When you're finished, click the Done button back in the Info window to get rid of the sizing and shaping controls.

Want to replace the text? Select Text Replace from the right-side menu in the Info window. Now, switch to a different application and type new text. Drag the text to the Drop Text Here area and the text automatically changes in the text track.

If you want your text track to move from one line to the next, you can *import* a text file as a QuickTime movie and then copy and add it as a text track:

1. Choose File⇨Import.

2. Select a text file with multiple lines — each paragraph, separated by a return, is treated as a new frame, with each frame lasting two seconds.

3. Select the entire QuickTime movie and choose Edit⇨Copy.

4. Switch back to your original QuickTime movie.

5. Hold down the Option key while accessing the Edit menu and choose the Add command.

Your multi-frame text track is added.

Translating QuickTime Movies

QuickTime is a great movie format. It's the sort of computer movie format that you could take home and introduce to your parents. It's conservative, efficient, and trustworthy, but capable of surprising you on a rainy day. Just the way a movie format should be.

But that doesn't mean you have to be exclusive with QuickTime. Play the field. Using QuickTime Pro Player, you can export your QuickTime movie into other formats, including the Microsoft Windows standard AVI (Audio/Video Interleave), MPEG, and DV Stream formats. (DV Stream is discussed in Chapter 4. MPEG requires third-party software, as I discuss in Chapters 16 and 18.)

Although many, many computer users have the capability to launch and watch QuickTime movies, it can be helpful to offer movies in both QuickTime and AVI. Almost all Mac users can play QuickTime movies (in most cases without additional downloads and installations), but Windows users can, by default, display AVI movies. For Windows users to play QuickTime movies, they need to install QuickTime for Windows. (Which is a good idea, but you can't always convince them of that.)

To translate your QuickTime movie into an AVI formatted movie:

1. **Choose File⇨Export.**

   The Export dialog box appears (see Figure 15-16).

2. **Select a location where you want to store the AVI file.**

3. **In the Save Exported File As entry box, enter a name for the file.**

   Note that it's recommended to end the name with .avi so that a Windows computer can identify the movie's file type easily.

Figure 15-16: Exporting a QuickTime movie as an AVI file.

4. In the Export menu, select Movie to AVI.

Note that the Use menu changes.

5. Make a selection in the Use menu.

You can select Default settings or one of the CD-ROM settings. The Default Settings are appropriate for a medium-quality Web movie; 1x CD-ROM is a lower quality CD or desktop movie, and 2x CD-ROM is a higher quality setting.

6. Click the Save button.

The Exporting Movie dialog box appears with a progress bar. When the progress bar indicates that the export process has finished, the dialog box disappears and the movie has been saved in its new format.

Chapter 16

Putting Movies on CDs and in Applications

C hapter 15 shows you some of the basics of creating QuickTime movies from your movies, including the built-in settings in iMovie and some tips for working with those movies within QuickTime. But there's a lot more you can do in the process of getting those movies out of iMovie and, after they're in QuickTime format, there's even more you can do to distribute those movies, whether through CD or the Internet.

Although iMovie, on its surface, makes it relatively easy to export your movies to QuickTime for different purposes, you'll find that fine-tuning that output takes a little know-how — a jump into the murky waters of QuickTime options. Don't worry, though, I'll be right there beside you in those waters, sitting on a raft with a little trolling motor hanging off the back. I may even be playing guitar and eating fresh avocado dip.

After you've tweaked your QuickTime movie output options, you have to do something with the resulting QuickTime movie. In this chapter, I cover both the advanced export settings in iMovie and some options for distributing that movie on a CD or as part of another application's document.

Putting a Movie on CD

One way to get your movie distributed is on CD — especially if you have a *CD-RW drive,* a special drive (either external or, in some rare cases, internal to your computer) that enables you to create CDs using special CD-Recordable (CD-R) or CD-Rewritable (CD-RW) media. These drives, sometimes called *burners,* cost a few hundred dollars and, in most cases, connect to a Macintosh through its SCSI, USB, or FireWire port. If you have an iMovie-compatible Macintosh model, you'll probably opt for either a USB or FireWire CD-RW drive, although some internal models (those that can be installed in the tower case of a Power Macintosh computer) exist as well.

A typical CD-ROM disc is a *read-only* technology, which means you can only read data from a CD-ROM, not write data to it. (Indeed, CD-ROM stands for Compact Disc-Read-Only Memory.) To create your own CDs, you need a drive that's capable of writing data to special CD-R (CD-Recordable) or CD-RW (CD-Rewritable) discs. You also need special software programs that enable you to create the disc and write data to it.

After you have these things, creating a CD that you can use to distribute your video project is simple. The main consideration is whether you want to create a simple CD-R that can be used by pretty much any Mac user (or, if you like, by both Mac and PC users) or if you want to create a special video CD. In most cases, you'll probably opt to create a CD-R because they're easy, cheap, and anyone with a CD-ROM drive and QuickTime can view your final product.

With a regular CD-R, all you're really doing is copying the QuickTime movie to a disc, which can then be popped into most CD-ROM drives and played back on the computer screen in QuickTime Player. Nothing special happens to the image or the format of the QuickTime movie — it's effectively the same as saving the file to a Zip disk or another removable disk, except that CD-Rs are cheaper, hold up to 700MB, and are a little easier to ship than other types of discs because they're so light.

A video CD also uses CD-R media, but it's written in a special format that requires some additional third-party programs and prep work. The result is a movie that's about the quality of a VHS tape but can be played back in some home DVD players as well as in most Mac and PC CD-ROM drives (if you have special video CD player software). A Video CD is similar to a DVD movie disc, except that DVD offers much higher quality. DVDs are prohibitively expensive to create, too, making it impractical for the home user. Creating video CDs isn't cheap — you need not only a CD-RW drive but also pricey MPEG encoding software and the full version of Adaptec Toast. But if you're willing to make the investment, creating a video CD can be quite a bit of fun.

Burning a CD-R

If you have access to a CD-RW drive, burning a CD with your QuickTime movie on it is fairly easy. This is a great method for distributing movies exported as QuickTime files, partly because CD-R discs are inexpensive (well under $1 per disc in bulk) and light enough to mail or hand out easily to friends. If you have a drive that's capable of writing to CD-RW discs, you can use the drive to write and, if desired, rewrite your QuickTime movie to a special erasable CD-RW disc. These aren't as good for distribution (CD-RW discs are a bit more expensive and less compatible with older CD-ROM drives), but the fact that they can be erased and rewritten to can give them an advantage over write-once CD-R discs.

In either case, the process of getting a QuickTime movie onto recordable CD media begins by exporting your movie to QuickTime. For now, export the movie according to the instructions in Chapter 15, selecting the CD-ROM Movie, Medium setting. (Later in this chapter, you find out how to tweak these settings to get the most out of your movie.)

With the movie exported, move on to your CD creation software. In most cases, this software is Adaptec Toast, which is the most popular way to create CD-R and CD-RW discs and move data to them (see Figure 16-1). (Toast got its name, by the way, from the fact that it's common to say you're "burning" a CD because the data is written to the CD using a small laser.) Another popular program is Discribe, a program made by CharisMac (www. charismac.com) and included with some models of CD-RW drives.

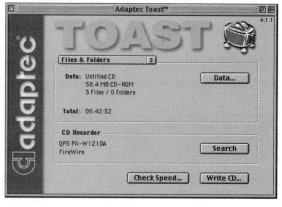

Figure 16-1: Toast is the most popular program for burning CD-R and CD-RW discs.

Following are instructions for using Toast:

1. **Launch the Toast program.**

   The main Toast window appears.

2. **Choose the type of CD-R you want to create.**

   The easiest option is to choose Mac Files and Folders from the Format pop-up menu in Toast. This creates a hybrid CD that can be read by both Macs and Intel-compatible PCs. (This may also be your only choice if you have one of the limited versions of Toast that tends to be included with retail CD-RW drives.)

3. **Drag your QuickTime movie from the Finder to the Data portion of the Toast window.**

   A little message appears saying "Drop files and folders here." When you drag and drop the QuickTime movie to that area, the Data section changes to represent the files that have been dropped. In some cases, the Data section indicates more files than you dragged (for instance, even if you drag only one file, you might see "3 Files" indicated on the screen). These extra files are shown because Toast is making editorial decisions about your movie, offering equal time to other movies. (I'm kidding — it happens because Toast adds important Mac OS system files to the disc.)

4. **If you want to customize the name of the CD:**

   a. **Click the Data button and view the data window.**

      In it, an icon representing the CD you're creating appears.

   b. **Click the disclosure triangle to see all items that will be on this CD.**

   c. **Click once on the name of the CD (probably "Untitled CD") and then wait a few seconds for the cursor to appear; now you can edit the name that the final CD will have (see Figure 16-2).**

   d. **Using this window, you can also add and remove additional files, either by dragging them in and out of the window or clicking the Add and Remove buttons.**

   e. **When you're finished, click the Done button.**

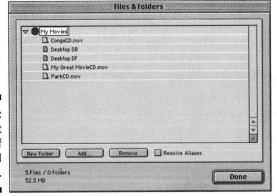

Figure 16-2: You can edit the name of your CD and file listing.

5. **Back in the Toast window, ensure that your CD-RW drive has been recognized in the CD Recorder section.**

   If it hasn't, make sure it's connected and turned on and then click the Search button. If Toast still doesn't find the drive, you may have a configuration problem or need to re-install either the drive's software or your version of Toast.

6. If everything looks good, click the Check Speed button in the Toast window.

This lets you test the speed of your Mac and hard disk to ensure that Toast can read data quickly enough to complete the CD write process successfully. (To properly burn a CD, the software must be able to send a continuous stream of data to the drive, which means it must be able to load the data from the hard disk and move it on to the CD-RW drive in a timely manner.) If your Mac or drive has trouble with the test, Toast may recommend you choose a lower speed setting for writing your data.

Now, you're ready to write the data to disc. Here's the process:

1. Click the Write CD button in the main Toast window.

The Writing dialog box shown in Figure 16-3 appears, unless you don't have a recordable CD in your CD-RW drive, in which case you are prompted to insert one.

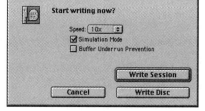

Figure 16-3:
The Writing
dialog box.

2. From the Speed menu, select the speed at which you want the drive to write the CD.

If you had trouble with the Check Speed test discussed previously, this is where you can choose a slower speed for the write process. If everything checked out during the Check Speed test, select the highest speed listing on the menu.

3. Decide on the Simulation Mode or Buffer Underrun Prevention options.

The Simulation Mode goes through the entire process of writing to a CD-R disc but without using the laser. That way, you can see whether any errors would have occurred during the write process without losing a CD-R disc in the process. (After a CD-R disc is written to, even if an error occurs, the disc cannot be written to again. If you're writing to a CD-RW disc, you have to erase it and start over.) The Buffer Underrun Protection option (a new feature in Toast 4.1 and higher) causes the disc to be written in such a way that errors are less likely, but it's also less-compatible with some CD-ROM drives and makes it impossible to use the CD as a master for mass duplication. (You know, just in case you were planning to run off 10,000 of the suckers.)

4. **Select Write Session or Write Disc.**

If you choose to write a single session, you can write additional sessions to this disc, if desired, in the future. The sessions can get a bit confusing because each new session you create on a CD-R disc has its own icon — when you mount a multi-session CD, you'll often see two or more CD icons on the desktop. Still, it's one way to take full advantage of a CD-R. If you choose Write Disc, your data is written to the disc and the disc is closed to any further additions. In either case, the Toast window changes to reflect that the CD is now being written to (see Figure 16-4.)

Figure 16-4:
Data is
being
written to
the CD-R.

When the write process is finished, assuming you encounter no errors, a dialog box appears.

5. **When asked whether you'd like to verify the CD, click Verify or do nothing.**

The CD is read and verified. Then, you see a dialog box with one option, an Eject button.

6. **Click the Eject button and the newly written disc comes flying out of your drive, ready to use.**

Now you can send the CD to anyone who has QuickTime on his or her Mac (or PC, if you have the full version of Toast and were able to create an ISO-9660 formatted disc).

Creating a video CD

Perhaps a more exciting approach to putting your movie on a CD is to go through the hoops required to create a video CD, or VCD. Video CD is a special format that you can play back in some commercial DVD players (that hook up to home entertainment systems) as well as on most PCs and Macs with video CD player software. The video plays back from the CD at near-TV quality, looking about as good as a VHS tape. (Not nearly as good as a DVD, mind you, but impressive nonetheless.) Using the VCD format, a single CD-R can hold about 70 minutes of video.

Creating a video CD, however, requires some investment. You face two hurdles. First, you need to translate your QuickTime movie into the MPEG 1 format, which is something QuickTime Pro can't do on its own. The solution is to use a third-party program, such as Terran Systems Media Cleaner Pro. Second, you need the full version of Adaptec Toast or a similar application that supports Video CD creation. Most versions of CD-R software that come for free with CD-RW drives do not support the Video CD format.

Another program, m.Pack from Asarte, has been bought by Apple but, at the time of this writing, not re-released. It's likely that video CD (as well as DVD) creation software will be available from Apple by the time you read this, so check Apple's Web site (www.apple.com) and retailers.

Mac HFS versus the Files and Folders option

One point of confusion in your quest to master CD-R burning may be some of the obscure terminology used in burning programs. Although they've improved, the issue of properly formatting the CD can make things a little sticky. Here's the skinny.

ISO-9660 is the standard format for PC-friendly CDs. Macs can also read ISO-9660 CDs with (usually) no trouble, although the Mac interprets them as PC media and uses its little PC icons to represent the CD on the desktop. Likewise, you can make hybrid CDs that show up as Mac CDs on Macs and PC CDs on PCs, but you have to copy your movie to the CD twice.

For Mac-only CDs, you'll often find two possible settings: Macintosh HFS or Mac Files and Folders. (I've seen this called Build a Mac HFS in some programs.) Macintosh HFS is used when you already have a Mac volume that you'd like to burn in total to the CD — this is the old way to create CDs. You begin by partitioning your hard disk to create a 700MB (or so) volume and then arrange files on that volume. Next, you arrange the files on that volume as you'd like them to be burned onto the CD-R. This helps you to know exactly how many files will fit on the CD-R *before* you start the burning process. Plus, when you copy files to the formatted volume, they're placed on that volume contiguously; when the burner reads them, it's much less likely to encounter errors. Then you use the Macintosh HFS setting in the software to move the entire volume onto the CD-R. (A twist on this is to use Apple's Disk Copy utility to create a disk image file that can be used to represent a volume.)

None of this is necessary because Mac Files and Folders enables you to simply drag-and-drop files and folders to Toast to create them. But Macintosh HFS is definitely an option if you're serious, but if you're serious about reliably burning jam-packed CD-Rs.

Here are the steps for creating a Video CD:

1. **Export your movie from iMovie to a QuickTime movie at full DV quality.**

   To save space, you can export the file at 325x244 pixels resolution because that's close to the resolution used by video CDs. To do this, you need to use the Expert feature in iMovie's Export Movie dialog box, described in the next section of this chapter, "Expert Exporting for CDs." The key is to avoid adding any compression at this point.

2. **Using Media Cleaner Pro or a similar utility, translate the movie into MPEG 1 format and crop the movie to 325x244 pixels if it isn't already at that resolution.**

   See Chapter 18 for more on Media Cleaner.

3. **Open the full version of Toast (Version 4.0 or higher) and choose Format⇨Video CD.**

4. **Drag the MPEG 1 file to the Data area on the CD.**

   You can click the Data button to give the CD a name.

5. **Follow the numbered instructions regarding writing data to disc in the "Burning a CD-R" section.**

   You'll want to use the Check Speed feature and then click the Write CD button to make your final choices. Select Write Disc and the Video CD information is written to the CD.

That's it — you have a video CD. Now you need a video CD player application (try Video Player 3.1 from `www.daemon-info.com`) to view the Video CD in full-screen glory on your Mac.

Expert Exporting for CDs

Although iMovie makes exporting to QuickTime easy enough, by default you really have only one built-in choice that's appropriate for creating CD-based movies: CD-ROM Movie Medium. It's a fine choice — certainly a law-abiding one — but that doesn't mean it's the best choice in every situation. Fortunately, you can tailor the export so that it works better under different circumstances. You may decide that you want to try to make your QuickTime movie a little larger, use a different codec for compression, or tweak other settings to get better quality before you burn the movie to a CD. Or you may need to go the other direction — for a very long movie, or for multiple movies, you may want to make the image size smaller and compress the movie more so that it fits on a CD.

Video CD instead of DVD?

As mentioned, putting together a DVD movie-mastering system is expensive (thousands of dollars), even though the price of DVD-RAM drives is coming down. Soon, it may be more affordable to create DVD movies than it is today, although it continues to be slight overkill for home movies and small business projects. (Rumors of a lower-cost Apple solution abound and may be fulfilled by the time you read this.)

Fortunately, you can use video CDs in some DVD playback devices, even those designed for home entertainment systems. This means a video CD created from a home or organizational iMovie can, in some cases, be played back in a standard DVD player. The problem is that not all DVD players support video CDs (check the DVD player's documentation — video CD support is becoming more common in newer models). According to the Video CD FAQ at

`http://www.geocities.com/Athens /Forum/2496/vcdfaq.html`

most Panasonic, RCA, Samsung, and Sony models play video CDs. You can also get dedicated Video CD players for home entertainment systems, as well as add-ons for Sony Playstation or Sega Saturn gaming devices that will play back Video CDs.

If you want to create either video CDs or DVDs without the hassle and expense of doing it yourself, plenty of service bureaus will do it for you. The CD Studio (`www.thecdstudio.com`), Taomedia (`www.taomedia.com`), and A's Photo Video Lab (`www.photovideolab. com`), among many others, offer CD and DVD mastering services.

To see the Expert settings when outputting from iMovie:

1. **Choose File⇨Export Movie.**

   The Export Movie dialog box appears.

2. **Choose Formats⇨Expert.**

   The Expert QuickTime Settings dialog box appears, as shown in Figure 16-5.

There's a lot to do in here, so pull up a chair and get comfortable.

Figure 16-5:
Here's where you can dig into the Image and Audio settings before you export.

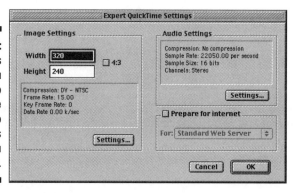

Image settings

For starters, you can set the size at which you'll export your movie. Then you move on to the settings for compressing the exported video:

1. **On the left side of the Expert QuickTime Settings dialog box, determine the size of your movie.**

   In the Width and Height boxes, enter the number in pixels you'd like to the final QuickTime movie to be.

2. **If you want to make sure the movie is proportional to a standard TV image, click the 4:3 box.**

3. **Dig into the video compression settings by clicking the Settings button.**

   The Compression Settings dialog box appears.

All these elements work together, so before we get in too deep, you should look at the different codecs and the settings you should use with each. For a CD-targeted QuickTime movie, you'll likely choose from Animation, Cinepak, DV, H.263, Sorenson Video, or Video. Each has strengths and weaknesses, as follows:

- ✔ **Animation.** The Animation codec, at its highest setting, offers compression rates that aren't much better than None, so the movies are generally too large for CDs. Still, it's worth mentioning because it's a popular way to archive video clips or to export them for loading into other applications, such as Media Cleaner, for fine-tuning the compression. At lower quality settings, it's a lossy codec, best suited for computer-generated images (titles, screen captures, and slides).

- ✔ **Cinepak.** You may opt to use Cinepak, especially if you're sending your QuickTime movie to an older Mac or PC, because Cinepak has been around for a while and is more compatible with older versions of QuickTime. That said, it isn't the best available codec for CD-based movies because it creates larger files and can be lossy. For best results, use a lot of key frames (one or two per second) and a high data rate limit (150 KB/sec or higher). Expect a 320x240 movie at 15 fps to take up about 12MB per minute.

- ✔ **DV-NTSC, DV-PAL.** Choose a DV codec if you want your files to be about the same size and quality as they are in iMovie itself. This isn't great compression (requiring about 100MB per minute of video for 320x240 at 15 fps) and, for playback, Sorenson is comparable in quality. Some third-party applications work best with DV-compressed video, however, especially if you're going to add special effects or do further editing.

✔ **H.263.** iMovie uses the H.263 codec as the default choice for three reasons. It's a sophisticated codec that gives good results, including better quality at about half the storage space as Cinepak. You can set a slightly lower key frame rate (1 per second or so), if desired, which also results in a smaller file. And H.263 compresses a little more quickly than some of the other codecs. At 320x240, a 1-fps QuickTime movie takes up about 6MB per minute.

✔ **Sorenson Video.** For all practical purposes, Sorenson Video is the codec to beat. It's a very good but demanding codec — you need QuickTime 4.0 or higher to play it back as well as a high-speed PowerPC-based Power Macintosh. Most G3 or G3-based Macs can play back Sorenson-compressed QuickTime movies very well. Be prepared to wait, though — compressing with Sorenson takes a long time. At 320x240, a 15 fps Sorenson movie can vary in its bandwidth requirement, but you can easily limit a Sorenson-compressed QuickTime movie to 150K/sec (10MB per minute). That would fit about 60 minutes of video on a CD, at very pleasing quality levels. One caveat: If you don't limit Sorenson movies to 320x240, 75-150K/second and keep to one key frame per second, they won't play back smoothly on pre-G3 Power Macs (see Figure 16-6).

Figure 16-6:
Close to ideal Sorenson codec settings for CD-targeted QuickTime movies, as long as you can deal with 10MB/min storage requirements.

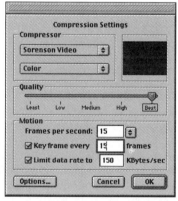

Sorenson-compressed video *doubles* well during playback. If you have a 320x240 clip compressed using Sorenson, choose Movie⇨Double Size to play back the movie at 640x480. The movie should offer surprisingly high playback quality.

✔ **Video.** The Video compressor is another older codec that still has a little life in it. It creates large files with mid-level quality, but it compresses very quickly and plays back well on older Macs. At 15 fps, a QuickTime movie compressed with the Video codec takes up about 30MB per minute.

With all that under your belt, you're ready to set your compression options. Here's what to do in the Compression Settings dialog box:

1. **In the Compressor portion of the dialog box, use the top pop-up menu to select the type of codec to use for the video portion of the QuickTime movie.**

2. **Select the number of colors the movie should use.**

   In some cases, you can also use the Quality slider to set a quality level that you'll be happy with.

3. **In the Motion section, you can select the number of frames per second the movie will be.**

   For CD-based movies, somewhere between 12 and 24 fps is probably adequate. I generally choose about 15 fps, but you might go higher if you absolutely need the best quality and playback will occur on a very fast machine.

4. **If you check the Key Frame check box, you can then enter how often a key frame should be placed in the movie; if you click the Limit check box, you can limit the data rate to a certain number of Kilobytes per second.**

   For CD-based movies, playback is often limited to 300K per second for compatibility with older drives.

5. **After you've set these options, click OK to close the Compression Settings dialog box.**

Next, it's on to audio settings.

Audio settings

QuickTime and iMovie give you more than just video exporting and compression to think about — you have compression settings for audio to consider as well. Lowering the quality levels of your audio is one way to make your QuickTime movies a little smaller in size, although it's worth emphasizing that the video compression is *much* more important if file size is your main issue. For QuickTime movies you plan to put on CD, you don't have to compromise your sound settings too significantly. (It's a slightly different story for Internet movies, as you see in Chapter 17.)

1. **In the Expert QuickTime Settings dialog box, click the Settings button in the Audio Settings portion of the window.**

   The Sound Settings dialog box appears.

2. **From the Compressor menu, you can choose the type of audio codec you want to use.**

3. **In the Rate portion, you can select a different frequency for the audio; you can also select whether to store the audio as 8-bit or 16-bit and whether it should be Mono or Stereo in this dialog box (see Figure 16-7).**

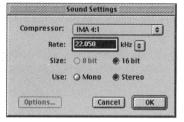

Figure 16-7:
The Sound
Settings
dialog box.

For QuickTime movies destined for CD, I recommend leaving audio at 16-bit and Stereo sound, although you can use Mono if space is a premium. (I only recommend 8-bit sound for the smallest movies, perhaps those sent through e-mail. Note also that most modern codecs work only on 16-bit audio.) 22.050 is a good kHz rate for CD-oriented movies — this is about FM radio quality. If you like, you can bump that number up to 44.100 kHz (CD-quality), although it adds to the size of your QuickTime movie. Or you can save some storage space by changing the rate to 11.025 (AM radio quality).

For compressors, you have four practical choices for CD-bound movies:

- **µLaw.** Although not highly recommended, the µLaw format (said "mu-law" thanks to the Latin character µ) compresses quickly and does minimal damage. It also does minimal compression — only about 2:1.

- **IMA 4:1.** This is easily the most recommended option for CD audio. It compresses quickly at about a 4:1 ratio and works well with Macintosh native sound in AIFF format. It also works fine for both spoken audio and music, making it a good all-around player.

- **QDesign Music 2.** If you have only music behind your movie, you might consider using QDesign Music 2, a codec that, as the name implies, is aimed mostly at compressing music. If you select this codec, note that you can click the Options button in the Sound Settings dialog box and choose a target data rate (between 8 kilobits per second and 48 kilobits per second) to fine-tune the quality versus storage tradeoff.

- **Qualcomm PureVoice.** If you happen to have no music and not much ambient sound in your movie, you might consider this codec, which works best for compressing speaking voices. It's aimed more squarely at the Internet because it can heavily compress spoken audio and works only with Mono settings. Still, if you need to squeeze a lot of talking-head movies onto a training CD, this may help make them fit. Note that selecting PureVoice activates the Option button in the Sound Settings dialog box, where you can choose different compression rates (9:1 or 19:1) as well as an option for Internet streaming.

4. **After you've made your settings in the Sound Settings dialog box, click OK.**

   You're back to the Expert QuickTime Settings dialog box, which displays a full report of your audio and video compression settings.

5. **If everything looks good, click OK.**

   You're back to the Export Movie dialog box.

6. **Begin the export process, as described in Chapter 15.**

Movies in Other Applications

After you export your movie to your hard disk in QuickTime format, you can do quite a bit with that file. In addition to distributing your QuickTime movies on CD or on the Internet, another popular approach is to include QuickTime movies within other application's documents. Two interesting places for QuickTime movies to pop up are AppleWorks and Microsoft PowerPoint, where you can incorporate video into your presentations, either for stand-up discussions that you give or for standalone presentations.

With most QuickTime-enabled applications, adding a QuickTime movie to a document is simple. In AppleWorks, for instance, you can add QuickTime movies to pretty much any document type — a word processing document, a slide in a slide show, or even a multimedia field in a database. In many of AppleWork's modules, you can simply drag-and-drop the movie's icon onto the document window to place it. You can also use the File⇨Insert command to add QuickTime movies in some windows (see Figure 16-8).

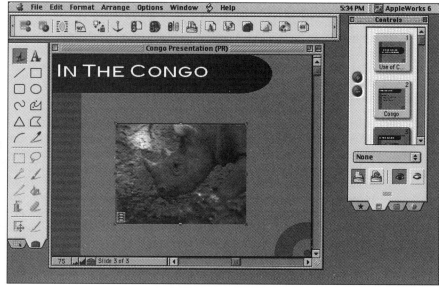

Figure 16-8:
Adding a
QuickTime
movie to a
presentation
slide in
Apple-
Works 6.

AppleWorks 6 offers special controls for QuickTime movies in the
Presentation module. In the Controls window, click the small tab that sports
the Play button. You see options that dictate whether or not a QuickTime
movie includes QuickTime Player controls, is played automatically, and is
played in its entirety before the slide is advanced (see Figure 16-9).

Figure 16-9:
The
QuickTime
controls in
AppleWork's
Presentation
module.

In Microsoft PowerPoint 98 and 2001, the commands to add QuickTime files to a presentation are Insert⇨Movies (for adding an entire movie) and Sounds⇨Movie from File (to add audio from a QuickTime movie). You then use an Open dialog box to locate the movie and add it to your slide. During the presentation, clicking the still poster image of the movie starts it — you can display it right there within the slide, making your sales or educational point in full-blown multimedia.

Other applications work well with QuickTime clips and QuickTime movies. Macromedia Director, for instance, is a popular application for creating professional-level multimedia presentations that include QuickTime clips. Included on the *iMovie 2 For Dummies* CD-ROM is a demo of MovieWorks Interactive, a program that enables you to build interactive projects. These projects can include buttons and other controllers that enable you to present multiple clips in a single project and enable the viewers to select which clip they will view next (as well as select other information, such as sound, text, and graphics).

Chapter 17

iMovies Online: The Internet and Apple's iTools

*I*t can be argued that what defines an advanced civilization is its capability to bore others with its own version of history. Witness Cleopatra's needle, the Aztec ruins of Latin America, and the American obsession with home movies of the mid-to-late-20th century. With iMovie and the Internet, the 21st century beckons, as a new era of worldwide personal history distribution is finally upon us. You can document your life with iMovie and distribute the result directly to millions around the world. Perhaps, with all this publishing power in the hands of individuals, we'll learn to use it for good instead of evil. If not, I hope we can at least learn to keep things *brief.*

Currently, the main limitation for posting movies on the Web is that Internet connections are slow for most users — anyone accessing the Internet through a modem, even a high-speed modem, is limited in the size and quality of QuickTime movies that he or she can realistically download. Because movie files require a lot of storage space, they also require a lot of *bandwidth* (the speed, or size, of an Internet connection). The bigger, longer, and higher quality the movie, the more bandwidth it requires. When people talk about the potential that *broadband* connections give us (faster connections into homes and offices everyone), one of those advantages is the ease with which we can download space-hogging movies.

So, for now, if you plan to distribute your movie to friends, family, or colleagues over the Internet, consider two things. First, do you plan to send the movie through e-mail or will you make it available on a Web page? And second, does your recipient's connection to the Internet offer enough bandwidth for a high-quality movie, or should you sacrifice some quality and size to keep your recipient from wasting a lot of time downloading your project?

In this chapter, you look at sending movies through e-mail, posting them on the Web, and using Apple's iTools for a whole host of movie distribution magic. Along the way, you see some tricks for making your movie as svelte and fast moving as possible.

Sending Movies in E-Mail

If you plan to send your movie as a QuickTime movie through e-mail, just remember that most people, even with high-speed connections, prefer not to download mail messages more than a few megabytes in size, tops. If you're sending a quick, small movie, that's okay. If you have a larger project that you want to make available over the Internet, I suggest creating a Web-based movie, as discussed later in the "Putting Movies on the Web" section.

Exporting the movie

For e-mail, you need to keep the movie short and its file size small. The first step is to tightly edit your movie and seriously consider how long it should be. For a typical e-mail movie, I recommend no more than three minutes. Even with a very small picture size (160x120 pixels) and iMovie's standard compression settings, a three-minute movie takes up about 5MB, which is the upper limit for sending a video as an attachment. (You can make the file even a bit smaller using the advanced export settings discussed in the section "Expert Exporting for the Internet.")

Got it chopped down to Hollywood-trailer length? The next step is to export the movie. One way to do this is using iMovie's built-in e-mail export option. Here's how:

1. **With the movie open and ready for export (see Chapter 14), choose File⇨Export movie.**

2. **Choose Export To⇨QuickTime.**

3. **Choose Formats⇨Email Movie, Small.**

   If you're sending this movie to someone who doesn't have QuickTime 4 or higher, turn on the QuickTime 3.0 Compatible option.

4. **Click the Export button.**

5. **Type a name, choose a place on your disk to save the movie, and then click Save.**

   The export process begins.

Attaching the movie

After you've exported your movie, it's easy enough to send it through e-mail: You simply attach the movie document to an e-mail message. Both the message and the movie are sent to your recipient, who can then download the message and attachment and use QuickTime Player to view the movie.

Most important, though, is the golden rule of sending e-mail attachments: Make sure your recipient knows it's coming and wants it. Don't send the message until you've told them to expect it and they've agreed to receive it.

Avoid sending unsolicited attachments, even to friends, for two reasons. First, a large e-mail attachment can take a long time to download and may block your recipients from receiving other e-mail or cost them money in per-minute Internet charges. (Just think if someone sent you a 5MB e-mail message that you weren't expecting. Might it not annoy you?) Over even a high-speed (56K) modem connection, a 5MB attachment can take 20 to 25 minutes to download. (Note that it can't hurt to put the approximate size of the download in the subject line, because some recipients have set options that enable them to download large messages at their leisure.)

Second, some Internet-borne viruses show up as e-mail attachments, so many savvy Internet users are wary (rightly so) of unsolicited attachments. Clever viruses look like they were sent by friends (by exploiting security holes in the address book features built into e-mail programs). If your recipient doesn't know the attachment is coming, he or she might toss the message and delete the movie just as a precaution.

The process of attaching a file to an e-mail message is easy. In most e-mail programs, you either drag the QuickTime movie's icon to your message composition window or use a Message⇨Add Attachment command (or something similar). In Outlook Express 5.0 or Microsoft Entourage, for instance, you can do either — you can drag a file to the Attachments area of the message (see Figure 17-1) or choose Messages⇨Add Attachments. (You can click the Add button in the Attachments area of the composition window, if you like the idea of yet another option.)

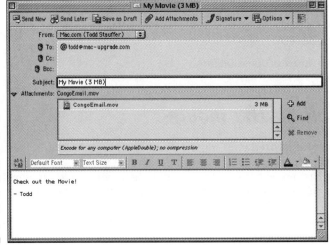

Figure 17-1:
A QuickTime
movie
attached to
a message
in Outlook
Express.

Encoding the attachment

The way e-mail works is a little odd. All e-mail messages, even if they include an attached file, must be sent over the Internet as plain text. For plain e-mail messages, this isn't much of a problem because they're basically text already. Attachments (such as QuickTime movies), however, are *binary files,* which means they include 1s and 0s that make up computer data, not just simple text.

The solution is to *encode* attachments, following a process that turns a binary file into a text-only representation of that file. The attachment is then sent across the Internet as if it were one long text message. When the message reaches the recipient, it's decoded back into a binary format so that it can be used as a data file.

Sure, that sounds simple. (Does it?) What's worse, though, is that different computing platforms tend to have different methods for encoding. So, you need to make sure you're selecting the appropriate encoding for the type of computer you're sending the movie *to.* Here's a list:

- ✔ **AppleDouble.** If you tend to send e-mail attachments to both Windows and Mac users, AppleDouble is probably best, as long as your e-mail program supports it. AppleDouble is a Windows-compatible format that also happens to work well for Mac recipients.

- ✔ **MIME/Base 64.** If you happen to be sending to a Windows user, this is the most compatible format. As a bonus, if you don't have an AppleDouble option, most Mac users can also read MIME/Base 64 encoded attachments.

✔ **BinHex.** If you know you're definitely sending to a Mac user (particularly a Mac OS 9 or earlier user), you can use BinHex, which is the Mac-only format. Windows e-mail programs often can't read this one. (PC users *can* decode these files with Aladdin Expander for Windows, a freeware add-on available at `www.aladdinsys.com`. If you have PC-using friends, encourage them to download it so they can decode and decompress Mac files more easily.)

✔ **UUEncode.** This format is common for sending to Unix-based computers, although many Windows-based e-mail clients and e-mail programs written for Mac OS X can handle it.

Where you set the type of encoding can also vary from program to program. In Outlook Express and Microsoft Entourage, you can select the encoding type in the Attachment portion of the composition window by clicking the italicized text below the Attachments list (see Figure 17-2). In other programs, you often choose the encoding method from the Preferences dialog box, most likely accessed at Edit⇨Preferences.

Some e-mail programs automatically attempt to compress your movie file using a special file compression utility. (This is a little different from QuickTime compression because it can compress any type of file into a special archive file designed for transporting over the Internet.) Most Mac e-mail programs default to StuffIt format compression, but many Windows and Unix users can't decompress StuffIt without Aladdin Expander (`www.aladdinsys.com`) installed. If you have the option, turn off any file compression that your e-mail program performs when you're sending QuickTime movies, unless you know that all your recipients are Mac users. Figure 17-2 shows that Outlook Express offers easy access to the File Compression option.

Figure 17-2:
In Outlook Express 5, it's easy to alter both encoding and compression options.

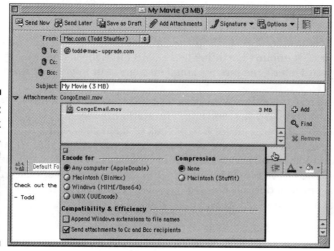

Sending the movie

After you've attached the movie and made your encoding decisions, you're ready to send the movie:

1. **Enter an e-mail address in the To section of the composition window, along with addresses in the CC section if desired.**

   In most e-mail programs, CC recipients automatically receive the attachment, too, so make sure they definitely want it before you add them. (Whether or not your CC recipients receive attachments is an option in Outlook Express and Microsoft Entourage.)

2. **Click the Send Now button in your e-mail program.**

   Assuming that you're connected to the Internet, your message and movie are sent on their merry way.

Putting Movies on the Web

Movies you put on the Web can be a little bigger than e-mail movies, both in screen size and in the amount of space they take up for storage. You don't want them to be too much bigger, though, because people with slow connections will still be forced to wait while the movie is downloaded. And if you plan to post the movie to your own Web site, you also need to consider any limitations that your Web provider places on downloads — some have an upper limit on the number of megabytes that can be accessed from your Web site per month, for instance. For home movies, you're not likely to hit that quota, but for an organization or business, you should at least discuss the possibility with your provider.

It's also common for ISPs to limit the amount of storage space you can use to store your files online (Earthlink has a 6MB limit, for instance) so you need to keep your QuickTime movies small enough to fit in your allotted space.

Aside from size considerations, you also have two approaches to adding a QuickTime movie to your Web site. The standard way is to simply make it downloadable through either a hyperlink or a special command that embeds the movie in your Web page. (The movie looks like it's part of the page when your visitor views the movie on your site.) In this case, your recipient has to download the entire movie file before it begins to play. (A special case, called a fast start movie, doesn't have to completely download, but the recipient still waits for most of the movie to download before it begins.)

The other way is to create a *streaming* QuickTime movie, in which only a very small portion of the movie has to be downloaded before it begins playing. The movie then continues to play as the rest of the data for the movie arrives almost simultaneously with the playback. Streaming QuickTime movies are generally of lesser quality and size and require a special Internet server (a QuickTime Streaming Server) to work correctly. Still, if your Web provider offers a QuickTime Streaming Server, you can create a streaming-capable QuickTime movie using iMovie.

For either type, you need to look at the prep work for creating and exporting the movie and then move on to how you can put the movie on a Web page.

Exporting the movie

iMovie's built-in Web-oriented export options compromise between the size of an e-mail movie and a CD movie, compressing it at 240x180 pixels and 12 frames per second. This makes for a decent looking movie that can be downloaded fairly quickly by average modem-based Web surfers — each minute of video is about 1MB.

iMovie gives you two Web movie presets, Web Movie and Streaming Web Movie. Which one you select depends on whether you want a regular Web movie or one destined for a special QuickTime Streaming server. When you select Streaming Web Movie, a *hinted* movie file is created. This type of movie file includes information (*hints*) that makes it possible for a QuickTime Streaming Server to stream the file, piece-by-piece, to the recipient, playing each in almost real time. (If this sort of movie is placed on a regular Web server, it acts like a fast start movie.) The hints compensate for the fact that different packets of data might take different routes on the Internet and arrive out of order. The hints tell QuickTime Player what bit of data is supposed to come next, so it can be rearranged and played in QuickTime Player as the rest of the movie downloads.

Using one of the presets (either Web Movie, Small or Streaming Web Movie, Small) is simple:

1. **With the iMovie open and ready for export (see Chapter 14), choose File⇨Export movie.**

2. **From the Export To menu, choose QuickTime.**

3. **From the Formats menu, choose Web Movie, Small or Streaming Web Movie, Small.**

   If you're sending this movie to someone who doesn't have QuickTime 4 or higher, turn on the QuickTime 3.0 Compatible option, which causes the exporter to use IMA audio compression instead of QDesign. The file will be a little larger.

4. Click the Export button.

5. Type a name and choose a place on your disk to save the movie and then click Save.

The export process begins. Note that for movies destined for the Web, it's best to use no spaces when naming the movie, although you can use the underscore character, as in **congo_web.mov**. (I suggest keeping the names all lowercase, too, because some Web servers are case-sensitive.) Also, make sure you end the movie's name with the three-letter .mov extension so that Windows and Unix computers recognize the file as a QuickTime movie.

HTML for a Web movie

Now you're ready to add the movie to a page on your Web site. Two approaches are available. You can create a link that causes the QuickTime movie to be downloaded to the user's computer, so that the user can view it in QuickTime Player. Or you can embed the movie in the Web page, so that it's displayed directly within the Web browser.

For a basic download link, use HTML's anchor tag and a URL that points directly to the location of the QuickTime movie on your Web server. Here's the code you add to your page for a linked movie:

```
<a href="congo_web.mov">Download the Congo movie (1.2MB)</a>
```

That's it. This link instructs the browser to look in the current folder on the Web server (the folder in which the Web page itself is stored) and attempt to locate the movie file. If you've properly uploaded the movie file to that folder, the Web browser downloads the file to the user's computer. You could also have a complete, or static, URL reference in the anchor tag, such as this:

```
<a href="http://www.mac-
        upgrade.com/movies/congo_web.mov">Download the
        Congo movie (1.2 MB)</a>
```

Note that, as a courtesy, you should include the size of the download in the text description portion of the link. Also, for maximum compatibility, remember to use the .mov filename extension. See Figure 17-3 to see how the link looks and works.

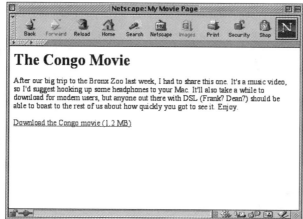

The other way to add a QuickTime movie to your Web page is to embed it in the page. You do this using the EMBED tag, which offers quite a few options and attributes. At the most basic, the EMBED tag tells the Web browser that it needs to load the QuickTime Plug-in, an extra bit of code that tells the Web browser how to play QuickTime movies from within a Web page. Next, the EMBED tag tells the plug-in where to find the movie file, whether the user sees a QuickTime controller (for play, pause, fast forward, and so on), and the height and width of the movie. Here's an example:

```
<EMBED CONTROLLER="false" HEIGHT="180" WIDTH="240"
       SRC="congo_web.mov">
```

The movie appears without a QuickTime controller and plays automatically when the page is loaded in a Web browser. If you want a controller to appear, change the CONTROLLER and HEIGHT attributes:

```
<EMBED CONTROLLER="true" HEIGHT="196" WIDTH="240"
       SRC="congo_web.mov">
```

Notice that I set CONTROLLER to true and added 16 pixels to the HEIGHT attribute. That alteration gives the movie area enough room to display the controller along with the movie. Figure 17-4 shows what a movie looks like when embedded on a page like this.

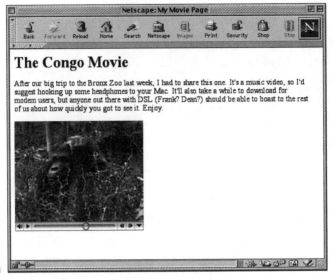

Figure 17-4:
A QuickTime
movie
embedded
in a Web
page.

The Embed tag offers a number of attributes. If you'd like the full details, check out the following address, where all the attributes are documented:

```
www.apple.com/quicktime/authoring/embed.html
```

Some interesting attributes include AUTOPLAY="False", which keeps the movie from playing automatically and TARGET="QUICKTIMEPLAYER", which causes the movie to appear in QuickTime Player (if your user has it installed) instead of within the browser window.

Here's another fun one: If you've ever headed to Apple's QuickTime site and played one of their movies, you know that you generally load a page that shows a still image and then you click that image and the movie plays. You can create such a clickable still image, too, but it takes some trickery. Begin by creating a QuickTime movie that has only one *frame* of video in it and save that movie as *moviename*_still.mov, where *moviename* is the name of the movie. (You can do this by creating a new iMovie project and importing a still image, as discussed in Chapter 11. Then export the movie to a QuickTime movie. Don't forget to use an image that's the same size as your full movie.)

Now, build your Embed tag so that it includes three important attributes. In the SRC attribute, put the name of your still movie. In the HREF attribute, include a reference to the actual movie file. The third attribute, TARGET, which is set to "myself", is the key: It tells the QuickTime plug-in that when the user clicks the still movie, the full movie file should load and play. Here's how it works:

```
<EMBED CONTROLLER="false" HEIGHT="180" WIDTH="240"
        SRC="congostill.mov" TARGET="myself"
        HREF="congo_web.mov">
```

You don't know HTML?

HTML (HyperText Markup Language), the codes used to create Web pages, isn't tough to master. Although it may seem at first glance to be a programming language, it's not, really. It's a *markup* language, one designed to add small codes to plain text to make that text more interesting. The codes add formatting (bold, italic, or heading formats), hyperlink capabilities, and images. You can even use special codes that embed multimedia files in the page, as you see in this chapter.

Ultimately, though, an HTML document — and, hence, a Web page — is simply a text document with these special codes. For instance, I can easily show you the entire listing that produced Figure 17-4. Interested?

```
<HTML>
<HEAD><TITLE>My Movie
    Page</TITLE></HEAD>
<BODY>
<H1>The Congo Movie</H1>
<P>After our big trip to the
    Bronx Zoo last week, I had
    to share this one. It's a
    music video, so I'd suggest
    hooking up some headphones
    to your Mac. It'll also
```

take a while to download for modem users, but anyone out there with DSL (Frank? Dean?) should be able to boast to the rest of us about how quickly you got to see it. Enjoy.</P>

```
<embed controller="true"
    height=196 width=240
    src="congo_web.mov">
</BODY>
</HTML>
```

HTML documents begin and end with `<HTML>` `</HTML>` *enclosing* tags. Within those tags, you find a `<HEAD>` `</HEAD>` section, where the `<TITLE>` `</TITLE>` appears, and a `<BODY>` `</BODY>` section, in which you put paragraphs of text (between `<P>` and `</P>`) as well as other tags, such as the `<EMBED>` tag shown in the example. After you create such a document, you save it as a Plain Text file (you can use SimpleText, for instance) and give it the .htm or .html file name extension. Now, upload it to your Web server computer using an FTP program such as Transmit (www.panic.com) or Fetch (www.dartmouth.edu/pages/ softdev/fetch.html).

Note also that this will probably make sense to your users only if CONTROLLER is set to false; otherwise your users will try to click the play button over and over and over again to get that one-frame movie to play. It may also help if the still movie actually says "Click Me" on it.

HTML for a streaming movie

If you've created a hinted movie file, you can place that file on one of two types of servers. The first type is a standard HTTP (HyperText Transport Protocol) server, which is just an annoying way for me to try to overwhelm you with fancy words while referring to a basic, boring Web server. A hinted movie on a standard Web server doesn't stream to the user, but it gets a fast start by beginning to play as soon as half or more of the movie has downloaded. (It downloads a buffer and begins playing that already down-loaded bit while the rest of the movie downloads. Sometimes this works; other times it stutters and stops if it plays faster than the rest of the movie can be downloaded.) Adding a hinted movie to your Web page is the same as adding a regular movie, as describe in the "HTML for a Web movie" section.

The other type of server is an RTP/RTSP server, or a Real-time Transport Protocol or Real Time Streaming Protocol server. If this type of server is avail-able, you need to store the files in whatever folder on your Web server is des-ignated for streaming movie files. Then, you access the file using a slightly different anchor tag that includes the "rtp://" protocol, such as:

```
<a href="rtp://www.mac-
          upgrade.com/streams/congo_web.mov">Watch the Congo
          Movie</a>
```

This launches the streaming movie in QuickTime Player, which is designed to play streaming movies and indicate to the user all the great things that happen when a streaming movie begins, such as "Negotiating" and "Buffering" (see Figure 17-5).

Figure 17-5:
QuickTime
Player when
viewing a
streaming
video clip.

Expert Exporting for the Internet

As with exporting for CDs, discussed in Chapter 16, iMovie doesn't give us many options for exporting for the Web. The basic Email Movie and Web Movie formats are okay, but you may want to do some tweaking.

The discussion in this section is compressed because the expert settings are discussed also in Chapter 16. The key difference is that you'll likely use differ-ent compressors for Web and e-mail video. In fact, I recommend the Sorenson Video compressor for all your Internet video needs, unless you're looking for compatibility with older QuickTime versions, in which case H.263 is a good compromise.

To begin, make sure your movie is arranged in a way that you find pleasing and satisfactory. Then:

1. **Choose File⇨Export Movie.**

   The Export Movie dialog box appears.

2. **Choose Export To⇨QuickTime.**

3. **Choose Formats⇨Expert QuickTime Settings.**

   The Expert QuickTime Settings dialog box appears.

Now you're ready to dig into the image and audio settings.

Image settings

Here's how to choose the image settings for exporting a Web movie:

1. **In the Expert QuickTime Settings dialog box, decide on a size for your movie.**

   The smaller the movie, the better, but remember that you're not forced to stick to iMovie's standard 160x120 and 240x180 settings. You can try 200x150 or 300x225 or anything you think may look good.

2. **In the Width and Height boxes, enter the number of pixels that you want for the final QuickTime movie.**

3. **Click the 4:3 box to make sure the movie stays in the correct proportions.**

4. **Click the Settings button in the Image Settings portion of the dialog box.**

   The Compression Settings dialog box appears.

5. **In the Compressor portion of the dialog box, use the top pop-up menu to select the type of codec for the video portion of the QuickTime movie.**

   For movies, I recommend that you look at one or two:

   • **Sorenson Video.** Sorenson Video is my top choice for Internet video. It creates very good video images in very small movie files. You can easily limit a Sorenson-compressed video stream to certain data rates. The only issues with Sorenson Video are that it takes quite a while to compress and doesn't work with QuickTime versions earlier than 4.0. Otherwise, it's highly recommended for Internet video.

   • **H.263.** The H.263 codec is okay for Web and e-mail movies, compresses faster than Sorenson Video, and is compatible with earlier versions of QuickTime.

6. **Select the number of colors the movie should use.**

   In some cases, you can then use the Quality slider to set a quality level that you'll be happy with.

7. **In the Motion section (below the Compressor and Color menus), select the number of frames per second that the movie will be.**

8. **If you check the Key Frame check box, you can then enter how often a key frame should be placed in the movie.**

9. **If you turn on the Limit check box, you can limit the data rate to a certain number of kilobytes per second.**

   This option is most important for Internet movies.

   What limits should you set? If you know that your users have modem connections, you can limit the data rate to about 5 to 10K per second. For higher speed connections, you can make it anywhere from 10 to 150K per second. (And if you're trying to cater to both types of users, you can export two different versions of your movie, if desired, and make them both available on your Web page.) Note that the dimensions of your movie and the data rate need to have some sort of relationship. At 50K per second, a movie that's about 180x135 looks good with the Sorenson codec and about 2MB per minute is required. At 150K per second, a 320x240 movie looks good in the Sorenson codec but takes a while to download — 10MB per minute of video.

10. **Click OK to close the Compression Settings dialog box.**

Next, it's on to the audio settings.

Audio settings

For Internet movies, you're more likely to want to compromise your audio quality a bit to make the file smaller because your Internet users aren't too likely to expect booming stereo sound in their stamp-sized QuickTime movie.

Here's how to choose the audio settings for a Web movie:

1. **In the Expert QuickTime Settings dialog box, click the Settings button in the Audio Settings portion of the window.**

   The Sound Settings dialog box appears.

2. **From the Compressor menu, choose the type of audio codec you want to use.**

   You have three practical choices for Internet movies:

   • **IMA 4:1.** This doesn't give great compression rates, but it's compatible with QuickTime 3.0. If you're exporting a movie for use with the widest variety of Internet users, IMA is probably the best choice.

- **QDesign Music 2.** QDesign Music 2 is good for compressing music and gives you extra options (click the Options button) for choosing a target data rate (between 8 kilobits per second and 48 kilobits per second) to fine-tune quality versus download speed. I'd stick to 8 to 12 Kbps for e-mail movies and 12 to 20 Kbps for Web movies.

- **Qualcomm PureVoice.** PureVoice is good for talking heads, especially if the background has little or no music. If you select PureVoice, the Options button is activated. Click it and you can choose different compression rates (9:1 or 19:1) as well as an option for Internet streaming.

3. **In the Rate portion, you can select a different frequency for the audio; you can also select whether to store the audio as 8-bit or 16-bit and whether it should be Mono or Stereo.**

   For QuickTime movies destined for the Internet, I recommend setting them at 8-bit and Mono for e-mail movies, 16-bit and Mono for modem Web movies, and 16-bit and Stereo for movies that will be downloaded using high-speed (DSL and cable) connections. 11.025 is a good rate for both types, although you can move up to 22.050 for higher-speed connections.

4. **Click OK.**

   You're back to the Expert QuickTime Settings dialog box, where you see a full report of both your audio and video compression settings.

5. **Turn on the Prepare for Internet check box and selecting the type of server you'll be using from the For menu.**

6. **In the For menu, select either Standard Web Server or QuickTime Streaming Server, depending on the type of server you're planning to use.**

   If you select Standard Web Server, the QuickTime movie won't be hinted. If you select QuickTime Streaming Server, the QuickTime movie will be hinted.

7. **If everything looks good, click OK.**

   You're back at the Export Movie dialog box.

8. **Begin the export process, as described back in Chapter 15.**

   When you're finished, you have a new QuickTime movie, ready to entertain the world!

iMovie and iTools

Apple's iTools — free tools that the company has made available on the Internet — are fun. They offer an easy way to get a free e-mail account (with a groovy @mac.com address), post a free Web site, and send special digital greeting cards (called iCards) that others can view over the Web. Along with all that comes the workhorse of iTools, iDisk, which gives you storage space you can use on the Internet.

iDisk and HomePage, tools for getting pages and images published and transferred online, work pretty well with QuickTime movies that you create in iMovie. After you have your movie exported as a QuickTime file, you can use iTools as a shortcut to getting it up on the Web or transferring it to a friend or colleague.

First, though, you have to sign up. If you haven't already, head to itools. mac.com or www.apple.com/itools/ and look around for the Free Sign Up button. You need to enter some info about yourself and download the Installer application. iTools requires Mac OS 9 or higher, which you probably have anyway because iMovie has the same requirements.

After you've installed iTools, you can sign in and use the tools any time — just head back to the iTools home page and click the Members button. You're prompted for your user name and password. Then, you have access to all your iTools stuff online.

Because iTools are really Web applications, it's important to realize that Apple can change them at any time. That's part of the reason why some of the instructions in this section are vague ("Look for the *xyz* button"). It's also the reason why you may come across an instruction in this section that doesn't seem to work. If that's the case, just stop and look carefully at the iTools pages — changes that Apple makes are designed to make things simpler and more powerful, so you should find the right button or command easily.

Uploading movies to your iDisk

One of the iTools is iDisk, an online storage space that, through a little bit of Mac OS magic, appears on your hard disk just like a network volume. You can use iDisk with your movie files in two ways. You can copy your movie file to your Movies folder (a folder already created right on your iDisk) for use with other iTools applications such as HomePage and iCards. Or you can copy your movie to your Public folder, where it can be shared with others. Anyone who knows your iTools user name can access your Public folder, so it's an easy way to make your movie downloadable to other iTools or FTP users. (It also means you shouldn't put any important financial documents in your Public folder; personal files should instead be stored in the secure Documents folder.)

Here's how to work with your iDisk:

1. **Sign into iTools at** `itools.mac.com` **on the Web.**

   You need to enter your user name and password.

2. **Click the Go button under iDisk or the iDisk menu item in the bar at the top of the iTools page.**

   The iDisk screen appears.

3. **Click Open my iDisk.**

   After a few seconds or more, depending on the speed of your connection (as well as how the Apple servers are feeling that day), your iDisk appears on the Mac's desktop (see Figure 17-6).

4. **Double-click the iDisk icon to open it, just as you would any disk that you're accessing over a network.**

Figure 17-6:
The iDisk icon and folder — note the folders that are automatically created for you.

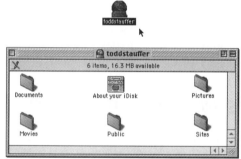

Now, you have two choices for your movie. You can drag it to the Movies folder, which then becomes automatically accessible for use with the HomePage and iCards tools. Or you can copy the movie to your Public folder, so that others can download it through iTools (if your friends have an iTools account) or the Web. Copy the movie from your hard disk to the iDisk just as you would to any other network or removable drive: Just drag-and-drop it on the folder where you want it copied. Now, wait — even with a high-speed connection, it can take a while to copy your multi-megabyte movie.

You have only 20MB of storage space to work with on your iDisk, and that includes everything stored in all the various folders. (As with most Finder windows, you can look at the iDisk window's title bar to see how much space remains.) If you want to store more files on your iDisk, Apple offers a pay-for-space option that enables you to upgrade to 200MB. See the main iDisk Web page (the one that appears when you log into iTools and select iDisk) for details.

If you choose to copy the movie into your Public folder, other iTools members can access that movie using the Open Public Folders tool on the iDisk page. For others who aren't iTools members, you need to take an additional step to share that Public folder on the Web:

1. **From the iDisk main page, click the Publish Personal Folder button. You can also head straight to the HomePage tool and select File Sharing.**

   A new File Sharing Web page has been created.

2. **Edit the text on the page, if desired, by clicking Edit Text. When you're finished, click Apply Text.**

3. **If you're happy with the page, click the Publish button.**

   If the publish process is successful, your Public folder is now available on the Web. You see the exact URL for the page on your screen.

   After your Public folder is published, others can access whatever is in your Public folder by heading to `http://homepage.mac.com/yourname/FileSharing.html` in a Web browser. (Note that *yourname* is replaced with your user name, such as `http://homepage.mac.com/stevejobs/FileSharing.html`.) Now others can download the QuickTime movie quickly and easily, without forcing you to design a Web site and all that jazz. Just drop a movie in your Public folder and it's available on the Web.

Adding movies to your HomePage

If you want to create a Web page that includes your movie but don't want to go to the pain and trouble of learning HTML, iTools comes to your rescue:

1. **Log onto iTools and select the HomePage tool.**

   The HomePage interface appears.

2. **Under the Create a Page heading, locate and click the iMovies button.**

   After the page refreshes, you see different types of pages you can create that enable you to display your movie on the Web. (Current options at the time of this writing include Theatre, Retro-TV, iMovie-Kids, and Drive-In.)

3. **Click a page option to begin building your page.**

   The page building interface provides a few buttons and options. Among them are buttons that enable you to Change Theme (change the type of iMovie page you're creating) and Change Text.

4. **Click Change Text and enter a title and short description for your movie (see Figure 17-7). When you're finished editing the text, click the Apply Text button.**

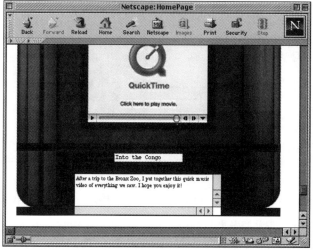

Figure 17-7:
Here I'm creating a Theatre page, and I've selected Change Text to edit the text.

5. **Click the Choose button under the QuickTime area.**

Another page appears, showing you the items currently in the Movies folder on your iDisk. The page gives you a number of options for accessing your iDisk, including an Update button (if you don't seem to be seeing any or all the movie files that you've uploaded) and an Open My iDisk button (if you need to open your iDisk and copy more movies to the Movies folder).

6. **Select one of the listed movies and then click the Preview button.**

You get a sense of how the movie will look when it's made available on the page you're creating. (Note that you'll have to wait for it to download, which may also help give you a sense of what your user's experience will be.)

7. **If you're happy with the movie as it stands, click the Apply button (see Figure 17-8).**

After you apply the selection, you're back in the template area.

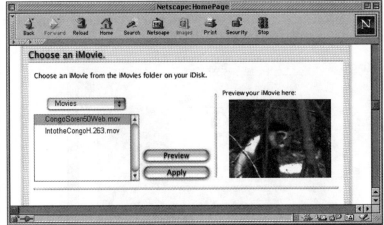

Figure 17-8:
Select and preview a movie from your Movies folder before you add it to your special iMovie Web page.

8. **Click the Preview button to see how the final page will look.**

9. **If you like what you see, click the Publish button.**

When you do, you get congratulations from iTools and see the name of the URL for the page that was created by this process. For instance, according to iTools, the page I created is located at `http://homepage.mac.com/toddstauffer/iMovieTheater.html` and can be accessed from any Web browser.

Pages created using the HomePage tools are stored in the Sites folder on your iDisk. If you know a little something about HTML, you can dig into those files and alter them as desired. And whether or not you know anything about HTML, you can head to the HomePage section of iTools and edit, create, and build links between all your pages, including those associated with movies.

Part V
The Part of Tens

The 5th Wave   By Rich Tennant

"What do you mean you're updating our Web page?"

In this part . . .

Sure, The Part of Tens appears harmless, but there's actually quite a bit of information packed into these mini-chapters. Turn to Chapter 18 for a look at some of the additional software, hardware, and accessories you can buy to turn working with iMovie from a hobby into an obsession. In Chapter 19, you can feed that obsession by adding some discipline and technique to the way you approach the making of your movies, including some specific advice for how to approach Web movie projects. Finally, Chapter 20 offers a quick guide to some of the most common troubleshooting problems with iMovie and how to get around them. Plus, you see how to dig through Apple's documentation and Web sites for even more info, if you need it.

Chapter 18

Burning Plastic: Ten iMovie-Making Purchases

*T*he whole point of that cool, cute little iMovie program is probably to get us to . . . buy more stuff. The more I think about it, the more outraged I become! Sure, iMovie is free with most Mac models and inexpensive with others. It adds untold benefits to beach-ball iMacs and cool portables and desktops in the Macintosh line-up. And, yeah, most off-the-shelf DV camcorders support it straight out of the box. But there's so much more you can do with your DV movies that, if you get carried away, you'll still find yourself spending tons of cash on your new DV habit . . . er, hobby. You know what that means: It's time to call your financial planner again and reevaluate your children's education.

In this chapter, you look at some add-ons and upgrades you may want to consider for both the software and hardware side of your movie-making experience.

QuickTime Pro

QuickTime Pro is the $29.95 upgrade to the standard QuickTime package that ships with modern Macs. QuickTime Pro is invaluable for anyone creating movies bound for the desktop, CD, or the Internet. By upgrading to QuickTime Pro, you add the capability to edit QuickTime movies after you've exported them from iMovie. Those additional capabilities include everything from easy cuts and export options to special effects such as transparency and graphical overlays.

Upgrading to QuickTime Pro is relatively painless — you do it straight through Apple's Web site. Visit www.apple.com/quicktime/ and follow the on-screen instructions for getting a registration code. After you have your code, open the QuickTime control panel and select Registration from the pop-up menu. (In Mac OS X, you can upgrade using QuickTime Player's own Preferences command.) Click the Edit Registration button and enter your personal information and registration number (see Figure 18-1 and note that the registration number I entered is fake).

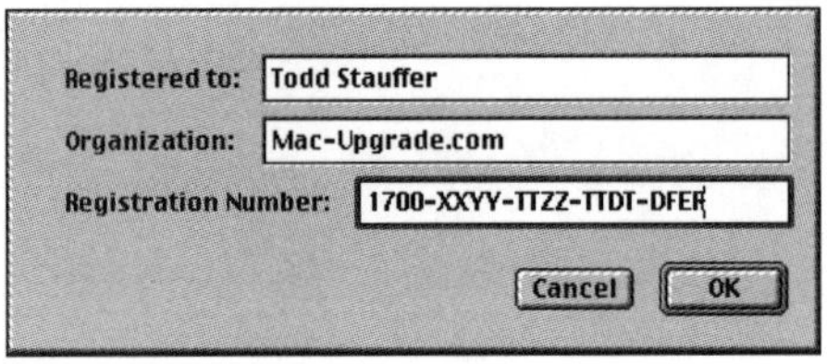

Figure 18-1:
The
QuickTime
registration
screen.

Registered to:	Todd Stauffer
Organization:	Mac-Upgrade.com
Registration Number:	1700-XXYY-TTZZ-TTDT-DFER

Cancel · OK

After you're registered, QuickTime Player Pro is augmented with many new capabilities, including those discussed throughout Parts III and IV of this book.

Media Cleaner or Cleaner EZ

If you're serious about QuickTime output, the solution is a Media Cleaner application. Terran Interactive (www.terran.com) makes Media Cleaner 5 and EZ, which both offer more sophisticated compression and output options than iMovie or even QuickTime Pro. Media Cleaner 5 is the more expensive option ($599), but it offers the capability to save files in MPEG-1 and MPEG-2 formats, suitable for video CD and DVD creation. Cleaner 5 can also process multiple files at once and offers other advanced settings.

Although Cleaner EZ ($99) doesn't offer quite the same level of options as Cleaner 5, it's still a great way to take exported movies and prepare them for CDs or the Internet. EZ can export files in Real media formats (for RealVideo players), as Windows Media files, and in more efficient QuickTime movies than are possible with iMovie alone. Cleaner EZ offers a friendly user interface and has wizards (see Figure 18-2) that walk you through the decision-making process on your way to a better video. In fact, I used Media Cleaner EZ for all QuickTime movies included on the *iMovie 2 For Dummies* CD-ROM. The output is much better and smoother than you can get from iMovie's Export feature alone.

Figure 18-2:
Media Cleaner EZ makes it easy to crop, compress, and output movie files in various formats for CDs or the Internet.

Adobe After Effects

Adobe has another contender that is at least worth your consideration — Adobe After Effects (www.adobe.com, $649). This high-end program works with exported QuickTime movies to clean up individual frames, add animated effects, change the look and feel of the image, and add special effects such as transparency and chroma-key backgrounds. After Effects is a complex program that I can't cover here. If you're creating video for an organization or business — or if you've reached the edges of iMovie's capabilities and want to move to the next level — After Effects is the choice for high-end effects (see Figure 18-3).

Figure 18-3:
After Effects
offers
amazing
capabilities
for pro-level
output, but it
can get a
touch
complicated.

RAM

Many Mac models that ship with iMovie pre-installed don't have enough memory to run iMovie, in my opinion. The minimum for success if 64MB, but the minimum for enjoying yourself while working with iMovie is at least 96MB and more likely 128MB or more. Fortunately, adding RAM to pretty much any iMovie-compatible Macintosh model is simple. I can't give you complete instructions here, but all modern Mac models include information on upgrading RAM in their included manuals (usually with helpful drawings, too). It's an upgrade that almost any Mac owner can perform.

Here's a quick look at the types of RAM:

✓ **iMac DV and Power Macintosh G4 (and blue & white G3).** iMac models have a special door on the bottom of the case that enables you to easily add a second RAM module; desktop models have a fold-open "door" that enables you to access the system internals and add quite a few RAM modules. Current iMac DV and Power Macintosh G4 models accept a type of memory called PC-100 SDRAM DIMMs (dual inline memory modules). Most Mac retailers offer RAM that's compatible with the iMac DV and, currently, not very pricey compared to other RAM types.

If you don't get RAM from a Mac retailer, make sure it meets these specifications for the iMac DV (2000 model) or Power Macintosh G4: 64-bit bus, non-parity, 168-pin, 3.3-volt, unbuffered, PC-100 compliant, and 8 ns refresh rate.

✓ **iBook and PowerBook.** Year 2000 model iBooks and PowerBooks that include FireWire ports use the same type of RAM for upgrading: one PC100 SDRAM in the form of a SO-DIMM (small outline DIMM). These smaller DIMMs aren't compatible with other Mac models, so make sure you order RAM that's specifically for Apple's portables. In both models, you upgrade by lifting the keyboard out of the front of the portable and adding the module in the space underneath the keyboard.

Hard Disk Upgrades

One of the issues you'll run into when working with iMovie is the need for more storage space. Depending on your Macintosh model, you may come across a few different solutions for adding storage space — for instance, you could add a removable storage drive as discussed in the next section. With certain Mac models, though, you might also consider an additional hard disk, which can be either internal or external.

If you opt for an external drive, your best bet is a FireWire-based hard disk, which is compatible with any iMovie-compatible Mac, because FireWire is a requisite of iMovie. FireWire-based hard disks are external boxes that can enclose disks ranging from 5GB all the way to 30GB and beyond. They tend to be a bit more expensive than internal disks, but they're the only viable solution for iMacs, iBooks, and some PowerBook models. (You can replace the disks in these models, but doing so requires some serious computer surgery.) You'll also find USB-based hard disks available as external options, but they're very slow and not recommended for transferring DV files.

In fact, depending on your Mac model, you may have trouble importing video from your DV camcorder, through your Mac, and out to a FireWire-based hard disk. In some cases, the fact that both the camcorder and hard disk are using FireWire can cause interruptions in the transfer. In that case, your best plan is to keep enough space on your main disk for transferring footage (either to or from the camcorder) while moving other clips and data to the FireWire drive in between transfer sessions.

Power Macintosh G3 and G4 models have space inside their cases to accept internal hard disks, although the type supported differs. Power Macintosh G4 models all support a second ATA/IDE hard disk, which is installed (in slave mode) above the original hard disk in a special bracket. Some Power Macintosh G3 models support a second drive, but only if the drive has the special bracket installed above the original hard disk inside the Mac's case. (Open your case and look at the hard drive, which is located in the bottom-rear corner of the case, near all the expansion cards. If a bracket is above the hard disk, it supports a second ATA/IDE drive.)

If your Power Macintosh G3 doesn't support an ATA/IDE drive, you can still add either an ATA expansion card (Sonnet Technology's Tempo, for instance, from www.sonnettech.com) or a SCSI expansion card, which enables you to install internal SCSI drives. In some Power Macintosh G3 and G4 models, a SCSI card is pre-installed. SCSI drives are a bit more expensive, especially for higher capacity drives. They can offer better performance than ATA drives (depending on the model), so they remain the preference of many die-hard Mac creative professionals.

Removable Storage

As mentioned in Chapter 16, a CD-R drive that enables you to store data on a CD can be a nice addition to your movie creating arsenal, whether you use the CDs for backup, distribution, or both.

Another option is a DVD-RAM drive, which tends to be more expensive but offers you the capability of writing a much greater amount of data (4.7GB or more) to a single disc. This makes it a realistic media for backing up larger quantities of data, but DVD-RAM media is expensive and isn't compatible with DVD-ROM drives. CD-R and DVD-RAM drives are available in both internal and external models, with FireWire external versions recommended for their speed and flexibility. Most internal versions come with new or special-order Macs, such as the DVD-RAM drive that comes installed as standard equipment in some Power Macintosh G4 models.

CD technologies aren't your only option. Although Iomega Zip disks, limited to 100MB and 250MB capacities, are popular for backing up and distributing regular data, they're a bit too small for digital video. Other removable disk models — such as the Iomega Jaz (www.iomega.com) and the Castlewood Orb (www.castlewood.com) drives — offer capacities of 2GB or higher per cartridge, making them more viable for backing up your digital video projects.

Steadying Equipment

One of the most important steps to getting good video using your camera is to lock it down. Put your camera on a flat surface or a tripod, or hold it steady and firm while filming. But sometimes, you just have to move. How do you keep your shots from bouncing all over the place?

One of the solutions is a *stabilizer,* a device that makes it possible to move with a camera without having the camera reflect every step you take and every bump that courses through your body. Glidecam (www.glidecam.com) makes a number of stabilizers, with prices starting at a few hundred dollars. Figure 18-4 shows a modestly priced model.

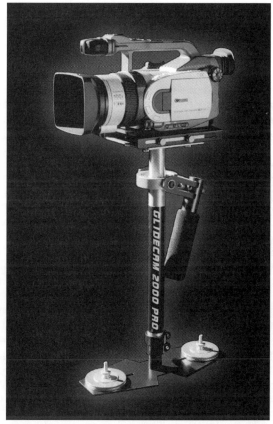

Figure 18-4: The Glidecam 2000 Pro ($369) offers stability while you're moving.

Photo courtesy Glidecam Industries, Inc.

Most stabilizers work either by anchoring your camcorder to your body in some way (some inexpensive stabilizers simply extend a bar from the camcorder to your chest) or by adding counterbalance weights to the bottom of the stabilizers. With these weights, it becomes more difficult to move the camera around in a jerky fashion — like a golf club or a croquet mallet, the weight at the bottom causes for a smoother swinging motion at the top. (Golf and croquet metaphors? I say . . . sherry, anyone?)

At the high-end, you can get steadycam stabilizers as well as specialized cranes, harnesses, and many other stabilizing products. For starters, visit an online video accessory store such as www.bhphotovideo.com or www.studiodepot.com. For individual manufacturers, see www.steadytracker.com, www.hollywoodlite.com, and www.videosmith.com, among others.

Lights

If you'll be shooting organizational or corporate video and don't have your own studio (or if you'll be doing a lot of shots in the CEO's office), you might consider a portable lighting kit. Lighting kits can range from a few hundred dollars to thousands. At the low end, though, you can get some simple kits that give you a key, fill, kicker, and maybe even background light, all of which you can set up, filter, and work with to get the best lighting possible for your shots.

For starters, it's recommended that you get a *tungsten* lighting kit, because these tend to be less expensive and well suited to digital photography. One of the manufacturers mentioned most often is Lowel (www.lowel.com), which makes lightweight Tota light kits for traveling and quick setup. Other companies that offer such kits include Smith-Victor, Cool-Lux (www.cool-lux.com), and NRG Research (www.nrgresearch.com). Best of all, some of these light kits start at well under a thousand dollars, giving you options within the budget of a small organization, company, or serious hobbyist.

Also, check your camera manufacturer (and third parties) for keylights that fit your camcorder's accessory shoe, including very bright lights that can be added to the top of many camcorders. These lights offer a nice, portable compromise, especially for documentary footage or newsgathering.

And don't forget the importance of fill lights or reflectors. Most photography stores and Web sites sell reasonably inexpensive fill reflectors that can be held close to your subject and used to fill in shadows and other irregularities that the key light (or sun) is causing. Popular reflectors are available from Bogen Photo Corp. (www.bogenphoto.com), Visual Departures (www.visualdepartures.com), and Photoflex (www.photoflex.com), among others.

Camera Filters and Lens Adapters

Most camcorders have a built-in lens that can't be changed — but that doesn't mean you can't accessorize it. Your manufacturer likely offers lens adapters (for wide and telephoto, for instance) and special filters that can help you get better shots.

Chapter 1 mentions the necessity of leaving a UV filter on your camcorder lens at all times. But there are other filters, too, and you'll find them interesting additions to your shooting experience. Here's a quick look at some of the filter types you may encounter:

- **Ultraviolet (UV).** These filters cut down on the amount of UV light, which reduces haze.

- **Neutral Density (ND).** Often described as sunglasses for your camcorder, these filters enable you to shoot with more open exposures even under outdoor lighting conditions. This adds to your ability to shoot a narrow depth of field (items not in immediate focus get fuzzy, such as with film).

- **Soft Focus/Diffusion.** Soft focus filters make things a touch more fuzzy, giving the image a less harsh focus and more of a light, airy feeling. This is the filter they would use, for instance, to film Audrey Hepburn.

- **Center Spot.** This is a special-case diffusion filter; it blurs the edges a bit but keeps a center area of clear focus. A center spot is a great tool for making your video look more film-like.

- **Polarization.** A polarization filter (or polarizer) changes the angle at which light comes into the lens, making it possible for you to shoot through a glass window or see beneath the surface of water, for instance. A polarization filter can reduce glare and reflections, especially under bright light conditions where the sun reflects off windows or metal.

- **Color correction.** Filters exist for all sorts of color-correction situations, usually to compensate for different light source temperatures. These filters are pretty specialized and sophisticated — for regular shooting, you're better off white-balancing your camera with care.

- **Special effects.** Tons of filters exist, so I'll go ahead and drop the rest of them into this category. From sepia tone to fog, mist, and star effects, you can trick your camera into seeing a wide variety of things.

When it comes to filters, the main name you'll hear is Tiffen (www.tiffen.com), a company that not only makes the bulk of filters used in photography but also offers adapters and, in some cases, lenses. Also check your camcorder's manufacturer (Canon, Sony, JVC) for lens and filter add-ons.

Another Camcorder or a DV Player or Controller

Finally, what's the ultimate purchase for an iMovie videographer? What could be better than a MiniDV deck that lets you play back and record to MiniDV from the TV or another analog device? For instance, Sony makes the DHR-1000, a device that's basically a MiniDV VCR. This is a great convenience for playing back footage, moving quickly through tapes, cloning (copying from one DV tape to another for backups or to correct time code problems), and studio display of your work. Such a device is also expensive, with a suggested retail price of more than $4,000.

Sony (`www.sel.sony.com`) also makes the DVMC-DA2, which takes analog input and translates it to FireWire-based DV data. It's a great go-between for attaching your VCR to your Mac and getting analog video into iMovie. Its only drawback is that it costs $500.

The best solution may be to get another inexpensive DV camcorder. (Or, if you already have an inexpensive DV camcorder, maybe you could get a more expensive one.) A second camcorder can be used for cloning, playback, and analog-to-DV conversion (if it has analog inputs). Best of all, it's also a camcorder, just in case your first one breaks, or you want to get two shots, or you decide to loan one to your brother-in-law!

Chapter 19

Ten Tips for Better Movies

- -

In This Chapter

▶ Plan your shoot

▶ Get permission

▶ Get handles

▶ Shoot to edit

▶ Set up for film-like shooting

▶ Check your lighting and shadows

▶ Get really good audio

▶ Shoot good action scenes

▶ Shoot video specifically for the Web

▶ Keep your cool when editing for the Web

- -

The best way to get a good looking movie is to *shoot* good looking footage before you ever get the video out of the camcorder and into your Mac. To do that, you can start with some of the basics discussed in Chapter 2 and move on to some of the add-on options discussed in Chapter 18. In this chapter, I talk about some tips for getting good footage and managing your sessions with the camcorder.

Plan Your Shoot

Maybe you're thinking: "What else should I plan? I have a camera, I bought iMovie, and I had a nutritious breakfast this morning. What more do you want?" By *planning*, I mean two things. The hardest video to edit is video you never get into your camcorder. It's a matter of physics. To get all the footage you need, it's important to plan your shooting so that you have extra tapes with you. Perhaps even more important, you should have an extra battery or two for your camcorder. If you use your camcorder with its LCD active or with external accessories such as boom mics or lighting, you're likely to use up the battery life of the camera before you even manage to record an entire tape's worth of footage.

The other part of planning is the tactical part — thinking about the shots you want to get before you go out to get them. For home video and family travelogues, most of the story unfolds on its own. For almost any sort of video, though, keep in mind the three major types of shots — establishing, middle, and close-up — and remember to "tell your story" by getting these shots as you're working the camera. Remind yourself, for instance, to get that sweeping, establishing shot from the top of a San Francisco hill before you start shooting middle and close-up shots of the family climbing on a trolley car.

For news, organizational, or corporate projects, planning may involve *storyboarding,* the process of planning your shots on paper to make sure you get everything you need to edit your project in the end. A typical storyboard includes quick drawings of the type of shot you want to get. Next to that shot, write in the idea or narration that should accompany it, along with notes regarding the length of time for the shot and the music or graphic effects you plan for the shot.

For an important project, storyboarding helps to ensure that you get all of the footage you need for the video. That way, you won't have to call back the CEO (or your paid actors) and ask to re-do a shot or fill in with additional comments or narration. A storyboard also reminds you of the direction of the project and can help you communicate that direction to your producers, bosses, and anyone else you want to convince of your wonderful concept.

Get Permission

Ever wonder why producers sometimes use that little fuzzy-blob effect on people's faces during the real-life cop shows or in documentary films? Sometimes it's because they didn't get a *permission release* from that person.

In a number of situations, it's important to get permission before you shoot video or display that video publicly. For the most part, the legal need to get permission from people refers to situations where you stand to make money (or otherwise commercialize or widely distribute) from the presentation of your video. So, if you're shooting home video and you get the faces of strangers in your video, it shouldn't be a problem.

If you plan to use the video in a commercial setting or long-term archival or documentary setting, consider getting signed permission release forms. Generally, a form that has the person's name, contact information, signature, and a paragraph or so outlining that he or she is granting you the right to use his or her image is sufficient. You can get standard forms from organizations that support video professionals.

None of this constitutes legal advice, though. If you're in doubt about whether or not to get releases from your subjects, consult an attorney. (And, no, your hairstylist doesn't count.)

Get Handles

Perhaps one of the most persistent amateur mistakes is to start the camera too late and stop the camera too early during a shot. Get used to the idea of adding at least a few seconds of footage on *either side* of the action of a particular shot whenever you can.

This does two things. First, you'll have more footage to work with when you decide, in iMovie, to cut your clips down to size. You may end up using parts of the handle footage (a little extra walking at the beginning or even some ambient noise at the end) in your final version. On that same note, you should finish any camera movement or zooming and wait a few additional seconds of recording before pressing Pause — that way, you won't be forced to cut a clip short while the camera is moving or zooming, which usually looks pretty bad. Tape, as they say, is cheap.

Second, getting handles keeps you from making the mistake of getting extra audio or extra, unplanned movement in your shot. If you take a breath and wait a few seconds at the end of a particular shot, you are less likely to suddenly swing the camera down to the ground or start talking ("Yeah, that was great!") before you have the entire scene shot. Get all your on-camera helpers accustomed to the extra few seconds, too, so that they don't suddenly "break character" after doing whatever you asked them to do.

Bottom line: Don't be afraid to get *too much* footage. Within reasonable limits, it's always better to have a little extra video to work with when you're making your edit decisions in iMovie.

Shoot to Edit

If you've read through many of the chapters in the middle of this book, you're familiar with the editing choices you can make in iMovie. Armed with that knowledge, you can make some choices while shooting with the camcorder.

One of the more important things to remember is the freedom that iMovie 2 gives you regarding sound-based edits. In Chapters 8 and 13, I discuss the amazing new possibility afforded by iMovie 2's Paste Over command: intercutting. So what does this have to do with shooting? Quite plainly, you can think about shooting one scene that includes audio you'll use with another scene that includes only video.

For example, suppose you're shooting a narrative discussion with your city's mayor. With your camcorder, you set up your lights and camera and film the mayor's comments from start to finish. But that may not make for the most exciting video. The fact that you can overlay the mayor's audio with different video means you might consider going out and getting video shots of issues discussed during the interview, such as city council meetings, people in the streets, the new holiday decorations. Then, back in iMovie, you can use Paste Over and other Timeline moves to add that video over the video of the interview. (In other situations, don't forget to get reaction shots, such as shots of the crowd during a speech, and cut-in shots, such as a close-up of the evidence the cops found.)

Other edits to consider are transitions and cuts that take place between two subjects or of the same subject from different angles. To avoid jump cuts (cuts that change focal length or zoom without changing the angle dramatically), consider whether you're moving so that different shots are different enough in angle. Remember the 30-degree rule, which states that different cuts of the same subject should have at least a 30-degree change in camera angle.

Set Up for Film-Like Shooting

For many digital videographers, a key desire is to make the video look as if it were shot on film. Video can be a little harsh looking compared to film, which tends to blur more easily, especially when panning quickly. Likewise, film has a much more shallow depth of field than video, making it easier to use manual focus to bring attention to parts of your shot. By comparison, video tends to keep quite a bit of your shot in focus, which gives video a flatter quality compared to film.

A few remedies and tricks can be used to make your video look a little more like film, if you like. Here's a quick list:

- **Use a filter.** Possibly the easiest way to make something look a little more like film is to use a lens filter, as discussed in Chapter 18. Using a soft diffuse, center spot, or vignette filter can add an effect that's not unlike film, giving your video a slightly warmer feeling. With center spot, you can also focus the audience's attention a bit more because subjects in the center are less diffuse than video on the edges of the screen.

- **Pull back.** If you physically pull the camera back from your subject while using the focal zoom (not digital zoom) to zoom in on your subject, you can begin to create a shallower depth of field. You'll notice that items at distances much closer and much farther away from the camera begin to get a little blurrier. (Remember, though, that if you're trying to get a close-up and you don't have a detachable microphone, the best solution is to forget about depth of field and get the camcorder as close to your subject as possible.)

✔ **Lock it down.** Shots that shake, rattle, and roll look like video; shots of beautiful vistas, multiple cuts from different angles, and shots that are steady look more like film.

✔ **Manual focus.** If you work with a locked-down (tripod or steady) camera on set shots — like they do in the movies — you can also switch to manual focus and use it to your advantage. Although a camcorder often has to find its subject to automatically focus the camera, using the manual focus mode enables you to focus on items that aren't in the very middle of the frame or are well in the foreground or background.

Check Your Lighting and Shadows

Lighting is incredibly important for getting the best shots, and you should remember that your camera doesn't see light in exactly the same way that you do. Just because *you* think a scene — especially an indoor or night scene — is well lit doesn't mean your camera sees it that way.

The answer is to use add-on lighting when you can, as discussed in Chapters 1 and 18. Beyond that, knowing your camcorder well can help — learn the settings for low-light, low-contrast, and other settings. Although your camera likely has an Auto exposure mode, learn the other exposure settings, especially those for bright sunlight and snow-blind situations. And anytime you change lighting situations, consider using the white balance feature of your camera to make sure colors are as true and vibrant as possible.

Finally, one quick, easy way to make your video look more professional is to minimize shadows, particularly when shooting people in close-up interviews. Use either a simple reflector or a fill light to fill in faces and even out lighting. In other instances, take note of where shadows fall and make sure you're not seeing confusing shadows, moving shadows, or your own shadow in the frame.

Get Really Good Audio

Suppose for the moment that you have the basics of using a tripod (when possible) and otherwise minimizing the shaking and zooming that can plague amateur video. The other hurdle to get over in the pursuit of good video presentations is getting good audio. Crisp, clean audio — especially when spoken — is key.

In general, the trick is to get the microphone as close to the subject as possible. If you're filming a close-up and interviewing your subject at the same time, you'll probably get good audio from your camcorder. If your subject is across the room, though, the audio requirements may call for a different solution. In that case, you may want to use a boom microphone, a handheld microphone, or even a small, clip-on lavalier microphone that you attach to your subject's clothing. See Chapter 1 for more hints on buying and using audio equipment.

Just as important is keeping out unwanted noises. Editing out unwanted laughing, sneezing, cursing, commenting, or horn honking is difficult, requiring a program other than iMovie. The best plan is not to record those sounds in the first place, if you can help it. Consider the placement of your microphones and how directional they are. Above all, as the director, keep control of your set.

Action Tips

The race goes by and you miss it. The UFO flies by and all you get is a shaky blur. How are you supposed to effectively catch action scenes on tape?

The most important consideration is knowing where the action is going to happen and being ready for it. If you'll be panning to shoot the action as a footrace or horse race or football play comes by you, be ready to turn your body (or the tripod, if you're not holding the camera) smoothly and deliberately. One way to do this is to stand with your feet facing the *midpoint* of the action, so that your body is twisted toward the beginning of the action. As the action comes by you, you can twist without moving your feet, thus making it less likely that the camera will bounce as you step. You should also do everything you can to keep from changing the tilt of the camera as you're panning because only a slight tilt can have an effect on the final image, especially during fast moving scenes.

Other considerations include focus and exposure settings. Some camcorders offer special settings for action exposure, which you may want to use if you plan to shoot an active scene. Likewise, stay on the ball with focus: If you know that your subject won't be moving much closer or farther away from your camera lens, you may be able to use the camcorder's focus-lock feature to lock it to a particular focus. This keeps the camera from seeking focus at an inopportune time.

Shooting for the Web: Less Movement

If you plan to shoot video that will be compressed and turned into a QuickTime or similar format movie, remember a few tips while filming. Because of the way compression works, movies that make the jump most successfully to CD or Web playback are those with fairly little movement. The reason is simple: The more each frame of video in your project changes, the less effective the compression scheme. And less effective compression is more *lossy,* which means the image suffers.

The best Web video is probably the most boring. If you have a close-up of your subject as he or she is talking, only fairly small portions of the video — the area around the mouth, for instance — change dramatically. This is a good thing — the more talking head video you can get, the better, as far as the Web is concerned. In fact, the only thing better than talking head video is still frame video (like a slide that you've imported) that has no changes from frame to frame. Close-ups also make more sense for Web video because they're easier to see and watch in the small windows that today's Web video offers.

Aside from getting close up, you should also note other movement in the frame that may need to be rendered at compression time. Instead of shooting your subject in front of a waterfall or a gaggle of angry professional wrestlers, make sure your subject has an unmoving background, such as a brick wall or a single-color backdrop. Any unnecessary movement must be rendered and compressed, affecting both the size and quality of the image.

Editing for the Web: Stay Cool

When you're editing an iMovie project destined for the Web, you have to keep your cool. What does that mean? It means you can't do all the crazy titles and effects you can do if you're outputting to a TV.

Specifically, for Web video, you should avoid transitions, rolling credits, and other extraneous movement and effects, all of which compress poorly and end up muddied in the resulting Web or CD-ROM video. Stick to straight cuts between clips or, if necessary, simple transitions. (Often, a fade or wash doesn't look good but a quick wipe works.) If you do use titles, avoid those that fly by or scroll; titles that simply appear and disappear are best. And titles should be larger than you might otherwise use for TV-bound video because your viewer is looking at a smaller image.

In my experience, it's tough to get titles to look good when you export an iMovie project to QuickTime. Part of that reason is simple: The compression techniques that work well for video often don't work well for titles because the two are different animals.

One trick can get you around this. If you create your movie so that it doesn't include opening titles and closing credits, you can export it using standard QuickTime settings discussed in Chapters 14 through 17. Then you can create a *second* iMovie that includes only the title sequences you want to create. (It may help to add a few seconds of black frames between the titles and closing credits, just to make them easier to edit.) You can then export the credits to the same-size (in pixels) QuickTime movie, but use a compressor such as Animation that's friendlier to computer-generated graphics. After the credits are exported, use QuickTime Pro or another QuickTime editing application to paste the credits back into the QuickTime movie. The result? A movie that's just as effective for Web and CD playback, but with better looking credits. (Another solution, mentioned in Chapter 18, is to use Media Cleaner 5 or Media Cleaner EZ, both of which do a great job compensating for credits when compressing QuickTime movies.)

Chapter 20

Ten Troubleshooting Tips

*i*Movie 2 has gone through some significant enhancements, upgrades, and bug fixes to make it a reliable, mostly bug-free application. That said, DV editing places strong demands on any computer. Despite the power and capabilities of today's Macs — including iMacs and iBooks — digital video editing requires a lot of RAM, a strong processor, and reasonably close attention to the condition of your hard disks and other storage media. If you're having trouble getting iMovie to work the way you expect it to, there may be a simple solution. Read on.

Dropped Frames and Import Issues

If there's any consistent complain from iMovie users, it's likely to be issues with dropped frames or frames that show *artifacts,* "noise" or other anomalies that affect the quality of the image. For the most part, the transfer process between your camcorder and your Mac should go without a hitch. If it doesn't, look at the following import issues and how to address them:

✔ **Poor image quality.** If you note that the image quality in the iMovie Monitor appears less than ideal or you feel that the movie, when displayed full-screen on your Mac's monitor, doesn't looks its best, this happens by design. iMovie doesn't show all the video information that remains part of the underlying clip, for the simple reason that most Macs aren't capable of processing that much data quickly enough. The real test of this issue is to connect an external TV monitor to your camcorder or preview your imported and edited clips on your camcorder's LCD display. If the quality is better on the TV or LCD display, that should allay your fears. If not, move on to some of the other issues in this section for possible remedies.

Choose Edit➪Preferences and click the Playback tab. You see options that enable you to select whether Smoother Motion or a Better Image are displayed in the Monitor during playback. Neither of these settings enables you to see the full quality of your video images — only a TV can reflect that completely.

If you're still having trouble, turn off File Sharing and turn off AppleTalk in the AppleTalk control panel. If you have more than 64MB of RAM, disable Virtual Memory in the Memory control panel (see the "Sound Trouble" section).

✔ **Dropped frames.** If you're seeing problems with the video you're importing from your camera, it could be the result of one of three major issues. First, Apple recommends that you have no DV devices, except the camcorder, connected to your Mac. Likewise, it's recommended that you capture directly to your Mac's internal hard disk instead of to a FireWire-based external hard disk. Capturing to a FireWire disk isn't always a problem, but some camcorders (some Canon models, for instance) don't capture well to FireWire disks. Also, some FireWire disk drives are slow compared to internal disks and can be too slow to write the captured video data quickly enough.

If you're importing to your internal disk, you may still have a problem — a fragmented disk. If the disk drive you're attempting to write to has significant fragmentation or other errors, it could affect its capability to capture video. Run the disk defragmentation tools in a program such as Norton Utilities or MicroMat TechTool Pro to ensure that the disk is working at maximum efficiency.

✔ **Distorted video.** There's a special case in which video can appear to be distorted as you import it into iMovie — the video appears elongated (people are taller and skinner than any human really should be) after it reaches iMovie. This likely means that you've recorded video using the camera's 16:9 aspect ratio option — this is a movie-theater's aspect ratio, not the standard 4:3 ratio for television. Unfortunately, there isn't a lot you can do about this because iMovie is incompatible with footage recorded at 16:9. Other programs, such as Final Cut Pro or Adobe Premiere, support the editing of such footage. The best plan if you work exclusively with iMovie is to make sure your camcorder is always set to record at the 4:3 aspect ratio.

✔ **Failed import.** Apple notes that the Energy Saver features of your Mac should be turned off when working in iMovie, and that no FireWire devices should be plugged in or unplugged while iMovie is importing or exporting video. If importing fails, look to these two culprits. Also make sure that your camcorder is plugged into a wall outlet. And finally, make sure enough disk space is available for the imported video. Remember, DV requires a lot of available disk space.

Memory Errors

iMovie 2 requires a Mac with 64MB of RAM, and that requirement is a bare minimum. If you plan to use iMovie 2 extensively, I recommend upgrading to 96MB, 126MB, or more RAM, if you can. In Chapter 18, I discuss buying and installing RAM.

If you have only 64MB of RAM, I recommend that you close all applications before launching iMovie and then work only with iMovie until you're ready to quit. It can also be advantageous to restart your Mac immediately before working with iMovie because that avoids problems that can occur with *memory fragmentation* in Mac OS 9.*x* and earlier. (When memory becomes fragmented, it's sometimes difficult for iMovie to receive the full amount of RAM it requests from the Mac OS, forcing it to run with less memory.)

What is fragmentation?

Fragmentation occurs as files are written to, deleted from, and rewritten to a disk. Over time, as some files are deleted and others overwritten, the operating system is forced to break up large individual files and store them in smaller gaps on the disk. This slows things down because the disk must jump around to different locations as the data is saved.

Picture a public library where about 20 percent of the books have been checked out and kept forever by patrons. Although the library now has about 20 percent of its space free for new books, that space is not *contiguous,* or located in a single part of the library. Small gaps exist where individual books have been removed from shelves throughout the building. When you delete files, save more files, delete again, and so on, you create this same situation on a disk.

Small gaps exist through the entire disk, even if a large percentage of it is free space.

The Mac OS can deal with all these different bits of data reasonably well, but it's inefficient to when the OS is forced to jump around to different parts of the disk to save or load a single, larger file. With large DV files, the problem can be more pronounced as the disk jumps all around trying to load or save the continuous stream of data. The solution is to use a utility program to *defragment* the drive, shuffling the current crop of data around so that larger contiguous spaces result. Then the disk can again save files efficiently, at least for a while. You should run such a utility program regularly, especially considering how demanding DV is and how often you'll be saving large files as well as individual clips.

If iMovie complains of memory-related problems during operating, quit iMovie, restart your Mac, re-launch iMovie, and use it without opening other applications. If you receive repeated complaints, it's possible you may need to install more RAM.

If you have more than 64MB of RAM and Mac OS 9.*x* or earlier and continue to receive complaints, you may need to set iMovie's memory partition to something higher. (In Mac OS X, assuming you have a future, compatible version of iMovie, memory is managed by the operating system, making this step unnecessary.) Here's how:

1. **Quit iMovie.**

   Skip this step if iMovie isn't currently running.

2. **Locate the iMovie icon in the Finder.**

   Make sure it's the original iMovie application icon and not an alias.

3. **Choose File⇨Get Info or press ⌘+I.**

   This opens the Get Info window.

4. **Choose Show⇨Memory. In the Preferred Size entry box, enter a new, larger number.**

   Note that the iMovie-suggested number is around 28000 or higher, depending on a few different factors. If you have more than 64MB of RAM installed, consider changing the Preferred Size number to 35000, 40000, or even higher. Note that the higher the number you enter, the less RAM you'll leave available for other applications when iMovie is launched.

5. **Close the Info dialog box.**

   The memory changes are noted and you can now re-launch iMovie.

Realize that iMovie won't get the full preferred size block of memory if other applications are already running and the requested amount isn't available. If you still have trouble after changing the Preferred Memory number, try restarting the Mac and launching iMovie before launching any other applications.

Camera-Related Error Messages

Error messages regarding the state of the camera generally point to some problem with FireWire. You've either unplugged the camcorder from the Mac's FireWire port or plugged in or unplugged a FireWire device while the camcorder was connected. You may also see an error if another FireWire device was accessed (perhaps by a File Sharing user or by another program running on your Mac) while the camcorder was being accessed.

If trouble persists, check Apple's list of compatibility issues with specific camcorders and devices at `www.apple.com/imovie/shoot.html` and ensure that your device is compatible. You should also check `www.apple.com/firewire/` to make sure that you have the latest version of the FireWire system software and any related Mac updates.

Help Trouble

iMovie occasionally loses track of its own help files: You choose Help⇨iMovie Help from the menu and, instead of the Help Viewer, see an error message. The first step is to open the System Folder on your Mac and then open the Help folder. If you see the iMovie Help file in that folder, iMovie Help is installed. If you don't see that folder, you need to locate it. If you've recently installed a clean copy of the Mac OS, you may have a Previous System Folder, in which you'll find a Help folder, inside of which may be the iMovie Help folder. If that's true, drag the iMovie Help folder from its current spot to the Help folder inside the active System Folder. You should now be able to restart iMovie and access its help system.

If you can't locate the iMovie Help folder, you may need to reinstall the help system:

1. **Insert the iMovie CD and double-click the Install iMovie icon.**

2. **Click Continue, Accept the agreement, and then click Continue again on the Read Me screen.**

3. **At the Install iMovie screen, select Custom Install from the pop-up menu.**

4. **Deactivate the Application option (by clicking the check box to remove the check). Activate the Application Help option.**

5. **Click Install and the Help files should be installed.**

6. **Return to iMovie and test to see whether the Help system works.**

If you still can't get Help to open, try rebuilding the desktop:

1. **Restart your Mac (in the Finder, choose Special⇨Restart).**

2. **As the Mac starts up, hold down the Option and ⌘ keys until the Mac desktop appears.**

   A dialog box appears asking whether you want to rebuild the desktop.

3. **Click OK and the desktop is rebuilt.**

4. **When the process is concluded, return to iMovie and see whether the Help system will open.**

If none of these is successful, you may need to reinstall the Mac OS or iMovie. These are drastic steps, though, so consider a workaround first. If you choose Help⇨Help Center from iMovie, the Help Viewer loads, displaying the types of help available. If iMovie Help is listed, click it. Now you can get help. It's an extra step, but I've seen it work when Help⇨iMovie Help doesn't.

Slow iMovie Startup

iMovie has to load audio resources as it's launched, and each additional sound effect delays iMovie as it opens. If you've added files to the Sound Effects folder in the Resources folder inside the iMovie folder, that could be the cause of the delay. Remove some of the sound effects files to see if iMovie launches more quickly. (Chapter 12 discusses adding sound effects in more detail.)

Note, too, that turning off Virtual Memory in the Mac OS 9.*x* Memory control panel will also cause applications, including iMovie, to launch a bit more slowly. The advantages of turning off Virtual Memory outweigh this negative, though, as long as more than 64MB of RAM is installed in your Mac.

Sound Trouble

If you're having trouble with sound input, you may not have the correct input device selected in the Sound control panel. Apple recommends that you *hide* iMovie before changing the sound device if you're having trouble switching. Select the iMovie icon or name in the application menu (at the top right of the Mac OS 9.*x* title bar) and choose Hide iMovie. Open the Sound control panel and change the sound input device, if necessary.

If you're recording audio from within iMovie, the program automatically stops recording after about ten minutes. This happens to keep you from accidentally recording until the disk is full. There is no way around this limitation. You need to be aware of it and, if you're talking, stop talking before the ten-minute limit, stop the recording, begin a new recording, and resume speaking. You can also use a different application to record sound and then import that sound track into iMovie, using the instructions in Chapter 8.

If you hear problems with sounds that you're exporting to camera (notably pops and hisses), adding RAM and turning off Virtual Memory in the Memory control panel may help. (This is relevant only for Mac OS 9.*x* users.) Apple recommends that you turn off Virtual Memory only if you have more than 64MB of RAM (ideally 96MB or more) installed. Here's how:

1. **Shut down any open applications.**

2. **Open the Apple menu and choose Control Panels⊃Memory.**

3. **In the Virtual Memory section, click the Off button.**

4. **Close the Memory control panel.**

5. **Restart the Mac by choosing Special⊃Restart.**

After the Mac is restarted, Virtual Memory is off. Try exporting from iMovie again to see whether sound problems have been solved.

A sound-related issue appears to affect exporting (to a camera) in another way. If you notice stuttering or staggered video after a particular point in your exported movie, overlapping sound clips may be to blame. (I've noticed this happens particularly with music clips.) In iMovie, note whether two sound clips overlap one another on the Timeline — or have a slight gap — at the exact moment when the export problems occur. If so, try to align the audio clip more precisely or, if possible, re-record the audio clip without the break. Then attempt the export again to see whether the video (or audio) stops staggering.

Dennis's Font Fix

This tip is so-named for a reason — it was discovered by the technical editor, Dennis Cohen. (He's always figuring out stuff like this.) If you notice trouble with the way iMovie displays text on-screen — particularly the text on buttons and in the Timeline viewer — you may have a font conflict. The Lucinda Grande font (ID #1024) is embedded in iMovie 2. If another font is installed in the Font folder inside your Mac's System Folder (or elsewhere in the System Folder), it could be causing the visual glitches. In Dennis's case, removing the Curlz MT font, which is included with Microsoft Office 2001, corrected the problem.

If you don't have Curlz MT but still note trouble with fonts, look for another font that has the ID #1024. How do you know? Use a shareware program such as FontBuddy (http://hometown.aol.com/vjalby/FontBuddy/index.html) or FONDetective (www.primenet.com/~gswann/software.html).

Tape Trouble

The digital nature of DV tapes makes them more reliable than analog tapes, up to a point. When they do fail, they tend to fail a bit more dramatically than analog tapes. Instead of static or slight video imperfections in an aging VHS tape, a DV tape may begin to drop frames, drop pixels in the image, or even cause portions of two images to appear on the same tape at once.

You should take precautions to care for tapes properly. Remove the tape from the camera if you don't intend to use it for more than a few days. Store it in its plastic case. Tapes should be stored according to temperature ratings — car windows, glove boxes, and trunks are not recommended.

It's also recommended that you stick to a single brand of tape (especially MiniDV tape) because the lubricant used in the tape can vary slightly from one brand to the next. You should also use one record mode for an entire tape, avoiding a mid-tape switch from SP to EP, for instance.

If you're having trouble exporting from iMovie to a tape, first make sure a tape is actually in your camcorder. Some camcorders allow iMovie to go through the export process, even if a tape isn't in the camcorder. Next, ensure that enough time is left on the tape for the complete iMovie to be exported. Finally, check the tape and make sure that its small record tab hasn't been switched to Save.

The big test for a tape is to use a second tape. If you record (or play back) from one tape and note errors, try a different tape. If both tapes have trouble recording or playing back, you may need to use a special head-cleaning kit to clean the camcorder. Consult your owner's manual or camcorder manufacturer for recommendations.

Device-Specific Issues

A number of specific issues have been identified with various brands of camcorders and other devices. Apple keeps a running list at www.apple.com/imovie/shoot.html, so I won't regurgitate all of them here. However, it is worth noting a few tendencies for different brands and types of camcorders:

✔ **Canon.** Some Canon camcorders won't allow you to press the Pause button from within iMovie if the camcorder is currently stopped. Instead, you must press the Pause button on the camcorder itself to go to Pause mode. Also, iMovie may not correctly report that a tape isn't in the camcorder or that the tape is locked (the tab is moved to the Save position), so physically double-check the tape in the camcorder before exporting.

✔ **Panasonic.** With many Panasonic modes, the time code is off by one frame during playback. The camcorder and iMovie don't agree on the timecode, but according to Apple, this doesn't affect functionality.

✔ **Sony.** With some Sony models, iMovie may not properly report that a tape is locked if one is inserted. Check twice before exporting to tape.

✔ **European camcorders.** Many European camcorders, especially imported consumer models, have disabled DV-in capabilities. According to Apple, this is a limitation in the camera, not in iMovie. You have to upgrade to a more expensive camera or contact the manufacturer for advice if you can't seem to export to your European camcorder.

✔ **Digital 8 camcorders.** Many Digital 8 models don't report recording problems to iMovie, so you should check them manually for locked or missing tapes. Apple also notes that iMovie is compatible with only Metal Particle type Hi-8 tapes and won't work properly with Metal Evaporative tapes.

Exploring Solutions on Your Own

If you haven't found the answer to your troubleshooting question in this chapter, you can look in two other places. The first is in iMovie's Help system. Select iMovie⇨Help and you'll see the main list of contents. Click the Late-breaking News item to see information on compatibility or other bugs and workarounds that Apple has acknowledged and discussed.

The second place to look for answers is Apple's Web site. The Tech Info Library (`til.info.apple.com`) is where Apple places articles about known issues and problems with all of its computers and software. Type **iMovie** as a keyword to search for articles related to iMovie. Information and updates for iMovie are available at `www.apple.com/imovie/`. Finally, the AppleCare Knowledge Base at `kbase.info.apple.com` can provide some answers, but you need to sign in with a registered account (it's free).

Appendix

About the CD

● ●

*O*n the CD-ROM:

- ✔ Sample QuickTime movies, showing techniques and examples discussed in the book
- ✔ Utilities for editing and working with QuickTime movies, including effects packs, Mac Video Titler, and a streaming QuickTime server for Mac OS 9
- ✔ Sound utilities for creating effects or jazzing up your movie's soundtrack, including Felt Tip Sound Studio and Groovemaker

The CD-ROM is designed to be as friendly as possible and offers a complete listing of its contents. I also include a listing here of some of the best tools available on the disk, as well as some instructions for accessing its contents.

One of the main reasons I include a CD-ROM with the book is so you can see sample QuickTime movies of some of the techniques and issues outlined in the book. Beyond that, I also include some freeware, shareware, and demonstration utilities on the CD that may help you in your quest for producing the best iMovies and QuickTime movies possible.

System Requirements

Make sure that your computer meets the minimum system requirements listed next. If your computer doesn't match up to most of these requirements, you may have problems using the contents of the CD. Note that any Macintosh that's compatible with iMovie 2 should be fully compatible with the applications on this CD.

- ✔ A Mac OS computer with a PowerPC or faster processor.
- ✔ Mac OS system software 8.6 or later.
- ✔ At least 32MB of total RAM installed on your computer. For best performance, I recommend at least 64MB of RAM installed.

✔ At least 700MB of hard drive space available to install all the software from this CD. (You need less space if you don't install every program.)

✔ A CD-ROM drive — double-speed (2x) or faster.

All the software on the CD is designed to work with Mac OS 9.x (and some earlier versions, depending on the software's requirement). If you have Mac OS X, most of the applications should work from within the Classic environment, although there's no guarantee. (Also, you needn't install QuickTime 4.1.2 because Mac OS X has its own version of QuickTime.) QuickTime movies I've created and stored on the CD should be viewable from Mac OS X's QuickTime Player.

If you need more information on the basics, check out *Macs For Dummies,* 6th Edition or *iMac For Dummies,* both by David Pogue (both published by IDG Books Worldwide, Inc.).

Using the CD

To install the items from the CD to your hard drive, follow these steps:

1. **Insert the CD into your computer's CD-ROM drive.**

   In a moment, an icon representing the CD you just inserted appears on your Mac desktop. Chances are, the icon looks like a CD-ROM.

2. **Double-click the CD icon to display the contents of the CD.**

3. **In the window that appears, double-click the START.HTM icon.**

4. **Read through the license agreement, nod your head, and then click the Accept button if you want to use the CD.**

   After you click Accept, the Main menu appears.

5. **To navigate within the interface, click any topic to see an explanation of the files on the CD and how to use or install them.**

6. **To install the software from the CD, simply click the name of the software.**

7. **When you are finished using the interface, close your browser as usual.**

After you have installed the programs you want, you can eject the CD. Carefully place it back in the plastic jacket of the book for safekeeping.

What You'll Find

Each piece of software included on this CD-ROM has its own licensing agreement or a similar document that you should read to completely understand how it's being distributed and what you need to do to legally use the software.

In general, you'll encounter three different types of software on this CD:

- **Freeware.** With freeware programs, the author requires no payment for you to use the software on an unlimited basis. Note that not all freeware software is public domain software, however, and the author may make certain requirements — for instance, he or she may require that you keep the Read Me file intact if you forward the program to someone else.

- **Shareware.** Often called try-before-you-buy software, shareware programs are distributed for free but require a small licensing payment for you to continue to use them after a certain amount of time. Small companies or individuals often write shareware programs as reasonably priced alternatives to commercial software. If you find that you enjoy using a program, I encourage you to pay for the program and get a registration code. You'll generally find instructions for doing so in the program's installed folder. (Check the "Read Me" or "Register" documents.)

- **Demos.** Demonstration programs are generally either time-limited or feature-limited versions of commercially available programs. On the CD, I include a few such programs, such as Adobe After Effects and AudioFusion TWS by Syclone Multimedia. You probably won't get much actual use out of these demo programs without paying for the full commercial version, but they do give you the opportunity to see how they work and to get a feel for whether they will prove useful.

Shareware programs are fully functional, free trial versions of copyrighted programs. If you like particular programs, register with their authors for a nominal fee and receive licenses, enhanced versions, and technical support. Freeware programs are free copyrighted games, applications, and utilities. You can copy them to as many personal computers as you like — free — but they have no technical support. GNU software is governed by its own license, which is included inside the folder of the GNU software. There are no restrictions on distribution of this software. See the GNU license for more details. Trial, demo, or evaluation versions are usually limited either by time or functionality (such as being unable to save projects).

Following are the software programs included on the CD-ROM. They're arranged according to the categories used to catalog them on the CD itself.

Sample files

Whenever you see an icon like the one in the margin and the accompanying text refers you to a QuickTime movie, you can head to the Sample Movies section of the CD-ROM. There, you'll find individual Chapter folders, in which are stored sample QuickTime movies. To display one of the movies, simply double-click it from its folder on the CD-ROM. This launches QuickTime Player, enabling you to view the movie. (If you don't get great results when playing the movie from the CD-ROM, copy it to your Mac's hard disk first and then view it from there, where it should play smoothly.)

If you need to install QuickTime (all iMovie-compatible Macs should have QuickTime installed), run the QuickTime installer on the CD-ROM. Note that the QuickTime version included is version 4.1.2; if you already have this version or a later version, there's no need to run the installer.

Internet utilities

Microsoft Internet Explorer, from Microsoft Corporation (www.microsoft.com)
This very popular browser now comes as the default browser for Mac OS installations. It supports Java, multimedia, and special IE-only features such as Internet channels. (Full version.)

Netscape Communicator, from Netscape, Inc. (www.netscape.com)
The most popular Web browser, Netscape Communicator includes Java, JavaScript, multimedia, and support for special Netscape commands. (Full version.)

DV and graphics utilities

Adobe After Effects, from Adobe Systems (www.adobe.com)
Adobe After Effects is an advanced, professional-level application that enables you to edit, title, and control digital video files. Advanced special effects range from transparency and animation to color, lens, film-like, and other special effects. (Demo version; will not save or render effects.)

Commotion DV, from Pinnacle Systems, Inc. (www.pinnaclesys.com)
Another effects program, this one is designed specifically for use with DV files to edit their appearance and add effects to your movie. (Limited demo.)

GraphicConverter, from Lemke Software (www.lemkesoft.de)
This well-respected shareware application offers many of the features of high-end paint and photo manipulation programs such as Adobe Photoshop but at a much lower cost. This fully functional shareware version can translate between graphic file types, enabling you to create static frames for titles or add text and effects to still frames exported from iMovie. (Shareware version; requires registration.)

MovieTools, from McQ Productions (www.mcqproductions.com)
MovieTools offers some interesting capabilities for working directly with DV video files, including chroma key compositing, effects, resizing, image control, and film-look enhancements. (This demo version prints *MovieTools Demo* on each frame of the movie you're processing but is otherwise fully functional. Paying for the software and entering the registration code stops this printing.)

RotoWeb and RotoDV, from Digital Origin, Inc. (www.digitalorigin.com)
Like After Effects, RotoDV enables you to create effects, paint on video, animate, and remove defects from digital video files. RotoWeb is a less expensive version designed primarily for users who intend to create movies for Internet distribution. (Both are demo versions, so Save, Save As, and Make Movie commands are disabled.)

Sound utilities

AudioFusion TWS, from Syclone Multimedia (www.audiofusion.com)
AudioFusion gives you a virtual techno studio, enabling you to create original upbeat, modern sounding soundtracks for your movies. (Demo version; save commands are disabled.)

Felt Tip Sound Studio, from Felt Tip software (www.felttip.com)
This shareware application gives you a more robust solution for recording your own audio, whether it's narration or music. ($25 to register.)

Groovemaker, from IK Multimedia Production (www.groovemaker.com)
The remix studio is sort of a combination of AudioFusion and SmartSound — download royalty-free songs and then remix them using the Groovemaker interface. The music leans toward hip-hop and techno, but there's nothing to keep you from getting creative with other styles. (Demo version; save functions disabled.)

SmartSound For Multimedia, from Sonic Desktop Studio (www.smartsound.com)
Create royalty-free sound tracks with this unique software. Using some standard song styles and small, drag-and-drop elements, you can build big band, jazz, rock, salsa, and other soundtracks. The company also sells add-on CDs

that give you a broader library of royalty-free music clips. If you've ever spent more than thirty seconds playing around with a music synthesizer or keyboard, you'll love this program. It's tons of fun creating the perfect sound-track for your video. (Demo version; save functions disabled and only a few music selections are offered.)

SoundApp, from Normal Franke
This venerable audio conversion tool enables you to turn any audio file into an AIFF file, which you can then import to iMovie. (Freeware; no payment required.)

QuickTime utilities

Cool Stream, from evological (www.evological.com)
This QuickTime streaming server works in Mac OS 9.*x* instead of requiring Mac OS X, like Apple's QuickTime Streaming Server does. Use an existing Mac to stream QuickTime movies to one (unicast) or more (multicast) recipients. (Freeware; no payment is required.)

Effects Pack 1, 2, and 3, from Buena Software (www.buena.com)
These special packs are plug-ins for QuickTime Player, enabling you to add all sorts of transitions and effects to QuickTime movies. (Each pack is a time-limited demo; after a certain length of time, the effects stop working unless you've registered by paying the appropriate fees.)

MoviEffects, Mac Video Titler, from McQ Productions (www.mcqproductions.com)
MoviEffects and Mac Video Titler enable you to take QuickTime movies to the next level, especially if you're heavily compressing movies for CDs or the Web. (The full versions are a bit pricey for hobbyists but not a bad deal for organizations and corporations.) Create your titles outside iMovie, thus avoiding trouble with compressed lettering and bad looking fonts. Use MoviEffects for a slew of other options including more editing tools, film and aging effects, color, black-and-white, and many other controls. (The demo applications place *MVT2 Demo* or *MoviEffects Demo* on the clips you save; otherwise, the demos are fully functional.)

MovieWorks Interactive, from Interactive Solutions (www.movieworks.com)
Create interactive movies, adding buttons, still images, and controls to your existing QuickTime movies. Other versions of MovieWorks create CD-ROM interfaces and other interactive presentations that include QuickTime movies. (Demo version.)

QuickTime, from Apple Computer (www.apple.com/quicktime/)
Apple's QuickTime software includes QuickTime Player and necessary system software. Install only if you don't already have this version; newer versions may also be available at www.apple.com/quicktime/.

If You Have Problems of the CD Kind

I tried my best to compile programs that work on most computers with the minimum system requirements. In fact, the system requirements for iMovie are, in most cases, more stringent than the system requirements for the items included on the CD-ROM. But computers can differ, and some programs may not work properly for some reason.

The two likeliest problems are that you don't have enough memory (RAM) for the programs you want to use, or you have other programs running that are affecting the installation or running of a program. If you get error messages such as Not enough memory or Setup cannot continue, try one or more of these methods and then try using the software again:

- ✔ **Turn off any antivirus software that you have on your computer.** Installers sometimes mimic virus activity and may make your computer incorrectly believe that a virus is infecting it.

- ✔ **Close all running programs.** The more programs you're running, the less memory is available to other programs. Installers also typically update files and programs; if you keep other programs running, installation may not work properly.

- ✔ **Restart your Mac.** Sometimes simply restarting your Mac will clear out any fragmentation in system memory, allowing the installer (or the installed application) to launch and run smoothly.

- ✔ **Have your local computer store add more RAM to your computer.** This is, admittedly, a drastic and somewhat expensive step. However, if you have a Mac OS computer with a PowerPC chip, adding more memory can really help the speed of your computer and enable more programs to run at the same time.

If you still have trouble installing the items from the CD, please call the IDG Books Worldwide Customer Service phone number: 800-762-2974 (outside the U.S.: 317-572-3993).

Index

• F •

Notes

IDG Books Worldwide, Inc., End-User License Agreement

READ THIS. You should carefully read these terms and conditions before opening the software packet(s) included with this book ("Book"). This is a license agreement ("Agreement") between you and IDG Books Worldwide, Inc. ("IDGB"). By opening the accompanying software packet(s), you acknowledge that you have read and accept the following terms and conditions. If you do not agree and do not want to be bound by such terms and conditions, promptly return the Book and the unopened software packet(s) to the place you obtained them for a full refund.

1. **License Grant.** IDGB grants to you (either an individual or entity) a nonexclusive license to use one copy of the enclosed software program(s) (collectively, the "Software") solely for your own personal or business purposes on a single computer (whether a standard computer or a workstation component of a multiuser network). The Software is in use on a computer when it is loaded into temporary memory (RAM) or installed into permanent memory (hard disk, CD-ROM, or other storage device). IDGB reserves all rights not expressly granted herein.

2. **Ownership.** IDGB is the owner of all right, title, and interest, including copyright, in and to the compilation of the Software recorded on the disk(s) or CD-ROM ("Software Media"). Copyright to the individual programs recorded on the Software Media is owned by the author or other authorized copyright owner of each program. Ownership of the Software and all proprietary rights relating thereto remain with IDGB and its licensers.

3. **Restrictions on Use and Transfer.**

   (a) You may only (i) make one copy of the Software for backup or archival purposes, or (ii) transfer the Software to a single hard disk, provided that you keep the original for backup or archival purposes. You may not (i) rent or lease the Software, (ii) copy or reproduce the Software through a LAN or other network system or through any computer subscriber system or bulletin-board system, or (iii) modify, adapt, or create derivative works based on the Software.

   (b) You may not reverse engineer, decompile, or disassemble the Software. You may transfer the Software and user documentation on a permanent basis, provided that the transferee agrees to accept the terms and conditions of this Agreement and you retain no copies. If the Software is an update or has been updated, any transfer must include the most recent update and all prior versions.

4. **Restrictions on Use of Individual Programs.** You must follow the individual requirements and restrictions detailed for each individual program in the "About the CD" appendix of this Book. These limitations are also contained in the individual license agreements recorded on the Software Media. These limitations may include a requirement that after using the program for a specified period of time, the user must pay a registration fee or discontinue use. By opening the Software packet(s), you will be agreeing to abide by the licenses and restrictions for these individual programs that are detailed in the "About the CD" appendix and on the Software Media. None of the material on this Software Media or listed in this Book may ever be redistributed, in original or modified form, for commercial purposes.

5. **Limited Warranty.**

   (a) IDGB warrants that the Software and Software Media are free from defects in materials and workmanship under normal use for a period of sixty (60) days from the date of purchase of this Book. If IDGB receives notification within the warranty period of defects in materials or workmanship, IDGB will replace the defective Software Media.

   (b) **IDGB AND THE AUTHOR OF THE BOOK DISCLAIM ALL OTHER WARRANTIES, EXPRESS OR IMPLIED, INCLUDING WITHOUT LIMITATION IMPLIED WARRANTIES OF MERCHANTABILITY AND FITNESS FOR A PARTICULAR PURPOSE, WITH RESPECT TO THE SOFTWARE, THE PROGRAMS, THE SOURCE CODE CONTAINED THEREIN, AND/OR THE TECHNIQUES DESCRIBED IN THIS BOOK. IDGB DOES NOT WARRANT THAT THE FUNCTIONS CONTAINED IN THE SOFTWARE WILL MEET YOUR REQUIREMENTS OR THAT THE OPERATION OF THE SOFTWARE WILL BE ERROR FREE.**

   (c) This limited warranty gives you specific legal rights, and you may have other rights that vary from jurisdiction to jurisdiction.

6. **Remedies.**

   (a) IDGB's entire liability and your exclusive remedy for defects in materials and workmanship shall be limited to replacement of the Software Media, which may be returned to IDGB with a copy of your receipt at the following address: Software Media Fulfillment Department, Attn.: *iMovie 2 For Dummies*, IDG Books Worldwide, Inc., 10475 Crosspoint Blvd., Indianapolis, IN 46256, or call 800-762-2974. Please allow three to four weeks for delivery. This Limited Warranty is void if failure of the Software Media has resulted from accident, abuse, or misapplication. Any replacement Software Media will be warranted for the remainder of the original warranty period or thirty (30) days, whichever is longer.

   (b) In no event shall IDGB or the author be liable for any damages whatsoever (including without limitation damages for loss of business profits, business interruption, loss of business information, or any other pecuniary loss) arising from the use of or inability to use the Book or the Software, even if IDGB has been advised of the possibility of such damages.

   (c) Because some jurisdictions do not allow the exclusion or limitation of liability for consequential or incidental damages, the above limitation or exclusion may not apply to you.

7. **U.S. Government Restricted Rights.** Use, duplication, or disclosure of the Software for or on behalf of the United States of America, its agencies and/or instrumentalities (the "U.S. Government") is subject to restrictions as stated in paragraph (c)(1)(ii) of the Rights in Technical Data and Computer Software clause of DFARS 252.227-7013, or subparagraphs (c) (1) and (2) of the Commercial Computer Software - Restricted Rights clause at FAR 52.227-19, and in similar clauses in the NASA FAR supplement, as applicable.

8. **General.** This Agreement constitutes the entire understanding of the parties and revokes and supersedes all prior agreements, oral or written, between them and may not be modified or amended except in a writing signed by both parties hereto that specifically refers to this Agreement. This Agreement shall take precedence over any other documents that may be in conflict herewith. If any one or more provisions contained in this Agreement are held by any court or tribunal to be invalid, illegal, or otherwise unenforceable, each and every other provision shall remain in full force and effect.

Installation Instructions

The *iMovie 2 For Dummies* CD-ROM is designed to be as friendly as possible and offers a complete listing of its contents. To install the items from the CD to your hard drive, follow these steps:

1. **Insert the CD into your computer's CD-ROM drive.**

   In a moment, an icon representing the CD you just inserted appears on your Mac desktop. Chances are, the icon looks like a CD-ROM.

2. **Double-click the CD icon to show the CD's contents.**

3. **In the window that appears, double-click the START.HTM icon.**

4. **Read through the license agreement, nod your head, and then click the Accept button if you want to use the CD.**

   After you click Accept, the Main menu appears.

5. **To navigate within the interface, click any topic to see an explanation of the files on the CD and how to use or install them.**

6. **To install the software from the CD, simply click the name of the software.**

7. **When you are finished using the interface, close your browser as usual.**

After you have installed the programs you want, you can eject the CD. Carefully place it back in the plastic jacket of the book for safekeeping.

For more information, see the "About the CD" appendix.

YOUR ONLINE RESOURCE

WWW.DUMMIES.COM

Discover Dummies Online!

The Dummies Web Site is your fun and friendly online resource for the latest information about *For Dummies* books and your favorite topics. The Web site is the place to communicate with us, exchange ideas with other *For Dummies* readers, chat with authors, and have fun!

Ten Fun and Useful Things You Can Do at www.dummies.com

1. Win free *For Dummies* books and more!

2. Register your book and be entered in a prize drawing.

3. Meet your favorite authors through the IDG Books Worldwide Author Chat Series.

4. Exchange helpful information with other *For Dummies* readers.

5. Discover other great *For Dummies* books you must have!

6. Purchase Dummieswear® exclusively from our Web site.

7. Buy *For Dummies* books online.

8. Talk to us. Make comments, ask questions, get answers!

9. Download free software.

10. Find additional useful resources from authors.

SURF THE NET

WWW.DUMMIES.COM

Link directly to these ten fun and useful things at **http://www.dummies.com/10useful**

For other technology titles from IDG Books Worldwide, go to **www.idgbooks.com**

Not on the Web yet? It's easy to get started with *Dummies 101®: The Internet For Windows® 98* or *The Internet For Dummies®* at local retailers everywhere.

IDG BOOKS WORLDWIDE

Find other *For Dummies* books on these topics:

Business • Career • Databases • Food & Beverage • Games • Gardening • Graphics • Hardware
Health & Fitness • Internet and the World Wide Web • Networking • Office Suites
Operating Systems • Personal Finance • Pets • Programming • Recreation • Sports
Spreadsheets • Teacher Resources • Test Prep • Word Processing

IDG BOOKS WORLDWIDE
BOOK REGISTRATION

We want to hear from you!

Visit **http://my2cents.dummies.com** to register this book and tell us how you liked it!

- ✔ Get entered in our monthly prize giveaway.

- ✔ Give us feedback about this book — tell us what you like best, what you like least, or maybe what you'd like to ask the author and us to change!

- ✔ Let us know any other *For Dummies*® topics that interest you.

Your feedback helps us determine what books to publish, tells us what coverage to add as we revise our books, and lets us know whether we're meeting your needs as a *For Dummies* reader. You're our most valuable resource, and what you have to say is important to us!

Not on the Web yet? It's easy to get started with *Dummies 101*®: *The Internet For Windows*® *98* or *The Internet For Dummies*® at local retailers everywhere.

Or let us know what you think by sending us a letter at the following address:

For Dummies Book Registration
Dummies Press
10475 Crosspoint Blvd.
Indianapolis, IN 46256

™

**BESTSELLING
BOOK SERIES**